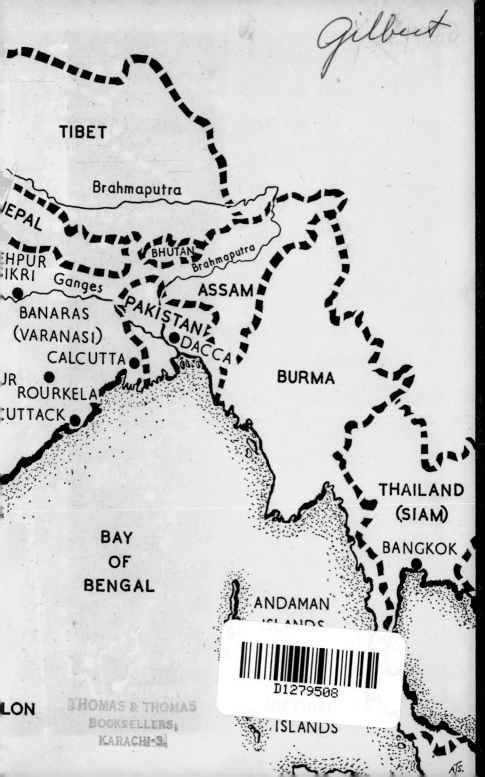

INDIA:
MIRAGE AND REALITY

by

PETER SCHMID

AUTHOR OF
" THE NEW FACE OF CHINA "

Translated by

E. OSERS

GEORGE G. HARRAP & CO. LTD

LONDON   TORONTO   WELLINGTON   SYDNEY

First published in Great Britain 1961
by GEORGE G. HARRAP & CO. LTD
182 High Holborn, London, W.C.1

© *English translation George G. Harrap & Co. Ltd* 1961

Composed in Bembo type and printed by
Morrison & Gibb Ltd, London and Edinburgh
Made in Great Britain

CONTENTS

ILLUSTRATIONS

Chandigarh : the Supreme Court building.

Every morning men and women wash away their sins in the Ganges at Banaras (Varanasi).

Every morning this sadhu in Banaras covers the entire distance to the Ganges on his stomach.

A brahmin at his morning devotions in Banaras (Varanasi).

A beggar dying near the bank of the Ganges without anyone paying the slightest attention to him.

Pilgrim in Banaras (Varanasi).

The Festival of Holi : even venerable pilgrims are not immune against attack from street urchins.

Indian Army personnel studying erotic tactics at the temples of Khajuraho.

Mysore : an Indian harvest thanksgiving festival in January. Cows are driven through fires for ritual purification.

When sacred cows collapse from weakness and old age their exalted status is no protection against the whip.

A bull with mutilated forelegs in the street in Calcutta.

Orthodox fanatics demonstrating in favour of a ban on the slaughtering of cattle in India.

Sivananda, the Yogi of Rishikesh, has his feet sprinkled with milk and strewn with flowers by his women followers every noon.

Yoga class in Sivananda's Ashram at Rishikesh.

Early-morning wrestling under Howrah Bridge, Calcutta.

Methods used by the sect of the Jains for observing the law against the taking of life.

Refugees from East Pakistan have settled down in the booking-hall of Sealdah station, Calcutta.

Between pages 48–49.

Typical Southern Indian landscape.

Straw huts of a primitive tribe in Orissa.

The women employed at the Bhilai steelworks take their babies along to the building-site.

Young Indian engineer at the Rourkela steelworks.

Peasants, their backs bent, planting rice.

A typical farm in Northern India.

Travelling on foot from village to village, Vinoba Bhave has carried his message of social rebirth all over the Indian sub-continent.

An evening with Vinoba Bhave.

Paper-makers in Jaipur.

The spinning-wheel, a symbol of India's liberation ever since Gandhi, provides an additional income for the impoverished peasant masses.

The palace of the Maharaja of Mysore.

The Maharaja of Mysore on an elephant hunt.

" Children by choice and not by chance " : a mobile birth-control exhibition.

Birth control is gaining ground : contraceptives on sale in the bazaar of Amritsar.

How rickshaw coolies live in Madras.

A pariah.

Brahmin children reciting sacred texts in a Sanskrit school at Madras.

Between pages 112–113.

Classical dancing : this young girl . . . wants to train as a professional dancer (*colour*).

Hindu architecture in a Moslem mosque : the famous mosque of Ajmer.

Outside the mosque at Delhi.

The Taj Mahal at sunset (*colour*).

The famous " House of the Winds " at Jaipur (*colour*).

Agra : view through a traceried window of Akbar's tomb at Sikandra.

One of the temples of Halebid, in Southern India.

The Ghats at Banaras (Varanasi) (*colour*).

Meditation beside the Ganges (*colour*).

An itinerant flower-vendor in Srinagar, Kashmir.

Floating homes in Srinagar, Kashmir.

Festival at the Mogul Gardens near Srinagar, Kashmir (*colour*).

Young girl and boats on Lake Dal, Srinagar, Kashmir (*colour*).

Idgah prayer in Srinagar, Kashmir.

Friday prayers in Lahore.

A temple festival in Kerala (*colour*).

Between pages 160–161.

Ritual dance at a Hindu festival at Quilon, Kerala.

Satyagraha in front of the Government building in Trivandrum, Kerala.

Co-existence of deities at Kerala : Stalin, Gandhi, Nehru, and the god Krishna.

Communist propaganda painted on a road surface in Kerala.

The Communists are fond of using traditional spectacles for their demonstrations in order to attract the public eye.

Unanimous vote for Tara Singh : a meeting of the Akalai Party, a Sikh secession movement.

A brahmin wedding : the final act of the ceremony.

People live on these boats near Dacca, East Pakistan.

Sikh meditating in the sacred lake of Amritsar.

Bazaar in Peshawar, Pakistan. Human features and handicrafts betray Persian influence.

The " Krupps " of Pakistan : hand-operated drills used by the warlike tribes for manufacturing their rifles.

Pakistani girls at the atomic physics laboratory in Lahore wear their traditional colourful Punjabi costumes.

Peshawar, Pakistan. Clash of two worlds : a woman in purdah below a poster advertising a Brigitte Bardot film.

Ambush in the streets of Katmandu : passers-by are given an injection against cholera by a team of the W.H.O.

Cow droppings for briquettes.   They are dried and used for fuel.

Street in Katmandu, Nepal.   The houses are decorated with fine wood-carvings.

Between pages 208–209.

CHAPTER ONE

Travel Thoughts of a Sahib

ON THE KHYBER PASS THE MACADAM STARTED
again—the Lord be praised ! This was the pass one had been
looking forward to with awe and terror throughout the journey :
the gateway through which, according to the schoolbooks, one
invading horde after another had poured into India from the
Central Asian cradle of human races. One had expected something wild, something romantic and dangerous. Yet here it was,
a modern metalled road, snaking its way up to the pass in coils,
two or three visible at the same time, and with a railway running
alongside. No ravine, no roaring waters, nothing romantic.
Only an army barracks on every prominent crag. Altogether
there was still a strong atmosphere of British Army boot-polish
about the whole of the Khyber Pass.

Behind me lay what I suppose I must call the roads of Afghanistan, even though my typewriter jibs at the word ' roads.' In
fact, my bones were still aching. As far as the Turkish frontier,
past Mount Ararat of Flood fame, the drive was fine—thanks, of
course, to the cold war. For wherever heavy guns can be moved
up towards the Soviet frontier a Volkswagen can manage
without difficulty. But in Persia my martyrdom started : deep
pot-holes in the road surface, or irrigation ditches, freshly dug,
carrying precious moisture right across the road. Or all at once,
just after accelerating a bit, comes a sudden drop down to a
dried-up ford strewn with boulders. No such thing as road-
signs. All you can do is pray, and brace yourself resignedly
against the bumps which seem to go right through you. And
then came Afghanistan. I had chosen the route through the

romantic but murderous north : at first between ruts and boulders over mule-paths and across streams ; steep drops down to the water and equally steep climbs up on the far sides ; down once more with wet, slipping brakes. And then through the desert, where the novice cheerfully digs himself into the deep sand with his spinning rear-wheels before he even knows what he is doing, and into furrows several feet deep ploughed by the heavy lorries. Poor little car ! But God and the Afghans are ever-present helpers.

Across the Khyber Pass—you console yourself—lies India with its good roads. What a joke ! True enough, the roads are metalled, but there are cows on them, and, what's more, sacred ones. These macadam cows, whose proper place would be on green pastures, all share a perverted predilection for standing in the middle of the road and gazing triumphantly at the rapidly approaching vehicle, which, of course, must freeze to a dead stop under the cow's basilisk-like stare. As a rule there is a cow-hand about, watching the scene with malicious pleasure, and without lifting a finger. In the course of my trip I tried out a whole range of dodges designed to drive a herd of cows off the road. My first experiment turned out rather expensive. I simply drove, ever so gently, into the hind-legs of one of the animals placidly walking in front of my car. But instead of making off at a trot it calmly sat down on the bonnet. The result was a huge dent and a crushed headlamp. Evidently this was the wrong method. A more elegant method is the indirect one—you creep up slowly alongside the cow and then accelerate ; the part of its belly which projects sideways thus gets a gentle shove, and if you are lucky you can see in your driving-mirror the beast kicking its legs in the air like a bonny baby. But this method, too, is not entirely free from risk. Because the cow may suddenly turn her head—" Hullo, who's tickling my belly ? "—and then its horn will go straight through your side-window. The only in-fallible method is patience. For a country which lives in an atmosphere of timelessness the speed of a motor vehicle is too fast, anyway.

Metalled roads ! Yes, a narrow central strip is metalled all right, but on either side of it is just a dirt-track with stones and pot-holes. And into that narrow, smooth strip in the middle everything is crowded : men, beasts, and vehicles. To begin with there are ox-carts. They are the delight of the artistically minded : with two wheels as tall as a man, and often of solid wood, they look as if they had only just been invented. A placid pair of zebus bend their necks under the yoke : their picturesque humps lend them an appearance of being predestined for their humble rôle, and their horns are spread out wide like arms opened in welcome. Comfortably they move along, in the middle of the road, as if on principle. They know their way, and if the weather is fine their driver will as a rule close his eyes for forty winks. Sounding your horn will not wake him up—at least, not for a long time. Then suddenly you will see a figure sitting up straight, and you can then start guessing : right or left ? If his short stick prods the ox on the right, the cart should be moving to the left ; if he prods the left ox it should move to the right. The rule of the road means nothing to the Indian peasant. A special treat is reserved for the motorist who catches up with a whole column of these carts. His honking will drive the nearest one off to the left, the next one to the right, while the third will probably go on hugging the middle of the road. It's no good losing your temper. Better save your curses for the moment when you find yourself behind such a cart on one of the narrow bridges built by the British many years ago. For miles you drive at walking pace, over some gigantic river-bed, with overtaking strictly prohibited. It is then that you realize, if you have not done so before, that the pace in India is determined by the ox-cart. And if you are wise you will adopt a cow-like mentality. You will find it useful also in your dealings with other animals of similar temperament. With the dogs, for example, which choose the middle of the sun-warmed road for their siesta just as if they were safely curled up in the corner of a settee. They are veritable suicides, those dogs. Lazily they open their eyes, almost inviting you : " Go on, run me over if you dare!" But who can dare? True, the dogs are not sacred, but only mangy, and strictly speaking you would be doing the poor animal a good turn by putting it out of its misery. But a dozen people would instantly appear from nowhere, declaring the miserable animal to have been their comfort in old age, the treasure of their family and of their country—and presently you would find them extorting from you a fabulous payment in compensation. I speak from experience : my bag after several months of motoring in India totalled two dogs, one small goat, one chicken, and one cyclist.

The cyclists are no less numerous than the cows, and, though belonging to the species of *homo sapiens*, they act even more stupidly. In India everything is overpopulated—including the bicycles. Almost invariably some friend is given a lift on the handlebars, and the lady on the carrier behind the saddle frequently has an infant strapped to her back. Thus no fewer than four immortal souls will wobble along a picturesquely undulating course in front of your approaching vehicle. More often than not there are two bicycles abreast (making eight immortal souls) ; instead of pulling in to the edge of the road in single file, as prescribed by the traffic regulations, they will fan out to both sides, leaving you the crown of the road. And as you nip cautiously through between Scylla and Charybdis, between murder on your right and murder on your left, you will make a surprising discovery. One would expect the Indians, those children of nature, to take to a bicycle with the skill and litheness of monkeys. Far from it ! These skinny fellows, even when not carrying a load, behave as if they had never ridden a bicycle before : their front wheel wobbles nervously, as though shaking with fever, and you can never be sure they will not suddenly . . .

Anyway, the cyclist I bagged—this happened much later, near Trivandrum—was alone. Which was just as well. He was cheerfully approaching me in the middle of the road, and must have been gazing inward, into his mystic soul, for he swung right across my path. Idiot ! I cursed, and jerked the car to the right. At the same moment he evidently realized his mistake, and likewise threw himself to the side. The bicycle was a twisted piece of metal : on the verge lay the young man, like Adonis felled by the wild sow. People immediately collected. I got out of the car, got him into the back seat, and off I drove to the nearest hospital. And then to the police-station, expecting the worst. In countries where motor vehicles are a rarity there is always a tendency to blame the motorist for every accident. If it were not for motor-cars people would not be run down : to be a motorist is a kind of original sin. Even if your victim threw himself in front of your wheels. That is why, as a rule, every traffic accident in Calcutta ends with the motorist being beaten up by the crowd and his car being set on fire, no matter whether he is guilty or not.

But I was lucky. For one thing, the policeman on duty spoke English, and for another a white sahib, or ' master,' still enjoys in India a degree of respect that is only rarely, as in other former colonial territories, mingled with hatred. My policeman was clearly so pleased to be able to talk at length to a sahib that I felt enveloped by a wave of good will. He certainly was a very easy-going guardian of the law. " We'd better drive out to the spot at once," I urged. But he dismissed the idea. " Let's have a cup of tea first." After that he calmly typed out my statement. " To-morrow morning will do," he replied to my renewed suggestion. After considerable pressure, at last I got him into my car and we drove off. The skid-marks were hardly visible by then. I was firmly convinced that any witnesses would as a matter of course take the side of their friend and give evidence against the stranger—if only because he was far more able to pay compensation. But not the people of Kerala. I found myself exonerated, and since the cyclist was reported by the hospital to have fully recovered I was allowed to move on shortly before midnight.

But I am anticipating. For we are still at the very beginning of my journey, and a great many wonderful experiences still lie ahead. Such as a drive through the old part of an Indian town.

That is a treat not to be missed on any account. You feel afterwards as if you had passed an advanced test in obstacle racing.

A slow-moving viscous mass flows through the streets, a kind of indefinable thick soup of vehicles : the ever-present ox-carts, the two-wheeled horse-drawn tongas, droves of cyclists and tinkling rickshaws. Everybody advances as best he can : left or right, it makes no difference ; a little shove here, a little bump there, what does one more dent matter ? An orgy of rattling, honking, bell-ringing, and shouting. For minutes on end man, beasts, and machines are completely interlocked—until a policeman, his arms raised in despair, appears on the scene, or until the jam sorts itself out by itself. Nobody minds : everybody has time. You never see a fellow-motorist tapping his forehead with his finger : every one is mad in India, anyway. In Germany, that country of dashing drivers, the town would look like a dump of scrapped vehicles in a day. But not, surprisingly, in India. I have seen there countless motor-cars which had broken down mechanically. But no crashes, in spite of the chaotic traffic. The reason ? Quite simply : the Indians drive carefully—unlike the suicidal Arabs or, even worse, the Japanese. I don't know if this is due to a sense of courtesy—either inborn or bred by the British—or merely to phlegm.

One point in support of the phlegm theory is the fact that all courtesy is suspended at night. It hardly ever occurs to a motorist to dip his headlights. For seconds the blinding lights torture your eyes, and the road ahead seems pitch-black. If a cyclist or a pedestrian were to step out just then—and that sort of thing is happening in India all the time—well, that would be curtains for him. Is this bad habit due simply to laziness ? Or to immaturity ? To an inability to put oneself in the position of another ? There are moments when a traveller begins to doubt the intelligence of the Indians.

Or at least their technical intelligence. After my rough journey through Afghanistan the oil seal of my left rear wheel had begun to leak. The easiest repair in the world. At the first

Indian garage I had the wheel repacked. But the leak was still there, and I was losing quantities of oil. Throughout my journey that seal was replaced about a dozen times, but the lubricant continued to ooze out. Near Calcutta one day my wheel suddenly parted company with the car and gaily streaked past me while I slithered along on three wheels before managing to pull up. Some genius of a mechanic had stripped the thread during the last repair. Motorists in India are never short of conversational topics : the misdeeds of Indian garage-hands would make a heroic epic. You can be sure that every repair leaves behind even greater damage. India is a land full of miracles, but to me the greatest miracle of all is the fact that motor vehicles run there at all. But then can one expect a nation which psychologically is still living in the age of the ox-cart to grasp the intricacies of a modern motor-car ? They may learn, parrot-like, to perform a few operations—but can they live with an engine and, as it were, feel its pulse ? Of all the Asians, only the Japanese have reached that stage.

Strictly speaking, a glossy piece of chrome and steel like a motor-car does not really fit into the Indian atmosphere. I am almost tempted to say that travelling by train is more ' in style.' Somehow the railway has become acclimatized. It is slow and ponderous. Whenever it runs across the wintry, arid landscape its drag raises up the dust, which wafts in through the window and presently covers faces and clothes, and settles in every crack. I can still see before me the Indian railway-stations which, like great magnets, draw the crowds from the towns : hundreds and thousands of brown figures in white shirts, with turbans, and in saris. I can see the coolies pouncing on me like a pack of hungry wolves the moment my taxi pulls up outside. Wearing red shirts and red turbans, they look like little devils, each with a numbered brass plate strapped to his arm. You want to hang on to your brief-case ? Impossible. No self-respecting sahib, or for that matter Indian, carries anything in his hand. Physical effort is unworthy of a man of position. Besides, the coolies are so cheap : two annas—about twopence—per load. And

I.—2

for all their emaciated appearance, they are a strong lot : they pile two or three cases on their head, without effort, and thus, like mobile turrets, they push their way through a sea of turbans.

The scene inside the station is like a seventeenth-century army camp. Piles of bundles ; cases bursting open, and only just prevented from spilling by bits of string ; metal trunks with padlocks ; clusters of live chickens ; bundles of sugar-cane ; huge melons stacked against the steel pillars. And spread out on the floor, around these possessions, whole families, from grandfather and grandmother down to the youngest infants. They have dossed down on the floor, pulled their loose garments over their heads, and gone to sleep. Have you ever seen people sleeping in the street ? Maybe in Naples—but that is a different kind of sleep. The *lazzarone* loves the sun and flourishes under it : his *dolce far niente* is the consummation of his existence. But the Indian sleepers have always seemed to me like exhausted troops, like soldiers utterly spent after a forced march, like men who are too tired to want anything except sleep. So skeleton-like are the legs sticking out from their rags, and so fragile are the bodies, that one is surprised to see them breathing. Others are dozing patiently, crouching on their heels, their soles flat on the ground. You try to do it ! It is not easy at all. Our Western bodies seem to have lost the deeper secrets of relaxed comfort, away from our instrument-made ease which begins not only with machinery but with the chair. I remember an English doctor in India who had a theory that the incidence of rheumatism and other joint troubles among our elderly people is due to our insufficient relationship to the ground as the zero-point of our system of co-ordinates.

These people wait as if they belonged to the place. When their train comes in, and their waiting is over, others move into their place. The people are temporary, but the waiting is permanent. Then there is the occasional sleeper who is not a traveller : dozing on the floor, without ticket and without money, his clothes in tatters, his most intimate parts exposed. Nobody jogs him. No policeman arrests him for indecent exposure or causing public annoyance. For, in point of fact, no one is annoyed. Not even if somebody, deciding that the lavatory is too far away, does his business in a corner. 'A call of nature' is what they call it : in India it comes into the same category as a sunset.

An Indian train is a kind of microcosm : a mirror of society. Our democratic Europe now only recognizes two classes, but on the other hand divides the smokers from those with clean lungs. This kind of trivial distinction is not made in India ; but instead there is a choice of four classes. Third class, needless to say, is out of the question for a sahib. For every stop means the influx of a further avalanche of human beings, coolies treading on each other's toes, and children climbing on passengers' laps. There is no defence, since your legs are wedged firmly, as though in a vice, between a mass of sacks and baskets. A sahib is expected to travel by luxury coach, with air conditioning, even though the nights are still cool—simply as a gesture of distinction. Personally I preferred going first class, if only because I was not keen on the company of snobs. In the first you meet the kind of people a traveller likes to talk to : professors, businessmen, engineers, senior civil servants. The compartments have an area of about 75 square feet, with three well-sprung seats allowing you to lounge in comfort. At night three more bunks are let down from the ceiling, secured with powerful chains, so that even the fat Sikh whose crash I had expected throughout the night succeeded in lowering himself and his massive body safely to the ground in the morning.

The barred windows provide a sense of security rather than of imprisonment : they are an indispensable protection against the noisy, bustling, demanding world outside. For the night is full of the arms of thieves ready to reach in through an open window and to lift the possessions of the unsuspecting sleeper. When life still bears the characteristics of a struggle you feel safe only inside a fortress. You fling your bedding on your bunk—for everybody in India carries his own sleeping-quarters like a snail—unroll your canvas bundle, and climb into your sheets and woollen blankets, which are all ready to receive you. And in the morning the whole equipment is just as easily packed up again.   Night travel is not only convenient, since long and dreary stretches of country which would take up a whole day's motoring are covered while you are blissfully slumbering, but it also engenders among the six sleeping companions a sense of common fate and an intimacy which is usually continued during the day in enjoyable conversation.   Occasionally it provides some mysterious experiences : one night, waking up at 3 A.M., I was startled to see, in the light of the full moon, an old man on the bunk opposite mine sitting in the lotus position in deep meditation, his eyes shut, his body rigid and motionless, as if all life had left it.

There is one item that I would advise any traveller to India to leave behind—his stomach.   Perhaps the fact that the Indians cannot cook is connected with their famous spirituality : certainly I was painfully reminded at every meal of the transience of all earthly pleasures, especially those of the palate.   There are many instances in colonial history when overlords and subject races have discovered certain spheres of kinship.   Thus the death cult of the Aztecs was somehow akin to the Spaniards' tragic outlook on life. In Indo-China Chinese refinement became so completely fused with that of the French that they can hardly be separated to-day.   Similarly, the puritanism of the British was ideally suited to India : it has protected the individual against the arbitrary despotism of politicians, generals, and policemen, but has handed him over to the tortures of the cooks. That is why, on balance, I prefer the French colonial system to the British, in spite of the political superiority of the latter. After all, a man does not suffer wrongful imprisonment more than once or twice in his lifetime, but he has got to eat three times a day.

The traveller in India cannot escape this culinary sadism, since with very few exceptions the price of an hotel room includes the main meals.   And the menu—God help us—is the same parody of an English menu from the Himalayas to Travancore. First a watery soup which tastes of nothing at all, followed by filleted fish, baked in a batter, as hard and dry as a rusk. The next course is chicken. To this day my stomach heaves when I hear the word ' chicken.' In India it is roasted and roasted until it has lost all definable taste, and it is served with a thin, much too salty, gravy. Finally there is a red jelly, tasting like toothpaste. There may be slight variations from one hotel to another and from one day to the next, but basically the sahib's food remains, unspeakably, the same. I don't know if it is merely the fault of the cooks : the European food was no better in luxury hotels, even when I ordered *à la carte*. Not for nothing is India the continent of ascetics.

On my travels, all over the world, I have always been passionately fond of the local cuisine. In a Turkish or Persian dump you may not find a clean spot to rest your weary head— but the kebab that is roasted for you on an open fire is delicious. Not to mention the wonders of Chinese cooking ! But in India you get curry, and again curry. Curried chicken for lunch, curried mutton or curried fish for supper. It all tastes the same ; it burns your mouth till your eyes water—and when all this magnificence reaches the end of its journey through your digestive system it still burns like brimstone. From sheer despair I eventually decided to go in for vegetarian dishes, which are not normally offered to a sahib at all. And lo and behold : they were excellent ! A delicious rice cake, for instance, baked deep brown, and filled with potatoes and vegetables. Or a tray with countless little dishes, each containing something different, enabling you to compose from them a veritable symphony of flavours. First a few lentils, then some vegetables, ground coconut, a red pepper, a little sour milk, all taken with chapati, the flat wheaten bread of India. I even believed that my vegetarian diet made me feel better physically : who knows whether the all-merciful idea that no living thing must be killed for food has not its origin in some secret purpose which makes the spirit willing and the flesh unpalatable ? Strict brahmins even avoid eggs, which, though not living things, nevertheless contain the germ of life.

It is the same in India as anywhere else in the tropics. The resident Europeans paint a terrifying picture of the dangers threatening unaccustomed stomachs, and at first you regard every mouthful as if it were poison, and every glass of water as if it were a cup of hemlock. Unless you rid yourself of this anxiety neurosis you are apt to end up like that diplomat who, upon returning to Switzerland, berated the hotel chambermaid for omitting to place into his bathroom a carafe of filtered water for cleaning his teeth. I very soon adopted the healthy fatalism of an old British colonel who recommended carelessness as the best form of natural immunization. Given its daily dose of microbes and parasites, the body immunizes itself in the end. Not only did I drink tap-water, but I even became an addict of pan, which is sold in India at every street corner like cigarettes back home.

Pan ! This Indian word has nothing to do with the frightening goat-like god of the Greeks. Fresh green leaves are stacked up on the stalls of the vendors, next to a selection of brown sauces which he carefully spreads on the green leaves with a spatula. A quantity of betel-nut is heaped on top and the whole thing rolled up into a package of convenient size for chewing. Now go ahead and chew ! But no grimacing, please ! Again, it is like all things Indian : at first you think it barbarous, hot, and revolting—like biting into laurel-leaves. Saliva pours into your mouth as though from a hydrant ; unless you swallow it at once a brown rivulet will trickle down your chin, and the dark-skinned fellows who are watching you curiously will split their sides with laughter. But presently you find the thing tastes very nice, and it becomes a necessity like tobacco—with the pleasant difference that it is not harmful but even conducive to the digestion. Before long you become quite expert at spitting the brown juice on to the pavement like the natives. Wherever you go in India the streets are spattered with these brown stains, just as though some monstrous carnage had taken place there.

But who knows ? A Persian poet, singing of the pan-tree, says that lovers have nurtured its leaves with their blood.

Hygiene is the enemy of the poetry of life. That is why I love old-fashioned Indian hotels. Naturally, technical progress has here too produced those modern multi-storeyed blocks where every guest, totally cut off from Nature, occupies his own numbered prison cell. But the old-type Indian hotel spreads itself out on ground-level. After all, there is plenty of land which costs nothing : hence the bungalows stretch out comfortably across the park, whose trees rustle through your open door. The servant's cat climbs over your furniture and makes friends with the guest. If you leave your breakfast unattended for a moment the ubiquitous ravens fly in through your open window and make off with your rolls. To become one with everything—that is India's religious principle. And that, no doubt, includes going shares with your brothers the ravens, and the dogs, and the buzzards which suddenly pounce from the sky to snatch the slice of chicken-breast from your plate. Everything here is hungry—man and beast—and all are mortal rivals, and at the same time companions sharing the same fate.

Even the hotel servants. Admittedly, they look anything but poor. They wear smart turbans with impressive starched tips at the ends, and they are dressed as if they were the personal body-guard of some maharaja. They populate the hotel in countless numbers, just as the ravens do the park. They circle around you, watching you, as polite relations will attend a rich uncle. The difference being that rich uncles are not really necessary, whereas servants in India are indispensable. The room servant, for instance, will touch neither your dusty shoes nor your soiled shirt. His caste—we shall discuss this strange institution presently—prohibits it, and you could kill him sooner than expect him to commit such self-abasement. That's what the boot wallah and the dhobi are there for—most contemptible creatures, handling what is unclean. They are all guilty of high treason, every one of these servants : they desire nothing more ardently than the return of the good old British sahibs. For their

stingy Indian masters to-day give them a great many more kicks
in the pants than Colonel Blimp would have ever dared to do.
But a sahib here has not only rights but also duties. A ' master,'
of course, is always rich—and therefore generosity is expected,
even demanded, from him. In other countries fraud is simply
fraud, the confidence trick of the rascal trying to part his victim
from his money. In India it is always accompanied by flattering
respect : as a sahib you are overcharged, and a superior being
does not, of course, haggle with a coolie or a driver over a few
annas. The gesture of those fellows is always the same : a
glance at the opened palm into which you have placed your
coins, followed by a glance at the giver, full of profound, pained
disappointment. " What ? " says the glance reproachfully, " Is
that all ? Is it possible that a master should be guilty of such
unworthy stinginess ? " Nothing is gained by making the gift
generous in the first place : the more open-handed you are the
richer you are bound to be, and the more suitable an object for
extortion. It is genuinely difficult to act humanely *vis-à-vis*
these rascals, since their insatiability—due, of course, to the
prevailing conditions—is ever ready to represent favour as a
right, and to demand instead of thanking. Not until the morning
of your departure do you realize to how many loyal souls you
have been near and dear. The room servant expects the lion's
share of your tip ; next, just outside your door, comes the head
waiter, followed by the boy who served your food at table.
Behind them three miserable creatures without uniform are
kotowing. One of them, it is explained to you, is the water-
bearer who had poured hot water into your tub every morning—
I am, of course, talking of a nice old-fashioned hotel. The next
man is known as the ' sweeper '—a somewhat euphemistic
description, since his duty every morning has been to creep into
your bathroom by a back door to remove the chamber-pots.
He only gets a few ridiculous annas, just like the third beggar,
also a lowly creature, who acts as the night watchman. When
all your change has at last disappeared, like corn gobbled up by
greedy hens, a last person suddenly hurries up and with a smile

presses a little flower into your hand : the gardener too wants his baksheesh.

Well, here's another piece of advice to the traveller : don't let it upset you ! In a European hotel they put a 15 or 20 per cent. service charge on your bill, and you pay up without demurring. And what about the delightful sense of being a sahib, a munificent patriarchal benefactor accepting the homage of his subjects ? In all conscience, who can say that he does not enjoy that flattery ?

CHAPTER TWO

Refuse-bins for the Living—
Fairy-tale Palaces for the Dead

THIS IS WHAT EUROPE MUST HAVE LOOKED like in the nineteenth century, at the beginning of the Industrial Revolution. Here in India it is not the town but the village that bears the typical features—the village with its pond where buffaloes cool their hot bodies, with its clay walls where lumps of cow-dung are dried to be used for briquettes, and with its artesian wells from which the women draw their jugs of water. A peaceful, soothing, and not too comfortable idyll.

The Indian metropolis has not yet any features of its own. But the small provincial capitals which crowd round the palace of a maharaja—they certainly have character. And the most beautiful of them cling to the hills and lakes of Rajputana, the wild and romantic region between Delhi and the Arabian Sea. As in early nineteenth-century Germany, princes and princelings used to reside here in their fairy-tale palaces, and the narrow little streets radiating from the palace gates were loud with the hammering of dozens of silversmiths and cobblers, with the rattle of looms, with the ring of coins of money-changers and usurers, and with the pounding of mortars in which apothecaries mixed their essences. From the ruler down to the artisan, everybody was part of one great family ; the small town was one great house. That is why Jaipur, the capital of what is to-day Rajasthan, still presents itself like a jewel. It is all of one mould— it was built from scratch in the seventeenth century, when the maharaja moved from his near-by mountain stronghold of Amber down into the more comfortable plain. A delightful pattern of white ornament, representing niches, pilasters, cornices, and consoles, cover the warm red of its walls, so that the houses look like plush sofas with crocheted lace antimacassars. The Indian everyday scene is, on the whole, far less colourful than our imagination pictures it. Only in Rajasthan are the saris of the women and the turbans of the men bright with gold and crimson. In the street are piles of marigold blossoms, oranges, pome-granates, and red peppers. There is colour everywhere, as though for a feast.

If the small towns resemble jewel-boxes the big ones resemble refuse-bins—grey, heavy, and tinny. Bombay or Calcutta—I can see before me the huge tenement blocks in overcrowded streets, façades of rusty railings, behind which stuffy darkness overspills from the rooms. Cartons, packing-cases with wood-shavings, suitcases, pots and pans, threadbare washing hanging on lines along the balconies, human bodies—everywhere life and decay, one within the other, the deposits of chance, jetsam washed up from the breeding-places of the villages, a crowded unorganic community of men without women. "The far too many"—it is difficult not to be reminded of Nietzsche's concept when faced with these human grains of sand in this urban desert. They stand around all day long. One squeezes oranges and pours out the ice-cooled juice for thirsty passers-by. Another may sell cheap fountain-pens. Yet another steals expensive ones. Within a week I twice caught a pickpocket who, as though stumbling, fell against my chest in order to snatch my ball-pen. Once caught they did not even try to struggle free, but stood apatheti-cally like tethered sheep. Even for roguery they lack vitality. Women and children, begging, will not be driven away by any amount of angry gestures or shouting. Persistently they will follow you with extended hands, without hope, without dignity, for mile after mile. Just like the rickshaw boys with their tall-wheeled vehicles who, for the sake of a few annas, puff out their lungs. "Nice girl, sahib," they whisper behind your ear. "Chinese girl, European girl—as you like."

Delhi, the capital of India, is something in between a jewel-box and a refuse-bin. It makes a tremendous effort to look Indian, but even Gandhi chided it with the fruitlessness of its attempt. Certainly there is nothing Indian about New Delhi, built by the British in the thirties. Connaught Circus, where dealers in clothes, jewellery, suitcases, and books hang about among classical columns, might, but for its human fauna, be in London. In the Government district the British architects combined domes and colonnades with the exotic elements of the Mogul style, and arranged the whole in gigantic vistas—a monument to a power which had come to be a little uncertain of itself, and required massive æsthetic reassurance.

In Old Delhi, too, there is nothing that is not much more beautiful in Agra, the rival capital of the Moguls. The Red Forts of Lahore and Delhi have suffered so much in an eventful history that they are but sad shadows of their former glory. What captivates the sightseer in Delhi is not so much that which has survived as the traces of tragic decay, where greatness has gone with the wind like the mouldering dust, and where the monuments of power—only seemingly everlasting—have passed away with it.

It almost seems as though there is something in the curse which is reputed to lie on Delhi—that the empire of every one is doomed who builds a new capital in this spot. It is fundamentally nothing but a huge necropolis, set up as a capital in countless ever-new shapes by foreign rulers, and razed to the ground again and again by the storm of new invasions. A drive out of the city along one of the roads offers a spectacle compared with which the Roman Via Appia seems reduced to village dimensions. Tomb follows tomb in massive tall cubes : tombs of kings, tombs of their servants, Persian, Afghan, Turkish—wherever the different rulers came from. The cities over which they once ruled have disappeared, or else survive only in outline, with walls overgrown by shrubs and with shattered gateways. One of these is Tughlakabad, created by the Mameluk ruler Tughlak in the thirteenth century. A capital of four miles in circumference, with a tall citadel and proud palaces, piled up within two years, like a temporary halting-place, without foundations,

of huge hewn blocks on rocky ground. Like men in fever
tossing on their beds, the great ones of this world looked around
for new centres of dominion, hastily ran up cities, and just as
hastily left them again. Muhammad, Tughlak's son, packed up
all that could be moved, and left for the South, to set up a new
capital in the Deccan. But, as well as a curse, there must have
been some magic in Delhi, which drew back those foreign
invaders from wherever they had moved their capitals. Perhaps
it was the secret of its situation : in the centre of the North
Indian plain, yet near enough the mountains beyond the Khyber
not to let the strangers wholly forget their origins. Even
Muhammad was to find his grave by the side of his father, placed
outside the walls of Tughlakabad like an outer bastion, a castle-
like resting-place without sadness, with crenellations and defences,
almost as though even the dead were ready to awaken at the
clash of arms and to hurry from their tombs to the battlements.

  Even Akbar, the first great Mogul Emperor—perhaps the
greatest of them all—had a share of this feverish restlessness.
Agra the magnificent was no longer enough for him. Twenty
miles away on a hill he built a new capital—Fatehpur Sikri—and
abandoned it again a few years later because there was no water,
and because the poisonous exhalations of the near-by swamps
spread epidemics among the palaces. It was a mistaken investment, the grandest in history. Contempt for worldly transience
can take two different forms : it may either renounce all ostentation and choose the life of the ascetic, or it may, regardless of
expense, build gigantic monuments without worrying overmuch
about the economic side of the enterprise. If it turns out to be
a failure, as in the case of Fatehpur Sikri—what more has been
lost than something transient ? Thus the glitter of Indian
palaces is more akin to the renunciation of the saint than would
seem at first sight : munificence as an active form of asceticism.
But we to-day can only be grateful for this mistaken speculation
of Akbar's which has left us a pure work of art, undefiled by
later use. How many secrets are revealed by its walls ! In the
bedchamber of the emperor the beams are as low as if the cares

of a whole empire had weighed them down. But close at hand
is the place of love : in the empress's bedchamber the artist's
chisel has coaxed from the stone plant and animal, blossom and
flowers. According to legend, Akbar chose the site of Fatehpur
Sikri in order to make his childless marriage fruitful by the
proximity to a saint. To this day childless women make
pilgrimages to the tomb of the saint in the forecourt of the great
mosque, and tie coloured ribbons to the traceried marble door-
ways as lasting tokens of their prayers. How different is the
origin of the Taj Mahal at Agra ! That famous mausoleum was
built by Shah Jahan, the grandson of Akbar, for his wife who
died in childbed while still young. Of her fifteenth confinement !
Behind the fairy-tale glamour lies the reality of a much-loved,
much-used, and much-abused wife.

I approached the Taj Mahal with some trepidation. Would I
be disappointed ? Would reality measure up to that dreamlike
poetry which imperfect pictures had nourished in our imagination
ever since childhood ?   At last I was standing before the tall
gateway topped by a row of delicate pavilions. I stepped into
its half-light, and immediately felt drawn by a radiant whiteness
ahead, which, as I penetrated farther, took on the shape of domes
and turrets and, upon passing through the second archway,
gleamed in front of me against a blue sky.

It is said that the Taj Mahal reveals its entire beauty only in
the full moon. Thus at every full moon there is a veritable
pilgrimage of sightseers to Agra. And that is a mistake. True
enough, the gleam of marble when the moonlight falls on the
façade may have its own magic. But the essential and deepest
experience of the Taj is one of colour, and therefore denied in
moonlight. The gateway and outer walls are built of that warm,
blood-red sandstone with which the Mogul emperors surrounded
their castles. It speaks of battle and power, of pride and heroism,
and the same spirit is conveyed by the green of the great old
trees around its battlements, by the lawns and flower-beds—
delight in earthy vitality. Let the eye drink its fill ! And then
suddenly the distant shimmering white against the blue sky comes

to you like a greeting from another world. In no other architectural monument has the transcendental become matter in such a miraculous manner as here. Right in the middle of turbulent life we are touched by the strange, delicate, and alluring magic of pure spirituality. Let us not forget it : this is a mausoleum.

And now begins a confusing pilgrimage. The transcendental is not unapproachably remote, not unattainable. As we approach, the mirrored image in a long strip of water grows to meet us, almost close enough to touch. We get closer, but—as with the child snatching for the sunbeam—the image withdraws itself. We pursue it, and the nearer we get the shorter is the magic carpet before our feet, the more persistently is the white mirage receding. At last it has disappeared, and the flight of steps, as though with a secret smile at having successfully lured us on, invites us to ascend. We leave our shoes in the care of a boy, and ascend the steps into the sacred place which now no longer tantalizes us as a distant mirage but receives us in its midst as something we have reached and achieved.

Why is it that, from Rome and Jerusalem to India, the most exalted places are desecrated by the most barefaced and shabby commercialism ? Doubly entombed, Shah Jahan rests by the side of his consort. On the upper floor, the marble ostentation of a flower-bed inlaid with precious stones covers symbolic nothingness ; below, in a dark crypt, the real bodies rest in modest sarcophagi. Both spots are guarded by a pair of gallant Moslems who leave nothing untried in order to extract some small coin from the visitor. First of all a flower is pressed into your hand so that you should place it on the imperial tomb—and one would only too willingly perform this duty with reverence and piety if one did not know that the same flower had already passed through dozens of hands, and had time and again been stolen from the patient marble. The second guardian of the tomb demonstrates to the visitor the remarkable acoustics of the cupola. At definite intervals he utters a shriek as if some one had plunged a dagger into his heart ; the note hangs trembling and echoing in the air, as though looking for a way out and failing to find it. This shriek mingles with the laughter of children, with the bright ring of girls' voices, and the darker notes of their fathers, producing a roar that crashes ceaselessly against the marble walls. Even when you have made good your escape into the sunlit greenness of the lawns and the deep red of the gateways this confused sound of human voices still comes over to you like the cries of the damned in hell.

One can only understand the sense of vitality expressed in the Taj Mahal if one compares it with Akbar's mausoleum at Sikandra. And yet power has already grown obese by ostentation. The eagles have been refined into peacocks : a ruler's aim is no longer to rule, but to please. It is a huge, massive structure, growing from its foundations in five floors of slender columns and pavilions. At first I did not understand the meaning of this piling-up, and curiously ascended the narrow little staircases until suddenly, beneath an open sky, a small courtyard opened before me with the emperor's sarcophagus at its centre. Again, as in the Taj Mahal, this is not the real sarcophagus ; that is reached only by a narrow little passage six floors farther down in the darkness of the earth. Now suddenly I understood the meaning of this gigantic structure : all that is earthly lies below the earth, but that which endures is turned towards the sky, the sun, and the winds. What more beautiful monument could there be to the universality of a great emperor ?

But at least Akbar lies alone. The tomb of his wife or wives is anonymous. Jehangir also buried his romantic mistress several miles away from his own mausoleum. But Shan Jahan already is more of a lover than a ruler : he rests united with his consort, and the mausoleum is hers, not his. Here we feel a softer form of life than Akbar knew, one which overlaid reality with the more refined pleasures of longing. In the evening before my departure I drove out once more to the Taj Mahal. The gathering dusk had extinguished the red and the green hues. But the dome floated high up under the departing sunlight, fragile against the pale silk of the sky, veined by the joints of the stone blocks, like the breast of a delicate woman.

CHAPTER THREE

Chandigarh : a Questionable Work of Art

*T*HIS GENTLEMAN YOU'RE VISITING—HOW MUCH does he earn?" the taxi-driver asked. For on arriving at Chandigarh, the new capital of the Punjab, I had discovered that the address in my notebook was incomplete. "He is a secretary," I said. "Then he'll be living in Sector 16, Block B," the Sikh answered knowledgeably. "Are you sure?" I asked in surprise. "Quite sure," he answered. "This is a damned logical city. All cooked up by crazy architects behind drawing-boards. 'Birds of a feather flock together,' these gentlemen told themselves. Or maybe it was the baboos. You know what a baboo is? That's what we call our senior civil servants who walk about with their noses in the air, and who look down on us ordinary mortals. These exclusive baboos thought it was a wonderful idea to live untouched and unseen by the common herd, among their own kind. Baboos to their right, baboos to their left, baboos opposite. So they divided the town into sectors, and each sector into blocks, and allocated each block or sector to people who earn the same salary, do the same work, have the same hopes and desires and the same worries. The Ministers all live together, side by side along one of the streets. Then there is the district of the judges. Their houses, compared with those of the Ministers, look almost grimly sober. And so on, all the way down through the official hierarchy. Over there, for instance, that group of plain bungalows is for the lowest category—the peons, who sit outside the offices ready to take in a cup of tea whenever a thirsty baboo rings the bell. As you know, our new Constitution has abolished castes. Indeed,

anyone driving an untouchable from his house is committing a
punishable offence. But the caste spirit has arisen in a new form.
Our baboos are the new brahmins."

The reason why the Punjab—the North-western Frontier
province—needed a new capital was, of course, the unfortunate
division of the sub-continent into India and Pakistan. Since
Lahore, the old capital, went to Pakistan that part of the state of
Lahore which remained with India needed a new centre—a
completely new town built on virgin soil, a city which, like the
great cities founded by the Mogul emperors, would testify to
the greatness of the country, to its universal spirit, and to its
splendid sense of progress. Le Corbusier was invited to act as
chief architect, and he was joined by other well-known architects,
including his cousin Pierre Jeanneret, the English architect couple
E. Maxwell Fry and his wife, and, of course, a vast team of
Indian assistants.

Architects in the past usually planned their cities from a
nucleus, such as a castle or a cathedral, around which the other
public buildings were grouped, surrounded in turn by a gradually
ending sea of ordinary houses. Nonsense, said Le Corbusier. A
city is like a body—with a head, shoulders, a trunk, arms and
legs. Chandigarh's head must be the Government buildings—
Parliament, the administrative blocks and the High Court. In
the shoulders are the homes of Ministers and judges ; farther
down in the trunk are the Town Hall and the Police-station ;
and industry and trade eventually are accommodated in the legs
right down to the toes. As for the various secondary schools,
hospitals, hotels, theatres, museums, libraries, railway and bus
stations, and so on, each of the 30 sectors will get their share.
The whole thing is criss-crossed by a network of streets, some of
them serving fast through-traffic, others slow local traffic, some
of them reserved for motor vehicles and others for ox-carts and
bicycles.

A glance at the town plan reveals the checkerboard arrange-
ment of the newly laid-out districts. Those who like living in a
street with an elegant name are disappointed in Chandigarh :

there are only numbers and letters, no more. For example :
Sector 13, Block B, D Street.

And if you happen to forget this code you just go on straying
about for evermore. To make matters worse, the Indians have
not so far set up any block or street name-plates, so that if you
ask the way every person you ask gives you a different answer.
As it happened, my friend did not live in the spot the taxi-driver
took me to. When I found him in the end—almost by a miracle
—he was greatly amused. " During my first few weeks here,"
he told me, " it frequently happened that I couldn't find my way
back home."

Anyone who likes modern architecture will be lost in perpetual
admiration over this ' city as a work of art.' But those who live
there do not find everything quite so admirable. Works of art
have a way of being rather impractical. The High Court, the
first of Le Corbusier's buildings to be completed and handed over
to its purpose, impresses the viewer by its tall monumental
gateway and the huge roof resting on vast arches. It had been
the architect's idea that this roof should trap the winds coming
down from the Himalayas, so that they would cool the building.
But the construction cost such vast sums of money, and the
estimate was so greatly exceeded, that the tax-payers were in an
uproar. Besides, in his anxiety to use the beautiful roof to
provide coolness, the architect had forgotten to screen the
building against the afternoon sun, which presently beat down
with splendid impartiality on judge, counsel, plaintiff, and
defendant, giving them a foretaste of hell. Whereupon they set
up such an infernal howl that an additional canopy had to be
built in a hurry—and this, of course, does not exactly promote
the æsthetic effect of the building as a whole.

Nor are the inhabitants of the residential blocks too happy
about the architect's ideas. The climate of Northern India is
cool in the winter—sometimes even cold—and terribly hot in
the summer, with temperatures rising to over 100 degrees in the
shade. For that reason traditional houses have a wide, open
roof terrace, to which every light breeze has free access. The

new architects—heaven knows why—decided to surround these
flat roofs with openwork walls, which do not stop the cold winds
in winter, but keep away any summer breezes. I visited a number
of buildings which seemed to me particularly beautiful, but
which their occupiers described as perfect examples of un-
thinking architecture. " The rain comes in from all sides," a
deputy departmental head who lived there explained to me.
" There is no way into my walled garden from outside, which
means that every day I have to wheel my bicycle right through
my living-room. The lavatory is on the first floor, and reached
only by an open staircase on the outside of the house. Whenever
my wife or daughter nip up there in their nighties they present
a fine spectacle to the passers-by in the street—and you know
how jealously women are screened from male glances in this
country." But there is an even weightier argument against
Chandigarh—an argument on the lips of everybody. " Even if
the city is the architectural wonder that many say it is," various
people ranging from a Member of Parliament to a small shopkeeper told me, " why should we Indians of all people build a
city like that ? We who have no money even for our most
urgent requirements ! Just look at the administrative block that
is nearing completion ! A nine-storeyed colossus of concrete
that will cost twelve million ! All around are wide open spaces—
in fact, as much room as you could wish for. The British, if
faced with similar conditions, would have built a large estate of
bungalows, which need no expensive lifts and, moreover, are
much safer in earthquakes. And, above all, they are very much
cheaper. But all the decisions about Chandigarh were made in
Delhi. Our province is now saddled with a huge debt because
of this boastful capital city which nobody really likes. We who
have to foot the bill were not even asked."

    In addition there is a nationalist argument. " Is there anything
Indian left in this architecture ? " a building contractor asked
me. " Nothing at all. It's a Western import which doesn't
really fit here." Most Indians vastly prefer the sham Mogul
architecture with its crenellations, domes, and roof pavilions

with which the British so generously furnished New Delhi. But their protest produces no more than a contemptuous smile from the architects of Chandigarh. " We do not ask for stylistic models," a young Indian architect told me. " We allow ourselves simply to be ruled by the material which we need : the brick which is kilned in the neighbourhood, the demands of a hot climate which forces us to provide a *brise-soleil* round the windows and projecting slabs in the façade to ward off the sun's rays and to provide shadow. The criticism which is showered on us doesn't worry us too much. People always grumble at first, but in the end they find we were right. Besides, we are learning all the time. From each completed block we draw our conclusions for the next. Perhaps we shall be working on this city all our lives. It continues to grow like an organism. The proof that we are right is that our way of building is now beginning to be imitated throughout India. Often, unfortunately, only in its outward aspects without functional understanding— but then that is the fate of modern architecture."

Functional understanding ? But surely the principal charge against the High Court and Administrative blocks was their pointless and expensive monumentality ? " We must not define function too narrowly," the architect met my objection. " Monumentality and beauty are functions too." This seems to have got us back to the revolutionary radicalism of the Bauhaus movement of the twenties, and very nearly to the classical concept. Chandigarh, it seems to me, is a fundamentally false work of art. Genuine style must spring from the spirit of a people, and reflect its way of thinking and feeling. In this sense the hollow, ostentatious architecture of Soviet Russia is much more genuine : it is the expression of a people whose psychological development has not quite kept pace with their headlong plunge into the machine age, and who have therefore fallen victim to a mania for the gigantic before developing a sense of form. Anyone wanting to see how the Indians react to the style of Chandigarh need only glance into the market-place, where battered crates litter the unswept pavement, where cows root about for food among the refuse-bins, where, in effect, after a few years the same slum atmosphere has arisen as can be found in the bazaars of the old towns.   Or I would invite the reader to accompany me to one of the Ministerial residences which look so wonderful from outside. In the living-room he will find the same primitive bench that is found in the homes of the peons ; on the walls hang the same vulgar calendars in crude colours, and on the window-sills figures of Hindu deities are displayed. In vain did Pierre Jeanneret design for his own house a set of original furniture made from native Indian materials—bamboo and hemp cord—with which these contemporary houses might be inexpensively and stylishly equipped.   But no Indian would dream of putting these crazy things in his living-room, beneath the pictures of Ghandi and Khrishna.   When I made these points to a young architect, he smiled.   " We know that India hasn't got the people yet who could intelligently occupy these houses. But by building them, nevertheless, we hope to develop a taste for modern living among the people. This city, in the final analysis, is a great educational experiment, and you can't expect an experiment to start with perfection. Come back in twenty years' time : Chandigarh is a city of the future."

CHAPTER FOUR

Banaras (Varanasi) : God is Improper

EVERY MORNING, AS THE SUN RISES RED ABOVE the haze of the flat horizon beyond the river, a sudden ripple runs through the recumbent crowds on the steps leading down to the Ganges. Only slowly are the blue shadows dragged out from their recesses, but the human figures scurry about with a lightness as though of spirits, who must go down to the gold-tinted waters for the blood which will turn them into live beings again for the day. On the bottommost step they crouch down, immediately above the water-level, their knees lapped by the waves, their devout faces turned towards the sun. With their palms they scoop up water and allow the drops to fall back in the morning breeze. The men fill voluminous shiny brass jugs and, standing up, pour the water over their bronzed bodies, which are naked except for a loin-cloth. The women throw themselves into the waves entirely, loosening their saris and disappearing in the waters. For a second or two they float below the surface like strange ornamental fish, their garments billowing out like fins, their long hair resembling some strange sea-plant reaching out for prey, but turning into disappointingly ugly strands when, puffing and snorting, they surface again. It is better to turn your head discreetly as they climb the steps once more. With their breasts and thighs outlined under the thin white cloth as clearly as if they were nude, they do not like being stared at by strangers. Now and again, perhaps, when youth still lends shapeliness to the figures, this self-denial may be hard, but as a rule it is not. In India, as anywhere else, religious devotion is more frequent among those of advanced years, and hence at this sacred river-bank shapeless pot-bellies and desiccated mummies are the general rule. Farther out from the bank, only a few yards from the bathers, a swollen corpse, covered with weeds, floats past ; a flock of pigeons has settled on those parts of the body which show above the water, rather like the crew of a submarine leaving port. I can hardly believe my eyes : I expect alarm, the arrival of the police, and attempts to identify the body. But no one seems to pay the slightest attention to the dead. The people go on diving, pouring water from their praying hands, even drinking it, or, in the traditional Indian manner, cleaning their teeth with a little stick. A paradise for microbes !

" Not at all," protested a student of the Hindu University, who was accompanying me. " Our laboratories have examined the water from the Ganges. It contains radioactive substances. That's why it is curative, and why, in spite of the circumstances— which admittedly may seem a little unappetizing—no one has yet been infected from it. The harmful germs are killed." Well roared, lion ! So the mystery has been scientifically explained ! After all, the most pious Hindus explain the sacredness of their cows from economic necessity. Why is the Ganges sacred ? Stupid question. Because water nourishes and cleanses, because the soul, coming to the river from the wintry, dusty, arid plain, breathes freely again among the green of trees and fields, and because the sweaty, unclean body finds refreshment in the water. What more is needed to feel respect for such a fountain of life ? And why do we need radioactivity for cleansing ourselves in the morning's early light of the filth of the night and of all that goes with darkness and shadows ? How elegant are the explanations of magic, and how clumsy those of science !

Walking through the narrow side-streets near the river-bank, my foot touched a bundle wrapped in red cloth and tied to a frame of bamboo rods, which had been dropped on the pavement —a corpse. How did it get there ? And then I saw a few men resting on the ground. They were on their way to the places of cremation farther down the river, from whence smoke and a smell as of roast meat drifted towards me. These places of cremation look considerably less romantic than one pictures them. The platforms on which the stakes are built are covered with crude, smoothed concrete, rather like an abattoir, to make for easier cleansing. Throughout the day these places are exceedingly busy, for to die in Banaras means a pass to a higher incarnation. Thus a vast number of old and sick people drift into the holy city in expectation of their end. And this end is as prosaic as the concrete structures where its last act is played out. Throughout a whole morning while I watched the cremations I saw not one wet eye, except, of course, from the smoke—not one distrait or even sad bereaved. The relations departed unfeelingly the moment their bundle had been handed over to the cremation squads and set down by the river's edge, its feet in the holy water. There was no indication whether the wrappings concealed a person taken in his youth, an old woman, or the father of a family in his prime. Only when the flames had licked over the dry wood, and eagerly consumed the butter which had been poured over it, were the wrappings turned into ash and the bare, dead flesh revealed in almost obscene nudity. While a cow comfortably chewed up the bast cords with which the body had been lashed to its bier, one of the cremation squad used a bamboo rod to stir the fire, much as a European boy roasts potatoes on a camp-fire. Since the abdomen was burnt more quickly than the bony parts of the body, he eventually inserted his pole into the thorax, and, like hay on a pitchfork, lifted the half-charred chest and bedded it down again where the flames burnt brightest. *Sic transit gloria mundi*, a Westerner might be tempted to quote. But here there is no wistfulness. The transiency of everything that exists, the senselessness of setting one's heart on earthly possessions—all these are sung to a child while he is still in his cradle. Why then should one mourn the dead ? And why preserve their useless remains in a grave and surrender them to the remembrance of those left behind ? Surely a grave would be an improper attempt to invest with artificial endurance that which is intended to be transient ? No, the ashes are swept into the Ganges, unfeelingly, by one of the cremation team, just as though they were refuse. Below the cremation places the bank of the Ganges is black with the ash of the dead. But even there people bathe—just as though this were a pure mountain stream. Delightedly they dive into the water and emerge again, blowing and snorting. Back to their homes they carry the large brass jugs, filled with drinking-water.

" Our cremation is a very venerable custom ; you need not turn your nose up at it ! " the student who accompanied me said in an almost offended tone. " Did I say anything about it being improper ? " I asked, smiling at this sudden revelation of the Indian inferiority complex. " Our Government is trying to modernize the methods," he added. " We are building crema-toria—they are more hygienic, and do not waste so much wood, which as you know is scarce in our country. But the people cannot quite get used to the idea. They want to be cremated in the old-fashioned way. Our people are very backward ! "

Mile after mile, in gentle undulation, the steep banks drop down to the river, and for mile after mile the steps of the ghats are crowded, all day long. Massive palace walls—as though the bathers were a besieging army—rise solidly from the banks, and the temples, which stand between them like curious pointed cakes, are almost crushed by this pompous show of worldliness. Only the mosque of the Mogul emperor Aurangzeb soars triumphant over the mass of the remaining architecture, standing with its minarets on a tall, rocky promontory, a monument to that fanatic on the throne who in trying to make Islam palatable to his subjects by fire and sword sealed the fall of his empire. It is a dark prison of God, devoid of all beauty. Walls, nothing but walls. As you step through the gateway you meet voidness without life. An idea of Nietzsche's came to my mind : " They made their God out of nothingness and so for them he became nothing." The solitude of God, the loneliness of man—these are the other side of the transcendental.

But down below, in the sphere of the immanent God of the Hindus, everything worldly is ennobled by his presence. And in turn everything divine is disfigured by its worldly associations.

That is the other side of the Hindu religion. Disgusting superstition side by side with genuine devoutness. For instance, take
that figure crawling towards the bank of the Ganges along one
of the narrow little streets. And I mean crawling. He is a
so-called saint, a sadhu. His hair, tied up in a knot behind his
head, is so matted with ash and cow-dung that it falls from his
head in long, light-coloured strands, like an uncared-for fur.
His face and body are also smeared with ash, and the pleasant
chocolate-brown of his Indian skin has given way to a dirty grey
from which his eyes and mouth stand out in repulsive moistness.
This strange creature pledged himself to make a daily pilgrimage
to the Ganges on his belly. He lies down flat on the hot pavement and, with his arms extended in front, pushes a piece of iron
as a marker as far as he can reach. He then brings up his feet and
throws himself forward again to his full length. The pavement
is damp and spattered brown with spat-out pan ; the steam of
urine rises from the corners in the walls. The nearer the sadhu
gets to the river-bank the more closely is he surrounded by
trampling feet, the more is he hemmed in on all sides by the
revolting lines of lepers who extend to the passers-by the stumps
of their limbs, begging for alms, by the sellers of flowers who
have piled their marigold-blossoms into heaps, by money-
changers, and by goats winding their way through the crowds
and nibbling at anything that is green. The penitent does not
allow anything to disturb him. His eyes, whenever they flash
upward during one of his forward leaps, seem in exultation ; as
for his mouth, it is difficult to decide whether it wears a smile or
the grimace of extreme physical effort. His path is now barred
by a small group : somebody has brought along a push-cart
with a child without arms and legs, and with a suffering face he
begs for baksheesh. Everybody knows as well as I that he is
probably a fraud, and possibly a criminal. He may be a member
of a gang which steals children, brutally deforms them, and then
exhibits them as a bait for sympathy. I decline to make a
donation, but everybody else pays up without mistrust. A
pious Hindu once told me that even abuse of the name of God

and cursing were better than indifference, since they at least show
some relationship to the Deity. A donor therefore does not
question the worthiness or unworthiness of the object of his
charity ; the giving of alms is pleasing to God, and that is
enough. It is an act of kindness bound to earn blessings for the
giver : it is a magic rite, no more. A few yards away there is a
roundabout with noisily happy children, for this is a feast day.
It is an old-fashioned affair, not powered by any machinery, and
without any music ; it is turned by hand simply. Almost
alongside it an emaciated figure is writhing on the ground—an
old man. He is dying, and has clearly been dying for some
hours. A dog is rooting about in the excrement into which he
has rolled in his agony. From their little wooden horses the
children call out delightedly to their mothers, who stand watching
them, only a few feet away from the dying man. Down the
steps to the river moves a stream of human beings, and a few of
them glance quickly at the dying man. But not one of them
would have interrupted his journey even for a moment to have
a closer look at him. Only the dog is interested in the dying
man. And why should anyone bother about him ? Karma ?
The one Christian character that is alive in even the least Christian
of us Westerners is that of the Good Samaritan. In Hinduism
every individual is alone with God. And if God has ceased to
help why should man interfere ?

"This is what our famous religiosity is like," my student
companion spoke up again. "Blind magic without heart.
India is not half so spiritual as everybody makes out—certainly
she is no less materialistic than the West. Just go and ask the
people here why they have undertaken their pilgrimage to
Banaras, why they perform their daily prayers so strictly.
Hardly one of them will give you an honest reply ; hypocrisy
is our national vice. Their true motive is not a wish for salvation,
but for much more concrete things—happiness, fame, power,
wealth, a multitude of sons who would bring honour to the
family. I don't suppose there is another religion that is so
intimately linked up with material interests as our oh-so-spiritual

Hinduism. If you speculate on the Stock Exchange you can pray to Lakshmi, and hope that she will magically affect the quotations. Everything is magic, or superstition, if we are to give it its proper name." I had long ceased to pacify my companion ; who was I to teach a Hindu tolerance ? Besides, our encounters offered little opportunity. Once more our way was barred. A man had placed a calf on the steps. Anyone wishing to know his future had but to grip its tail and, thus guided by the magical contact, fish out from a little box a strip of paper with the prophecy. The man seemed to be doing a roaring trade : those eager to know their future were elbowing their way to him. And there, at the next corner, was another ash-covered sadhu. He kept his mouth wide open and with a blade of grass held taut between his two hands forced his tongue into a variety of repulsive shapes. He was slobbering at the mouth. Another young man, whose features at a hundred yards betrayed the criminal, had managed to get about two dozen people to crowd around him ; he was wearing the pale orange garment of the Sannyasin, he had a rosary round his neck, and his hair was shorn in the monastic manner. His panacea against cough, diarrhœa, prickly heat, and puerperal fever was selling like hot cakes.

Where there is light there is also shadow. Where there is no shadow there is only pale grey half-light. I have never seen a feast of such orgiastic ecstasy and at the same time such revolting vulgarity as the New Year, named Holi, which under the Hindu calendar is celebrated in March. In the early morning, as I was making my way through the narrow little streets of the old city towards the river, three young men leapt out at me brandishing old bicycle pumps like guns. The moment they caught sight of me they filled them from a bucket which one of them was carrying, and before I knew what was happening to me I was being squirted at from all sides. " Mind my suit ! " I wanted to shout, but already my trousers were covered with red blots, just as if some schoolmaster had emptied his red inkpot over me. The triumphant shrieks of the first group brought out a second :

their bucket contained some blue colour which immediately
blended on me into a pleasant purple.   Before long a brilliant
yellow was added, and I shone in all the colours of the rainbow.
By then I had quite written off my suit, for in spite of all assurances
from the culprits the colours are not washable.   On this day
everybody in India wears his oldest clothes, and those who do not
are certain to regret it afterwards.   Holi is the feast of the street
urchins *par excellence*.   What a joke to ambush an elderly,
thoughtful pilgrim climbing the steps from the river, and to cover
him in bright colours as though he had been conceived by
Picasso !   No one is spared, not even the beggars.   And when
no victim is in sight one urchin will spray another.   The colours
are mixed as strong as possible—new ammunition can be
purchased at any street corner—and the boys stand their ground
heroically when their opponents fire a full charge of colour into
their faces from point-blank range.   When their high spirits
brim over they even tip their full buckets over each other.
After a few hours the whole world looks like a speckled Easter
egg.   The roadway is wet and shiny with purple, and dripping
and blinded vehicles cautiously grope their way along them.
Even the houses are decorated right up to the eaves, especially
in the narrow streets, where families fire at each other from their
windows across the roadway.   Never mind—after all, the
symbolic meaning of the exercise is the tarnishing of the old
Adam and all that goes with him, so that everything must be
cleansed and renewed for the new year.   Even the houses are
freshly whitewashed.   In the evening the Indians will put on new
snow-white clothes and visit their friends, rubbing red powder
into their foreheads, and embracing them solemnly in a feast of
all-uniting love.

While we are on the subject of love—no woman would
venture out into the streets during the Holi festival.   For squirting
bicycle pumps is by no means everything : Holi is a Bacchanalian
festival of sex.   The men run around in a trance of obscenity.
Phalli from rubber hose and long bamboo rods project from

their loins. They carry alarming little jack-in-the-box devices which they snap open before the eyes of the startled passer-by, revealing a monstrous erection. Little boys chase you, squealing, with pictures on which dwarf-like men expose giant-like genitals. There are not individuals any longer—only crowds, throngs, grunting, squealing, and caterwauling. Now and again a more reasonable stranger touches my arm : " Better get home—the people no longer know what they are doing." But I shake them off. I want to see the other side of holy India. Even if it were to prove really dangerous. Young lads around me leap upon one another like billy-goats, squealing with concupiscence. They tear their clothes off their bodies and, laughing, exhibit their bellies. Wherever I go the crowd follows me like a tidal wave. There is no hiding for a white man, no escape. In the end, when one of them attacked me from behind and, grunting, tried to press his excited body against me, I fled to my car as though it were an armoured fighting vehicle.

Hard as it may be to see anything divine in these orgies, there is nevertheless a religious meaning in them. After all, the Lingam, a representation of the male member, is one of the symbols in which the God Shiva, the creator and destroyer of worlds, is venerated in thousands and thousands of temples as the most sacred deity. True, hardly anyone considers this form of the phallus obscene : it takes the form of a round column about a foot high, which is strewn with flowers, and sprinkled with fresh water, and rubbed with liquefied butter. No more obscene is its female counterpart—a round, slightly elongated seat, a kind of bidet raised to a ritual image. Besides, not only in India is sex as a primeval force invested with divine significance. Wherever a peasant plants his seed in the furrow a mind not yet divorced from nature by tractors sees in the process a prototype of procreation. Fertility rites are at the root of all peasant religions. In this world the act of procreation is no more improper than death is terrible.

A little more questionable, especially for young ladies under twenty, is a visit to one of the famous temples on whose walls

the sculptors have set a monument to the art of love of their day.
It is left to the spectator whether he wishes to see in this unending
series of variations of embrace a symbol of tantric Yoga or of
plain obscenity.   True, at Khajuraho—which is reached in a day's
drive from Banaras—the ceremonial solemnity almost entirely
banishes all association with natural love-play.   At Konarak, on
the other hand, a temple situated in the magnificent solitude of
the eastern coast, the artist's fantasy had clearly been more
strongly influenced by down-to-earth reality ; indeed, his frieze
constitutes an almost complete manual for would-be courtesans.
But even here there is not for a single moment any suggestion of
vulgarity.   The faces of the men and women are rapt in bliss
in a way that makes the activity of their bodies seem no more
than an expression of a profound divine longing.   While I was
in Khajuraho a battery of the Indian Army was on manœuvres in
the neighbourhood, and one day, while I was strolling among
the temples, some groups of soldiers drifted past the embracing
figures.   I can well imagine the comments which any European
soldiers would make, faced with such pictures.   The young
Indians, however, regarded the scenes curiously but in silence,
without any sniggers, and almost solemnly.   " Why are you
taking photographs of this ? " a sergeant challenged me.   " Are
you trying to poke fun at our religion ? "   " Not at all," I
replied.   " I simply like them."   " But why do you like them ? "
the other persisted, suspiciously.   I was saved a reply, for an
elegant gentleman of intellectual appearance suddenly butted in.
" Because as he looks at these pictures one millionth part of that
infinite bliss that is expressed in them is passed on to him," he
said quickly.   I glanced at my rescuer in surprise and gratitude.
" These erotic scenes," he continued his unsolicited lecture,
" signify the moment of unparalleled bliss which is granted to the
master of Yoga—which is granted to him in every limb—nay,
in every hair on his body.   Do you know how many hairs we
have ?   Millions !   A million times the ecstasy of sexual delight—
that is what we experience when we become one with the deity.
I speak from experience :   my grandfather achieved it."   I had

…ndigarh : *the Supreme Court building with the roof that had been designed to* …*cept the cooling winds, and the roof canopy which had to be added subsequently to* …*d off the unbearable heat of the sun.* *A typical case of "drawing-board architecture."*

(above) *Every morning men and women wash away their sins in the Ganges at Banaras (Varanasi).*

(left) *Every morning this sadhu in Banaras covers the entire distance to the Ganges on his stomach.*

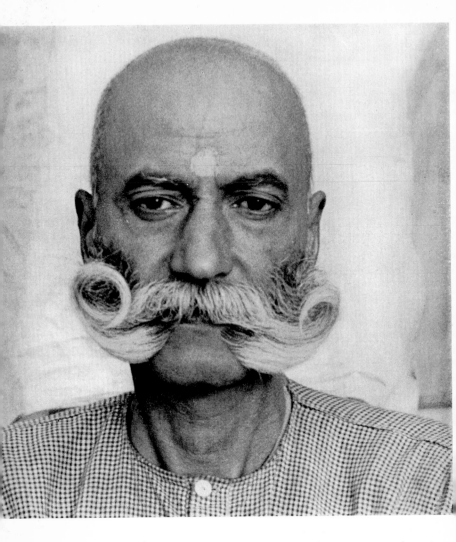

Pilgrim in Banaras (Varanasi).

The Festival of Holi: even venerable pilgrims are not immune against attack from street urchins.

Indian Army personnel studying erotic tactics at the temples of Khajuraho.

Indian harvest thanksgiving festival in January: cows are painted with bright ...urs and driven through a number of fires for ritual purification. This picture was taken at Mysore.

This is how sacred cows are treated when they collapse from weakness and old age.
Their exalted status is no protection against the whip.

A bull with mutilated forelegs in the street in Calcutta: no one releases the animal
from its sufferings.

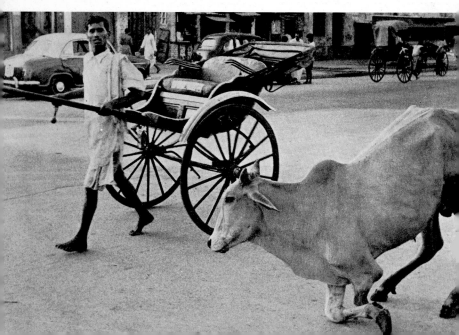

...der the banner of the sacred cow : orthodox fanatics demonstrating in favour of a ban on the slaughtering of cattle in India.

(Above) *Man turned God : Sivananda, the Yogi of Rishikesh, has his feet sprinkl* *with milk and strewn with flowers by his women followers every noon.*

(Right) *Yoga class in Sivananda's Ashram at Rishikesh. Yoga demands that e* *practitioner should stand on his head for about ten minutes every morning, to stimul* *blood circulation through the brain.*

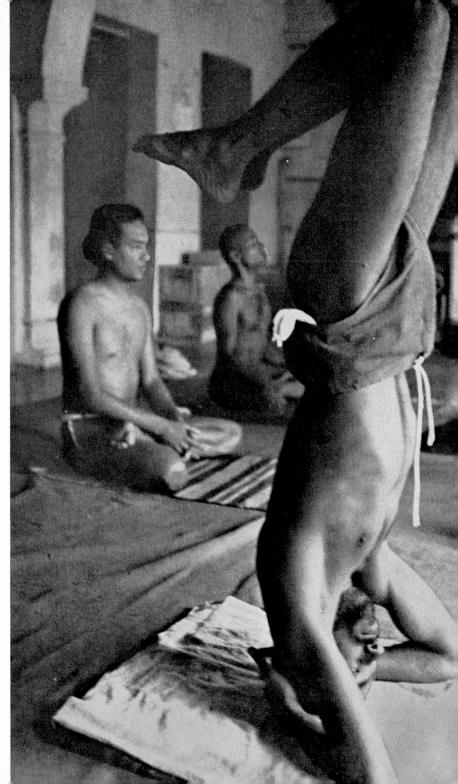

(Above) *Early-morning wrestling under Howrah Bridge, Calcutta.*

eft) A mask over their mouths—lest they should swallow an insect—and a mop by
ir hands—lest they should inadvertently step on some living creature: to such ends
does the sect of the Jains observe the law against the taking of life.

Sealdah station, in Calcutta. This is where the refugees from East Pakistan arrived
few years ago, and this is where they have settled down to this day—in the booking-h
of the railway-station. Anyone wishing to buy a ticket must clamber over th
possessions.

collected myself a little in the meantime. "And you yourself?" I asked. "If I had experienced it," the other said, almost solemnly, " I should not be standing here. But my grandfather was a holy man." A considerable audience of soldiers had collected around us, and they inspired the gentleman to further revelation. " Hinduism is eternalism," he cried. " Eternalism ! Do you know what that means ? I am not only I ; I am also you. I am the watch on your wrist. I am the stone beneath your feet. I am everything. There is no death, only transformation of the same divine substance. Do you believe that ? " I did not quite know what to say. The man was all too clearly showing the symptoms of religious mania. But the soldiers, all of them simple, healthy young men, nodded thoughtfully. " We believe it," they said.

CHAPTER FIVE

Cows—Sacred Sufferers

I̱T HAPPENED IN ONE OF THE MAIN STREETS OF Calcutta. Buses, filled to bursting-point, were roaring along. Taxis screeched to a halt as the traffic lights turned red. Here and there, wedged in among it all, was a tall-wheeled rickshaw, an anachronism, with a brown-skinned, kicking human animal between the shafts. Apart from myself, no one stopped to look at the bull which had turned into the avenue from a side-street and was reeling over the pavement. It was a young animal, and by some unknown accident it had been badly mutilated. Both its fore-legs had been severed at the knees, and on its stumps, now healed but far too short for its hind-legs, it tottered along awkwardly and painfully. It almost looked like an involuntary kangaroo. With its nose forced against the ground because of its disability, it rooted about hungrily among the refuse of the gutter, looking for dry leaves, but making do even with old newspapers which it crumpled up and swallowed down. At that moment a dainty young cow also turned the corner into the main street. To human eyes it possessed no particular charms : its hip-bones stuck out from its meagre body like ploughshares, and its skin had the matted roughness that comes from undernourishment and lack of attention. In fact, a real frump of a cow, which a well-bred European bull would have hardly thought worthy of a cursory glance. But our cripple was not so exacting. Though not prepared to share with her his old copies of the *Statesman* or the *Hindustan Times*, he was clearly stirred to love by the young animal. His nose gently touched hers, their bovine eyes met for a moment in devotion, and a soft, passionate lowing broke from his chest. No doubt the flirtation would not have ended so platonically—since Indian cows do not allow even the city traffic to interfere with their intimate affairs of the heart. But the legless bullock stumbled as he desperately tried to raise himself to the requisite height ; the stumps of his fore-legs gave under him as, impotently lustful, he collapsed on the pavement, half comically and half tragically.

Apart from myself, not a soul gave the poor animal another glance. Coolies, children, sadhus, old women—they all walked past the tortured animal with an air of perfect unconcern, and merely seemed amused at my own sympathy. Once again I felt the urge which I invariably experienced at the sight of the mangy dogs which roam about the railway-stations, markets, and restaurants in large packs—the urge to kill, to put an end to suffering. To kill in this case would not be brutal murder ; death would not come as a terrible experience but as a relief. But this is not the way the Hindu thinks. For a creature to suffer is Karma, the logical consequence of an unsuccessful earlier human existence. To shorten the torture of this reincarnation would mean interference with divine justice. You would not even do the poor creature a service, since you would deprive it of its merits with regard to a future incarnation. And while all animals are condemned to this kind of life, killing a cow out of compassion is downright unthinkable. For in India the cow is sacred ; to lay hands on a cow would be the worst possible sacrilege, murder of a deity. Thus every calf that is born has the dubious prospect of dying a natural death sooner or later.

Such a natural death can occur surprisingly quickly after birth. For instance, if the peasant demands all the milk of the mother cow for himself. In that case he simply ties up the cow's udder with sackcloth, and the poor calf starves. If it dies pitifully—too bad. That's the way of the world. No murderous blood has defiled the human hand. For that is all that matters : the refined sophistry of not committing the sin of killing outright. You may drag your victim to within an inch of death—provided

Nature completes what you have started you remain pure. I
have seen peasants beating unwilling oxen so unmercifully that in
our unholy Europe they would have been hauled before a court
for cruelty to animals. From the boxes of their carts they pinch
or twist the animals' tails to such an extent that many animals in
India have a mutilated tail, or no tail at all. And once an animal
has done its duty it is left to its own devices ; the cow whose
milk has dried up, or the ox that has become too old and weak
for work, is simply dismissed. Let them feed on old newspapers
and rags, let them roam the fields, furiously chased away by
other peasants, but never killed. Until eventually they die
somewhere by the roadside. The moment Nature has put an
end to their sufferings the taboo is lifted from them. Some
pariah—for no Hindu of caste would demean himself to touch a
dead animal—will strip off its skin, which, though it does not,
of course, produce first-class leather in view of the animal's
sufferings in its lifetime, is nevertheless useful. Shoes made in
India come almost exclusively from cattle-hide, and that is why
very strict Hindus decline to wear leather footwear, or even
belts, as sinful.

But not all cows have such a sad old age to look forward to.
Many a rich Hindu earns himself his treasure in heaven by
providing an enjoyable old age for the sacred animals. The cow
asylum in Delhi is situated on the outskirts of the city, and
reached only after a long drive through narrow, poor, and dirty
streets. But the moment you have passed through the tall gate
of the Gauschala—a word meaning something like Cow Hall—
you realize that you are in a kind of bovine grand hotel. With
patent pride, its director conducted me through its extensive
tree-shaded courtyards, where the silvery bodies of cows were
crowded around feeding-troughs, through large, clean byres,
where young calves turned their innocent faces towards us.
" In India the cow is a sacred animal," Mr Anand lectured me,
" because of its unparalleled economic importance. Primarily
it provides us with milk which, as we are vegetarians, is our only
source of animal fat and protein. And since we use practically

no horses—only the Moslems do that—if it were not for our oxen all our rural carts would be at a standstill, and not one plough would draw a furrow through our fields. Cow-dung is collected and dried. No doubt while travelling through our villages you noticed the cow-dung drying on clay walls. It is then used as fuel. Cow urine is used to fertilize our fields. The liquefied butter, which we make from the milk, nourishes not only us but also our gods, to whom we sacrifice this *ghi*. India's entire life depends on the cow. We revere it as our mother—and tell me : would you kill your mother ? "

Hastily and quite sincerely I assured him that I would not, and Mr Anand continued to explain to me the workings of his not very lucrative institution. " As soon as a peasant ceases to derive economic advantages from his cow or ox he is invited to bring them here. Sometimes the animal is not even old but merely sick, in which case we can still use it for breeding purposes. Have a look at our bull there—a first-class animal. Not quite so near, please—he is rather dangerous ! " The beast pawed the ground, lowered its horns, and uttered a strange sound, not unlike that of a turkey. I hurriedly retreated. " But does it pay," I asked, " to breed progeny from useless cows which surely do not belong to one of the best strains to start with ? " Mr Anand did not seem in the least surprised at my scepticism. Any Hindu who deals with cows treats Westerners from the outset with a kind of superior condescension, as a species of human being who cannot, with the best of intentions, be convinced of the excellence of the true faith. " Whether it pays or not," he said, " our cows here must feel absolutely happy—that's why they are also entitled to enjoy motherhood. Just look at that touching scene over there—isn't it wonderful ! " And he pointed to a still young cow with revoltingly white, totally blind eyes, bending over a young calf lying on the ground, licking its hide. It was quite true : economic considerations really are of no account in the Gauschalas. A list displayed in the gateway revealed that of the 1000 inmates only 10 per cent. were yielding milk. It did not say how many litres. From a profit-and-loss account sheet

I could see that about one-third of the maintenance costs were covered by the production of milk and butter, while the rest was provided by donations, and even a small Government subsidy. Above the doors of the cow-sheds, on the walls of the courtyards, were boards with the names of the generous donors. " Twenty years," was the answer to my final question as to the average age at which the inmates of the cow asylum departed this world.

When I had left, and was once more strolling among the wooden shacks, with their naked, undernourished children, I could not help shaking my head. What kind of country was this, where rich benefactors gave their money for the welfare not of children but of old cows ? But that is asking the question in a European way : India cannot be measured with a rational yardstick. The sacredness of her cows is far more than an absurd romantic caprice—it is a religious luxury bordering on economic disaster. There are in India 160,000,000 head of cattle— almost one to every two human beings. An Indian cow yields 180 litres of milk a year—compared with over 2500 litres of its Danish or Swiss sisters. If the Indian yield could be increased to even half the European figure millions of Indian children could drink their fill of milk. This is the problem which has for years been engaging the Ministries in Delhi, the agricultural experts of the United Nations, the Ford Foundation, and heaven knows what other aid organizations. In vain. Everybody knows the solution—a simple and obvious solution. To begin with, kill off all useless animals—which would be about 60 per cent. according to figures of the National Planning Committee— then feed the remaining 40 per cent. properly, and use modern methods to breed a healthy and economically profitable generation of cattle.

But this sensible solution, in support of which Premier Nehru himself has come out, is violently opposed by all religious Hindus. They not only demand the scrapping of such godless plans, but, on the principle that attack is the best defence, they demand a prohibition of the slaughtering of cows throughout the whole territory of India and the closing of all slaughter-houses which, in such cosmopolitan cities as Bombay and Calcutta, provide Moslems, Christians, and other blasphemous carnivores with beefsteak.   Anyone killing a cow, they demand, should be condemned to lifelong imprisonment like any other murderer. In the exemplarily orthodox Nepal the slaughter of cows is indeed logically punished by death.

While I was in Delhi there was an exhibition taking place, organized by the Action Committee in Defence of Cows, combined with a cattle show.   High Hindu dignitaries rode demonstratively in ox-carts through the streets of the capital, with large slogans carried in front of them, and subsequently presided over a mass meeting below a huge portrait of a cow surrounded, as though by a halo, by the rays of the rising sun. No fewer than 3,000,000 deities are incorporated in the cow, a young man at the exhibition explained to me.   An unending picture gallery illustrated the glorious part played by the cow in Indian mythology—such as the touching scene of the God Krishna being suckled by a cow.   When I informed my companion that Romulus and Remus were said to have been adopted by a she-wolf he nodded eagerly.   Here, he said, the difference between the violent Western soul and the gentle non-violence of India was clearly illustrated.   Even that traitor to the cow, Nehru, had in some pamphlet of his referred to the proud beasts of prey which the nations of Europe used in their heraldry— lions, wolves, bears, and eagles.   Why, even the cockerel of the French was an aggressive bird, whereas the cow, the idol of India, emanated nothing but self-sacrificing motherhood.   I thought of the ' peaceful ' bull in the cow asylum and held my peace.

This peaceful national symbol of India, the cow—if the pictorial posters at the exhibition were to be believed—had been surrendered to a terrible fate.   A big coloured map of India was covered with countless bleeding, parcelled-up carcases of cows— at all those places where a frivolous, irreligious Government had authorized slaughterhouses, where gentle Indian cows are murdered together with other non-sacred animals.   And in what a bestial way, too ! A model showed a huge circular saw towards which the poor animals were carried, strapped to a conveyor belt, to have their heads sawn off while they were alive.   When I remarked to my companion that I had not seen any such martyrdom at any slaughterhouse I knew he replied apologetically that the artist—no doubt in order to stir the spectator—had allowed his fantasy a little freer rein.   Altogether the exhibition was designed as propaganda, as the publicity campaign of a militant obscurantism.   There were arguments against an intensification of arable farming and vegetable-growing, because this would deprive the cows of their grazing. The final piece of the exhibition was a grotesque apotheosis of a cow, with a figure of Nehru, half contrite and penitent and half converted, kneeling before the animal.   Even if one feels respect for India's religiosity, one can only deplore the blind fanaticism of these cow-worshippers.   For it is their blindness in the face of their country's economic problems which, in the final analysis, plays into the hands of the enemies of all tradition— those who are only too ready to sweep all religious taboos on to the refuse-heap.

Fortunately, there is another kind of cattle in India apart from the cows, which is not surrounded by the odour of sanctity, and is therefore suitable for modern breeding—the buffalo.   They are known throughout the tropics—big, awkward animals with a shiny black skin lacking sweat-glands.   Because of this lack they spend hour after hour cooling themselves in ponds and streams.   Only their big waved horns and their nostrils show motionless above the surface of the water.   Obviously no one would think of declaring these idiotic, phlegmatic animals sacred.   The silvery zebu cows, with their delicately moulded heads and elegantly curved horns, may indeed radiate, to eyes symbolistically inclined, a kind of purity.   But the buffaloes, belonging as they do entirely to the realm of water, make up for their lack of spirituality by a much more useful quality— their milk is more plentiful, and is so rich that blobs of fat float on top, and in its raw state give it the taste of fresh nuts. Since, as I have said, old buffaloes may be killed and even eaten with impunity, agricultural reformers with a big sigh of relief have concentrated on this type of livestock. It is significant that one of the sights of the new India should be a dairy farm at Aarey, near Bombay. Hundreds of buffaloes lie here in clean, open sheds at the foot of a hill, on whose summit, like a castle, stands a modern pasteurization plant. From here tens of thousands of bottles of fresh milk are sent to Bombay every day, where their low price makes them accessible even to the poor. When I visited the dairy farm of Aarey hundreds of school-children and other spectators were crowding outside the gate, just as if this were the Taj Mahal or some other famous monument.

CHAPTER SIX

Between God and the Devil

THE SAINTS SEEM TO HAVE STRUCK A BAD PATCH in the India of the five-year plans. Ten years ago, on my first visit to India, I saw Ramana Maharshi, one of the last great saints, who was then dying. He had undergone an operation for a malignant tumour—without any anæsthetic at all. He had had the tumour cut from his living body, from whose sensations of pain his conscious mind had long severed itself. Of his weakened body there was then left only the radiance of his St Francis-like eyes. But even his end was no longer considered quite proper by some experts of the world of Yoga. Ramakrishna, it was explained to me, had categorically refused to submit to surgical intervention. He had allowed his body to be consumed by terrible tortures until he had died—or, more correctly, not died but departed. A true saint does not die : he sits down for his last meditation, and thus, erect, his body crosses the threshold of death. The last of the famous ones to depart was Aurobindo, the sage of Pondicherry ; and to this day no successor of similar status has been found. Can this possibly be due to the fact that intelligent young people in India are needed nowadays as engineers, physicists, doctors, or sociologists —in fact, that India's entire spiritual atmosphere is gradually extroverting itself from its century-old inwardness ?

Not at all, the experts assured me ; there are still great saints. Only they are not known. The world of Indian saints, I was told, is like an iceberg—only the tops are visible. The number of sadhus in this enormous subcontinent is estimated at 6,000,000. They all call themselves sadhus—from the true mystics who seek their God in retreats in the tropical forests of Kerala or among the icy wastes of the Himalayas, to the vagabonds, cheats, and criminals who don the pale orange garments of the Sannyasin so that they can cash in on the gullibility of the simple villagers, who enable them to live a life of lazy comfort at their expense. The boundaries between genuineness and deception are fluid : just as among us Christians, there are in India many naïve, unstable, or near-maniacally exalted spirits who are practically forced into deception by an unending demand which greatly exceeds their limited spiritual abilities. Strangely enough, this excites the irreligious rationalists far more than the pious believers. Premier Nehru has said in a speech that only 10,000 to 15,000 sadhus were real ascetics, whereas the vast remainder were merely " parasites and asocial elements." Ramana Maharshi, on the other hand, in spite of his great wisdom, never objected to such pious mountebanks settling at his Ashram—that is what the schools founded by famous Yogis are called—or to the fact that this Ashram thus became a place of unchecked money-making and other dubious practices. After all, in a world pervaded by the breath of God must not even deception, lies, and evil serve His revelation ? Where everything derives from the One, all moral opposites become meaningless. The mere fact that in our age the idea has been conceived of dividing the sheep from the goats—of dividing the true sadhus from the false and neatly docketing them in a professional register—is sufficient evidence of the metaphysical mist that has descended on the Indian mind.

Thus at six o'clock one morning—for pressure of work had compelled him to invite me at that early hour—I met Swami Ananda for breakfast at the headquarters of Bharat Sadhu Samaj, the Association of Indian Saints in Connaught Square, in New Delhi. This Association was founded in 1957 in order, as its statutes put it, " to unite all sadhus in constructive social work, with a view to the all-sided advancement of India and the improvement of the world on the foundations of truth, nonviolence, freedom from fear, and unity." In particular, these progressive sadhus undertake to support the five-year plan.

" How ? " I asked Swami Ananda, who was a member of the
Executive Committee of the Association. " By moral support :
by way of mass education, mass prayers, and cultural programmes," he replied promptly. These, in fact, are the words
in the statutes.   " Can you please give me an example," I persisted,
" of some such activity already in progress ?   You see, I am a
photographer, and I can't be satisfied with mere verbal information. . . . "   The other man thought hard. His small, perpetually
smiling face, surrounded by a grey beard and in constant nervous
motion, reminded me of a Pekinese. " Everything is in a state of
preparation," he said vaguely. " What ? " I feigned surprise.
" After two years—nothing but preparation ? "   He nodded.
" We are still busy compiling membership lists and organizing
ourselves," he added. That, indeed, seemed to be the sum total
of their activities. The work of Swami Ananda, like that of a
number of other orange-robed colleagues, consisted mainly of
scanning the Indian Press for articles about the Association of
Indian Saints and cutting them out. On the walls were propaganda posters for the second five-year plan. " Could you explain
to me how the idea of material progress in the sham *maya* world
can be of interest to a sadhu engrossed in contemplation of the All-
One ? " I pursued my questions. " Oh," he said, " there is no
contradiction at all. We belong to the world—that is the most
profound meaning of Hindu teaching. All men are brothers ;
our mission is love. Love for our fellow-beings, love for all
creatures, for the animals, for the trees and plants. We are all
one.   That is why a sadhu must work for the welfare of humanity. . . ."   " And also for that of the animals and plants," I added
logically.   " Yes, perhaps," Swami Ananda said, surprised.
" God is everything, the entire creation. When I am one with
Him I am myself the whole creation ! "   It was strange to hear
words of profound philosophy from the lips of a Pekinese,
thrown out casually, like small coins to a beggar. " Independence
did not bring us everything we had hoped for," Ananda chatted
on.   " No brotherhood, no spirituality at all. All the people
think about is filling their stomachs. The politicians have brought

nothing but dirt into our world. Now we sadhus must clean it. . . ." "How many members have you got?" I asked. "Five thousand!" "Women too?" "Women are nothing but trouble," the Pekinese remarked. "Otherwise we are tolerant and universal; every creed is represented—Buddhists, Jains, even Christians." And he pointed to a picture of Christ crucified hanging on the wall surrounded by a lot of other deities. "Christ too shed His blood for the welfare of humanity," he said.

In India the sadhus who support the five-year plan do not enjoy a very good reputation. "Those gentlemen organize conferences, get Ministers or even the President to make speeches for them, and generally throw their weight about," one of the best-known Indian writers told me, laughing. "Don't you believe that any of them would so much as lift a finger to do any real work. And what's the purpose behind it all? To lend a modern cloak to their discredited trade in order to get at the purses of devout supporters." Most religious people likewise have only a contemptuous smile for them. "They support the five-year plan!" scoffed the editor of a religious periodical. "They ought to see that the five-year plan was put into the service of God!"

True enough, the real saints are scarcely to be found in the association of sadhus. Most of them hide from the world, or are known only to a small circle of intimates. And if one meets them at all it is usually by chance.

One evening a friend in Banaras took me to the Hindu University, where we were going to visit an old retired professor who I thought could be useful to me in view of his connexions with leading figures of India's spiritual life. A young man, whom I took to be a kind of acolyte, opened the door. "Would you please take off your shoes?" he asked us, as we were about to invade the professor's study informally. This is not only a gesture of courtesy but almost of ritual in all religious homes in India : their purity is not to be defiled by the dust of the street.

The professor was one of those touching and helpful people

whom one encounters in India time and again—filled with real goodness and a readiness to help which seemed second nature, and did not shrink even from personal sacrifice. But I was unlucky : the great saints whose names passed between the professor and my friend as possible persons for me to visit all turned out to be unavailable. One of them had picked up the disease which was just then sweeping through the holy city as a result of a cargo of bad edible oil, and was hovering between life and death. Another had set out on a pilgrimage. Throughout our consultations the young man who had opened the door to us sat in silence in a corner of the room, and time and again I felt my eyes drawn to him. He had sat down in a chair and, in the Eastern manner, had drawn up his legs underneath him, so that his attitude was one of crouching rather than sitting. Thus he followed our conversation with a mute interest which was reflected in his features. But what emanated from this young man surpassed that which is psychologically comprehensible : I am almost tempted to say that the semi-darkness surrounding him was pierced by a radiant brightness. I could not avoid the impression that he was more than a mere acolyte—all too clearly he bore the marks of a higher rank.

" Oh, yes, he is a young Mahatma who has lived here as my guest for the past twelve years," the professor explained when I asked him about the young man, who had meanwhile left the room. " One of these days he is going to be a great saint ; he is striving for salvation in only his third incarnation, and I believe that he will make it this time." I was surprised at such certainty, and tried to explore the source of such extraordinary knowledge. " Why don't you ask him yourself ? " the professor suggested. He knocked at the door of the next room, asked for permission to enter, and we found ourselves in a strange monastic cell. The room contained nothing except one of those plaited frameworks which serve as beds in India. The walls were white and bare, and the lamp, flickering a little as the door opened, cast a tremulous light over its uneven surface. The Mahatma was crouching on the bed, engrossed in a Sanskrit text. I was afraid he might

resent our invasion. But he most willingly met our request for
a conversation, and I thus learnt his story—a story that might
come from a long-lost past when legends were real-life accounts.

Rishi Kumar, Son of the Sage, was the name he had chosen
for himself, or perhaps had been given by one of his teachers.
His surname was forgotten, buried in a forgotten past like all his
relationship to the world. Rishi Kumar had spent the customary
boyhood of a brahmin child, somewhere in a village in the
Central Provinces. The religious exercises which were the duty
of his caste had left a deeper impression on his mind than on
those of his playmates—but that for his parents was a cause for
joy rather than alarm. Then, when he was seventeen, he met an
old Yogi who had left everything in order to tour the villages as
a beggar. It was recognition at first sight : " This man is your
master, he will show you the way." Rishi Kumar faced his
parents : " I want to leave ; I want to follow the holy man."
For a moment the parents were silent. His father said nothing ;
his mother began to cry. He was an only son. He bowed to
the silent request and stayed at home. Until one night he felt
an invisible hand touch his head. " Go ! " a voice said to him.
" Go ! " And he obeyed, going out into the night without
farewell, following the man he had chosen as his Guru, or
spiritual teacher.

It is one of the mysteries of a mystic career that it invariably
starts by companionship with such a spiritual teacher. The
word ' teacher,' as we understand it, carries too much the
connotation of lecturing to be an adequate description of the
much more subtle influence of a Guru. A Guru need not speak
at all ; his example—but this Western concept, too, is too
moral—his mere presence, his exhalation, helps the incipient
Yogi to crystallize from within himself that which is divine in
him. Aurobindo, to whom Rishi Kumar's path led at a later
date, was undoubtedly a much greater spirit than that obscure
sadhu who first aroused him. But a man has only one Guru, just
as he has only one first love. The third station in Rishi's life was

Banaras.   There the professor found him, sitting on the bank of
the Ganges, and took him home with him.   For twelve years
Rishi Kumar had lived in the small room with the bare walls,
scarcely ever leaving it.   A single modest meal each day sustains
his body.   Three hours of sleep refresh him.   All the remaining
time is given over to meditation, reading, the recital of sacred
names.   He never leaves the house, not even to bathe in the
Ganges—for most sadhus a daily exercise.   " I do not go to the
Ganges, the Ganges comes to me," he told me, bursting into
immoderate laughter which rang clear like a bell.   Only a child
can laugh like that—so immoderately and so purely.   Had he
never regretted his choice, I asked him ;   had he never experienced
the temptation to yield to those pleasures which are not incompatible with normal religious observance—the pleasures of
a good meal or of contact with a woman.   He knew the
temptation, he replied, but it was so slight compared with
the bliss of Oneness with God that he found it easy to fend
it off.

As soon as our conversation drifted from the personal to the
philosophical sphere, where I had hoped to learn something of
the wisdom which is revealed in meditation, I was rather disappointed.   Strictly speaking, Rishi Kumar revealed to me
nothing that I could not have read in any moderately adequate
manual of Indian philosophy.   Yet the familiar acquired a
strange originality from the way it came from the lips of the
Mahatma.   Before every reply he would hesitate for a moment,
as if listening into himself or beyond himself, and he would then
utter the words, naïvely, as if merely repeating what he had just
heard from somewhere.   I understood that in India meditation
does not mean penetrating into new, unexplored regions.   After
all, the contents of the divine are known and have been revealed
in the holy writings since time immemorial.   Religious concepts
have become platitudes.   What matters now is not to discover
them but to realize them subjectively, to experience them con-
cretely.   That is difficult—much more difficult than it may
appear to us Westerners.   To the Christian religious practice is

made easy by moral action towards our neighbour. "Inasmuch as ye have done it unto one of the least of these my brethren, ye have done it unto me," is a more manageable path than the solitary God-seeking of meditation, as it has developed in the Hindu religion, where the moral and the religious constitute two separate worlds. Besides, the religious experience of an Indian saint, and possibly that of any saint, is beyond communication. One might even say that communication deprives it of its real meaning, since recourse to words involves the use of a medium which is no longer adequate to it. The most profound religious experience is so secret and so esoteric that any attempt to convert it into a message, any attempt to form a school, is fundamentally a threat to it. I realized that clearly on my visit to the Ashram in Pondicherry, whose centre now is no longer Aurobindo himself, but his grave.

A grave for an Indian saint ? Since when have Hindus been buried and not burned ? Well, Yogis are allowed this exception. Because, it is said, all that was worldly in them had been consumed in the fire of their spirit while they were still alive, their body being of unearthly character, might therefore, rigidified in the lotus position, be surrendered to the earth. In Aurobindo's case legend—if one may call officially attested facts legend—reports yet another phenomenon of the transience of the flesh. Whereas in the tropics dead bodies usually begin to decay straight away, the mortal coil of this particular Yogi resisted decay for 110 hours.

And now it rests under a massive stone slab, which in turn is buried beneath a mountain of flowers. It was a Sunday morning when I visited the Ashram, and a crowd of people were thronging the cool, shady courtyard, kneeling down by the grave, touching the stone with their foreheads, and remaining so for several minutes. Among them were many white faces ; not for nothing did Aurobindo write in English. His teaching aimed at a universal brotherhood, and therefore members of all nationalities are made welcome in this community. This universality could not have found finer expression than in the woman who

I.—5

had succeeded to the saint's position in the Ashram—that ' Mère '
whose portrait hangs in every room of the Ashram. It was for
her that the assembled disciples were waiting on that Sunday
morning.   Very shortly she would celebrate her eighty-first
birthday, and that Sunday she was to mark the occasion by
presenting a white sari or towel to every visitor. The Mère,
whose civilian name was Mme Richard, and who in the course
of an ordinary earthly marriage had known even the pleasures of
biological motherhood, was of French-Egyptian-Turkish descent,
and had, when she first joined Aurobindo many years before,
proved to be such a congenial disciple that within a short period
of time she rose to the position of a kind of *alter ego* of the saint.
There was an air of expectancy among the crowd in the courtyard. Aurobindo had shown himself but rarely to his admirers ;
during his last years he had scarcely spoken to anybody, and had
only occasionally allowed himself to be exhibited. Hence this
encounter with the Mère, even though not a word was spoken,
was an exceptional experience for the members of the Ashram.
" Her eyes give strength," whispered the owner of a printing-
works in Kanpur, whose acquaintance I had made in my hotel,
and who had brought me here. Meanwhile the frail figure,
supported by two woman assistants, had descended the steps and
had sat down in a chair. I found myself in a long queue, slowly
shuffling closer, and had plenty of time to observe her. She
wore an embroidered hood and a full Indian garment which left
only her face exposed. Had I ever seen such eyes before ? They
were totally different from those of Aurobindo : for there in a
finely moulded poet's face were eyes which seemed blind to the
outer world, which no longer seemed to take in material objects,
and which in their seclusion appeared almost haughty. The eyes
of the Mère, on the other hand, were innocent, soft, like those of
a child or a doe, but at the same time imbued with something like
omniscience. They pierced those before her like arrows ; one
felt overcome. But under those truly divine eyes was a mouth
which, it seemed to me, contrasted strangely with her spirituality.
Teeth like fangs poked out from between her lips. I could not

recall what they reminded me of until suddenly I thought of the leer of Rangda, the evil female demon of Bali. But by then I was past, clutching a towel in my hand, with the Mère's birth date embroidered on it. Talk of personality cult ! I thought to myself, and watched the crowd filing past her. The Ashram had a membership of no fewer than 1400 ; a mass presentation such as this must cost a pretty penny. The recipients reacted variously to their gifts, according to origin. The Indians walked away from their revered giver with dignity, yet with faces relaxed and cheerful. " After all, why the fuss ? " they seemed to say. The Europeans, on the other hand, especially the women, received their presents as though each were the veil of St Veronica—they pressed it to their bosoms, arranged their faces in solemn expressions, like girls making their first Communion, and strode away with eyes half closed and, it seemed to me, bated breath.

Even before, at Aurobindo's tomb, this demonstrative devotion of the European followers had annoyed me intensely. It is accompanied, in conversation, with a kind of sentimental hauteur which makes the interlocutor feel all the time that he is a most unspiritual Philistine. A former German lawyer, who for the past seven years has been in charge of the Ashram library—an extensive institution amply supplied with books, periodicals, and gramophone records—gave me some details about the conditions of acceptance. He had emigrated from Germany after Hitler's rise to power, and had gone to Tahiti with his family ; but that island paradise had not afforded him spiritual satisfaction. So off he went to India, to Aurobindo. Every applicant is closely scrutinized by the Mère herself. Her exceptional intuition, I was told, immediately perceived an applicant's spiritual calling, and promptly divided the spiritual sheep from the unspiritual goats. Her conditions of enrolment were these : an applicant must cut himself off completely from all past worldly connexions. His property and possessions were assigned to the Ashram, which for its part assumed responsibility for the physical and spiritual well-being of all its members until their death. And let no one imagine that in Pondicherry he would have to eat the pitiful bread of the ascetic. Aurobindo was a modern saint. Since the body, as he taught, was the residence of the supramental—that was his term for the mystic spirit, for the One behind the multitude of appearances—this vessel must be properly looked after. The disciples, therefore, are living very comfortably in private houses scattered throughout the city. Each one has his duty to perform in the community of the Ashram—either, as our German, in the library, or as an artisan, or as a teacher in the school, which is likewise run according to modern educational ideas. Freedom and absence of restraint are regarded as the best atmosphere for the formation of a young personality ; this is achieved by means of games and music—hence the extensive collection of gramophone records.

Was the Ashram a centre from which the practical application and propagation of Aurobindo's pedagogical ideas could spread to the rest of India, I asked. Well, I was told a little hesitantly, Nehru himself had been greatly impressed during a visit, and had asked how this school could be made to serve the nation as a whole. The Minister of Education had suggested that young teachers might spend some time at the Ashram as visitors, in order to acquaint themselves with its methods ; an idea which proved impracticable since what mattered most was the fundamental spiritual experience. Thus the Ashram lives and works only for itself; its schools are filled with the children of Ashram members. And the two million rupees which the maintenance of the Ashram costs annually, and which derive largely from donations by pious supporters, serve merely—not to mince matters—the spiritual masturbation of a small group.

This may seem a harsh word, but I believe it is not an unjust one. I was soon to find the malaise which I experienced in Aurobindo's Ashram confirmed by many people who had spent some time there, and had left it after the Yogi's death. Even during Aurobindo's lifetime, I was told, the Mère had proved a pernicious influence, because she had placed her unquestionable spiritual abilities entirely at the service of personal ambition. If anyone did not kotow to the Mère, one of the disillusioned told me, then his days in the Ashram were numbered. The old lady was quite clearly an Asurian, a demonic power—I thought instinctively of her Rangda teeth—who had merely assumed the mantle of the saint. A diplomat's wife, who was interested in spiritual matters and who had spent some time as a guest in the Ashram, told me she had felt from the very first days a strange mental depression whose cause she was unable to discover. One evening she had been gazing for a long time at Mme Richard's picture, which in accordance with the reigning personality cult hung in her room too, and suddenly the portrait had turned into a vision of a she-devil of terrifying appearance. She had felt waves of infernal heat closing in upon her, and had been forced to leave the Ashram and Pondicherry at once. It was also to be assumed, I was told, that Aurobindo had been bewitched by the Mère, since tantric Yoga was well known by its preternatural sexual capacity to be capable of providing unimaginable ecstasies. Indeed, the lady added pointedly, to this day, and even at the age of eighty, the Mère had not lost those skills.

I am reporting these remarks exactly as I heard them, without presuming to pass judgment. If true they reveal clearly that the saints are living, not within the safe shelter of solid piety, but buffeted by dangerous metaphysical gales. For in the spheres to which they have ascended they are exposed not only to divine influences, but also to diabolical ones, and the vanity which almost inevitably springs from the adoration of devout disciples only too easily opens the door to all kinds of dark powers. But if, on the other hand, these remarks are not correct, or only partially so, they represent nevertheless a characteristic feature of the world of Indian saints—their delight in slander. The saints discuss each other in exactly the same way as film stars do. Even when they praise one another it is to be silently assumed that the speaker occupies, or at least deserves, an incomparably higher rank. Krishna Menon, a police officer from Trivandrum who has risen to the post of sage, and who dispenses his wisdom

chiefly to wealthy foreigners, and is therefore regarded by
Indians as a prostituted saint, made a contemptuous gesture
whenever in my conversation with him the name of some rival
saint was mentioned. Without the least irony, he remarked that
among all people alive he was the only one who could interpret
the profound philosophical meaning of the Vedas, and must
therefore be counted among the greatest Mahatmas ever.
Evidently contact with the Last Things induces a downright
monstrous degree of uncritical self-adulation.

One need only look at what one of the best known among
living Yogis, Swami Sivananda of Rishikesh, says about himself
in a book published under his own imprint. He writes :

> Swami Sivananda's place in history must be compared with that
> of Buddha or Jesus. Historians will describe him not only as the
> greatest of all modern religious men, but also as an incarnate divine
> power who has wrought miracles in the hearts of men.

I would call Sivananda the Frank Buchman of Hinduism ;
his community of divine life has surprisingly many features
in common with the Moral Rearmament movement. Like
Buchman, he has understood the secret of publicity. The above-
mentioned self-advertisement continues :

> The twentieth century is the age of democracy. Sri Swamiji's
> religion, in order to spread, must reach the heart of every individual,
> not merely that of a king. That is why he addresses himself to every
> individual, by means of books, pamphlets, leaflets, gramophone
> records, and photographs, in order to win them over to the godly
> life. Moreover, the twentieth century is an age of science : people
> no longer accept a doctrine merely because somebody gave his life
> for it ; they must be convinced that it is true, useful and practicable.

Publicity is everything. While in Pondicherry cameras are
prohibited as though they were instruments of the Devil, and
a secret snapshot might mean the confiscation of the film—
almost as if you were inside the Pentagon—Sivananda only
blossoms out when he smells celluloid. As soon as he catches

sight of an unsheathed camera he will adopt a pleasing stance and a wise smile. He even maintains his own photographers, who take pictures of him engrossed in profound conversation with every distinguished visitor, and these pictures subsequently appear in his books. Sivananda is a publisher on a considerable scale. His Ashram at Rishikesh has its own printing-works, and the presses never stand idle. Its productions are launched upon the world by post, and every morning the saint himself spends several hours inspecting the addresses on the parcels, since these are often strangely mutilated by his acolytes. This publishing activity is financed by devout followers : in return for underwriting the printing costs a supporter is allowed to add his own biography to a commentary on the Bhagavad Gita or a practical manual of the godly life, much as a medieval patron and his family were shown on altar panels kneeling left and right of the Holy Virgin. This feverish publishing activity consumes 150,000 rupees [1] annually, and most of the printed matter is given away free. I left Rishikesh weighed down by a parcel containing at least twenty books, one tin of a tonic purée, and one small bottle of hair tonic, manufactured by the Ashram dispensary. But for my firm resistance I should have had even more to carry. Sivananda is a true genius of a giver. In his Ashram he has opened an eye clinic to which patients come from near and far to receive treatment free of cost. Anyone arriving in search of spiritual guidance is given food and shelter without ever being charged. When I asked Sivananda where all the money came from I received an evasive reply : " God sends it," he said. " It has never yet been short."

Sivananda's Ashram does not display that showy spiritual ostentation which makes such an unpleasant impression at Pondicherry. He himself lives in a modest little house above the bank of the Ganges ; his windows overlook the temples of pilgrimage which make Rishikesh, together with the near-by Hardwar, one of the holy places of Hinduism. It is here that the river leaves the mountains which gave birth to it ; for the first

<hr>

[1] A rupee is worth 1s. 6d.—*Translator's Note.*

time it is able to stretch itself, freed from the restraint of the cliffs, as a great new-born river in which men can swim and bathe. At the same time the fresh coolness of the mountains still dispels the summer heat of the plains : no wonder that a whole colony of Yogis has settled at this spot, dotting the banks with their houses. But no Ashram can compare in importance with that of Sivananda. From his small house, past which singing columns of pilgrims file reverently, the buildings climb up the steep slope below the pine-trees of the forest which has earned the Ashram the name of the Yoga-Vendanta Forest Academy. Sivananda can devote himself to his followers only in the evenings, when the entire Ashram, complete with disciples and visitors, assembles under the starry sky to enjoy the presence of the master with edifying talk and songs. Solicitous disciples warmly wrap him in soft blankets and bed him down on a low wall ; Swamiji is seriously ill with diabetes, and can only make his way from his house to the Ashram only with the aid of a stick and the support of loving hands. He is now only the spirit which hovers over the waters, while the teaching proper at the Forest Academy is done by two younger Yogis. He has said all there was to say. His aim—popularization of mystic wisdom— has become reality in his simple, almost childlike songs.

> Serenity, regularity, absence of vanity,
> Sincerity, simplicity, veracity,
> Equanimity, fixity, non-irritability,
> Adaptability, humility, tenacity,
> Integrity, nobility, magnanimity,
> Charity, generosity, purity—
> Practise daily these eighteen ' ities,'
> You will soon attain Immortality,
> Brahman is the only real entity,
> Mr So-and-so is a false non-entity.
> You will abide in Eternity and Infinity,
> You will behold unity in diversity.
> You cannot attain this in the university.
> But you can attain these in the Forest Academy.

Or an even more concrete recommendation :

> Eat a little,
> Drink a little,
> Don't take
> Strong coffee,
> But take
> Mild coffee
> Once a day.
> Be moderate
> In eating, drinking,
> In everything.

Thus Sivananda's community sings evening after evening in the moonlight. Those who imagine Indian Yogis to float only in the higher spheres can correct their mistake by looking at the above little poems. Sivananda, in effect, is not an esoteric saint, and does not wish to be one. Many of his colleagues therefore shrug him off as a charlatan. If one limits religiosity to a private mystic encounter with one's God, then indeed this publicity saint is a little hard to stomach. Sivananda, who in earlier years practised sucessfully as a doctor in Malaya, does not show any particularly holy features in his external make-up either. True enough, his fat belly is wrapped in the pale orange garment of the sacred order of the Sannyasin monks, but his solid bald head suggests much more the successful businessman, especially when he puts on his pince-nez. He looks what he is : a commercial traveller in divine wisdom. And if he did not make any higher claims one might even regard his zeal as meritorious. But what would one say if Frank Buchman were to declare himself to be Christ come again ? Sivananda claims nothing less : he is not merely the proclaimer of a God, but God Himself. " To recognize God," one of his disciples writes, " means to lose consciousness of one's ego and to fuse in the Self, which is the soul of souls, the life of all life, and the Being through which the unending number of things, both visible and invisible, exist." Why then should God not manifest himself in finite human

shape, since He stands behind every form and manifestation ?
I hardly believed my eyes when, after lunch, I was invited to
Sivananda's little house and encouraged there by the God
himself to climb upon tables and chairs in order to take pictures
of the homage which a group of women was paying at his feet.
God Sivananda had made himself comfortable in an armchair ;
a bowl under his feet received the flowers which the women
were scattering over them, and the milk which they proceeded
to sprinkle on them.   This spiritual harem was headed by Dr
Chellamma, an eye doctor from Madras, who like many who
obeyed the call at a more advanced age had at first led a normal
professional and family life.   At the age of forty, after her two
daughters had married, she had followed the bidding to higher
things.   Similarly, many wealthy and respected men leave their
homes after their children have grown up, and their parental
duty has thus been performed, to roam the country as pious
beggars.   Sivananda's books had opened Dr Chellamma's eyes
and brought her to Rishikesh, where she was now in charge of
the clinic as the master's closest intimate, and where—possibly
under the effect of Aurobindo's example—she had been groomed
as his successor and a Goddess in her own right.   What was
more, this had been done with all the full publicity drive
launched by an efficient publisher for a young author.   Dr
Chellamma had dropped her old name and assumed the pseudo-
nym of Sivananda Hridayananda—meaning ' heart of Sivananda.'
She too at times enjoys the honour of divine foot-washing, and
a collection of her love-letters to Sivananda has been published
by the Forest Academy.   " My lord, when I begin to read your
letters I so much lose myself in them that my heart-blood seems
to pulse through the lines of your holy words in order to absorb
the nectar which is contained in them " : could worldly passion
find more ecstatic words than this spiritual surrender ?

Among the devout ladies there was also an elderly person
dressed in the orange robe of the Sannyasin, whose thick accent
led me to suspect Teutonic origin.   I approached her and asked
her in German where she came from.   I could see the pleasure

produced by the familiar sounds, but instantly her spontaneous reply died on her lips. " A Sannyasin does not remember her origin," she said in atrocious English. " Everything that is past is expunged." With which she left me, haughtily, as if I had made her an indecent proposal.

A few days after my visit to the publicity God I was in Delhi facing an old woman whose name, admittedly, did not enjoy the world-wide reputation of Sivananda or Aurobindo, but was held in high esteem among the true experts on the world of Indian saints. Raihana Tyabji Sannidhi did not even belong to the Hindu faith. She was the daughter of a Moslem father, a judge of the Supreme Court, and had enjoyed such an excellent Western education that she spoke English like her mother tongue. Or perhaps not quite : " About the highest things one can only speak in Hindi ; in English they get quite a different meaning," she complained in conversation with me. I had been introduced by an American colleague. Raihana welcomed me with an almost embarrassing intimacy and called me " Brother Peter " ; she did not mind in the least that I arrived without appointment in the middle of a conversation she was having with a middle-aged Englishwoman. This woman was a meek and gentle creature, born in India and so closely linked up with the instincts and destinies of that country that in 1947, when India received her independence, she renounced her British citizenship and chose Indian instead. She was soon to learn that she had placed herself between two stools : the British regarded her decision as something very near to high treason, and the Indians could not overlook her white skin. She was compelled to work for an Indian salary in some administrative office, and eventually was pensioned off before reaching her retirement age. In short, she was no great personality—but she was typical of that large number of people who come to Raihana for help, consolation, and advice. Raihana does not maintain an Ashram of her own ; she lives modestly in the house of friends. She does not act the great philosopher, but confines herself to giving what spiritual advice she can : " A tap through which divine grace flows," is how she describes

herself.   At first sight one would scarcely credit her with any
saintly gifts, but a second glance reveals the unusual character of
the woman.   She is no beauty—on the contrary.   There were
large white blotches on her skin, both in her face and on her arms,
and these biological flaws were intensified by a definite will to
ugliness.   Her toothless mouth, disdaining dentures, had shrunk
to a grandmotherly shape, and her pointed chin gave her face a
sharp appearance.   But her forehead and the bold arch of her
nose might have belonged to a Renaissance *condottiere*, and in
her eyes there was less of dreamy inwardness than wide-awake
intelligence.   In younger years this woman had gained fame by
a book of mystic hymns, *The Heart of a Gopi*, which, alluding to
Krishna's divine love-play with the milkmaid, voiced the ardour
of such a divine bride.   Strangely enough, this book had been
not so much deliberate poetry as a kind of automatic writing—
just as though some divine power were speaking through her.
How was it that a girl brought up in the Moslem faith should be
engulfed by such distinctly Hindu visions ?   Her example proves
that tuition and instruction are far less decisive than the God-
laden atmosphere of India, which conjures up its appropriate
visions even from the subconscious of a person of a different faith.
But then Raihana is no ordinary Moslem, but a Sufi—a mystic
for whom all religions spring from the same ultimate origin, and
who feels at one with those of different faiths—whether Hindu
sadhus, Christian monks, or Zend Buddhists—in their striving
for union with the Godhead.

   This mystical Oneness, this fusion with everything, is no doubt
the root of that gift of clairvoyance for the sake of which so many
people visit Raihana.   As a young girl, she told me, she had
suddenly discovered that the sight of bare feet revealed to her, as
if in a flash of lightning, the fate of their owner.   To-day she
derives her understanding not from the feet but from the hands ;
these she scrutinizes, not palm upward, like the usual fortune-
tellers, but by studying their backs.   When I put her to the test
myself I learned that in some earlier incarnation I had lived in
China, and therefore still felt as strong an affinity with East Asia

as with the West—which is perfectly true. Moreover, her sharp eyes even read the errors and mistakes of my present existence from the backs of my hands, accurate to the year ; I prefer to be spared the details. Raihana does not presume to foretell the future : she is an adviser, not a soothsayer. She discerns trends and points them out to the individual, who must then make his own decision.

Oneness is also the ultimate meaning of her advice. Is not all despair and all grief due, in the final analysis, to the individual's isolation and seclusion ? Quite trifling things like domestic difficulties are resolved in her eyes into a kind of God-given pattern in which even evil has its place. Her house is surrounded on all sides by pitiful encampments of the casteless and gipsies, and the stench of carelessly deposited excrement penetrated to us through the window. " Disgusting," I said ; " why can't people show a little more self-discipline ? " Raihana sighed. " I have often wondered," she replied. " But I console myself with the thought that this desolate piece of land may one day become fertile as a result, and that the perfume of flowers will then replace the present stench. Besides, in a way I admire these people. They live on practically nothing ; they sleep in the open ; disaster cannot touch them since they have already suffered all those losses we civilized people fear, and have thus found security in nothingness."

When I asked Raihana to tell me something of her life she began her biography at a date 15,000 years ago. At that time, she told me, she had been a great miracle-worker, capable of curing the sick and raising the dead. The reverence of men had made her vain and selfish, with the result that she dropped many ranks in her subsequent incarnations. Ten thousand years ago she had sounded the lowest depths of demoniacal evil, being responsible for the unhappiness and destruction of hundreds of thousands. " And now I have to scramble up again from this terrible depth by devoting my life to helping others," she concluded simply. " I am still boundlessly self-centred and ambitious, and to be of service is good for me. In fact, I sometimes ask myself whether my new rôle of adviser does not spring

from mere selfishness, in that even under the guise of a humble
counsellor I am really seeking to dominate those I counsel." I
have never heard such words from any other Yogi—words of
such honesty and unvarnished self-knowledge. The Western
psychologist will have no difficulty in identifying the image of
thousand-year old reincarnations as a reflection of the unconscious
mind with its whole ambivalence of the divine and the diabolical,
which we have already encountered in the case Aurobindo's
Mère. All the saints, I believe, are ambitious for power, for to
become one with God is a piece of tremendous presumption !
The question is whether they disguise their superhuman claim
or sublimate it in such wonderful humility as does Raihana.
The extent to which the destructive devil still lurks in her
unconscious was revealed to me by a glance at the bookshelves
by her bed : from top to bottom they were full of thrillers. " I
read Agatha Christie for relaxation," she confessed to me.
Perhaps some readers will understand me if I describe this saint
with her detective fiction as my truest and finest religious
encounter in India.

CHAPTER SEVEN

Peas against Babies

*W*E ARE ENGAGED IN A HOPELESS RACE AGAINST our women—and for the moment they are still outpacing us," an Indian industrialist said to me in Bombay when I asked him what he thought was the most difficult problem of his country. " Our Government," he amplified his somewhat enigmatic reply, " is doing all it can to raise the Indian people from its century-old poverty. Our economic plans aim at increasing the agricultural acreage by irrigation and reclamation, and at increasing our crop-yields by modern agricultural methods. We are building power-stations and steelworks as the basis of industrialization. And yet we are getting poorer and poorer, because this increase in production is time and again swallowed up by an increase in our population. Our women bear too many babies ! "

It is not even known for certain by how much the population of India increases every year. The inaccurate statistics which underlie the economic plans put the figure at five millions— every year an increase as big as the population of Switzerland. But some critics shake their heads over this figure, and speak of six or even seven million. By the time the statistics are discovered to have been inaccurate, they say, it will be too late—by then the unexpected numbers will have become a disturbing factor beyond any control.

Statistics make boring reading, and there is almost a secret satisfaction in the knowledge that they may even be false. But in India even the optimistic official figures are alarmingly fascinating. Think of it : every seventh inhabitant of the world is an Indian, although India occupies only the 44th part of the surface of the globe. What a disproportion ! While on a world-wide average there are nearly 14 acres to each human being, the Indian is restricted to 2.5 acres, while the Russian can spread himself on 25, the American on nearly 8, and even the Chinese on 5 acres. Among the great nations, only the British and the Japanese tread on each other's toes to an even greater extent, but with industrialized nations this does not matter so much as in India, which is over 70 per cent. dependent upon agriculture for a livelihood. And, moreover, from that 2.5 acres the Indian collects a smaller harvest than anybody else ! His yield of wheat is a mere three-quarters of a ton, compared with four times that figure in Italy, three times that figure in Japan, and more than double that figure in China. The fact that India's cows give only a few drops of milk may be due to their sanctity—but why should the non-sacred Indian hens lay only a quarter of the eggs laid by hens elsewhere, and then only of miniature size ?

It is only the humans in India who are of rabbit-like fertility. In the United States there are 25 births a year for every 1000 inhabitants, in nearly all the countries of Europe this figure fluctuates around 15, and even in Japan, which a few decades ago threatened to explode, that figure of 15 seems to be the present level. But in India the figure is 40 per 1000 ! Why ? For one thing, people marry young. Even though the law nowadays forbids child marriages—which used to be contracted in the old days even between babes in arms—about half of all young girls still marry before reaching their fifteenth birthday. And every one of them, on average, gives birth to six or seven children. In the past starvation and diseases took a heavy toll of these births. But to-day, as everywhere else in the world, modern medicine has stopped up this safety-valve of nature. In the opinion of experts India's soil, properly farmed, could support a population of 450 millions. But if the population continues to grow at the present rate this limit will be reached in 1969. And what then ?

Birth control—or, as it is called here, family planning—has literally become a question of life and death for India. The

Indian Government, therefore, is tackling the problem with all the energy its urgent character demands. No fewer than 2500 birth-control centres are active throughout India to-day—most of them in conjunction with mother-and-child clinics. For above all, the campaign requires camouflage. "The women regard us with tremendous prejudice," I was told by the woman doctor in charge of the recently founded Family Planning Research Institute in Bombay. "There's hardly one among them who will overcome her shyness and fear, and will come to us for advice. Our work is felt to be something negative, a kind of attack on the very substance of motherhood. The Indian regards a large number of children as a kind of life assurance ; in his old age they will look after him, and he will rule them as the head of a great tribe. So long as that old-fashioned social structure is not changed a marriage producing a large number of children will continue to be regarded as a blessing. That is why we must get hold of the women in other ways, why we must gain their confidence before revealing our real intentions. Once we have achieved that, and have explained to them what this is all about, they are, as a rule, wildly enthusiastic."

The staff of the Institute have therefore thought up all kinds of allurements. In the morning free milk is handed out. There is a nursery where the children are not only looked after but also fed and medically inspected—all free of charge. For young couples there is a medical marriage consultation centre. These attractions have proved successful for that very class of the population that needs birth control most—the poorest. By working among these proletarians in Bombay the doctors and social workers are introduced to the specialized job which they will subsequently have to perform single-handed somewhere in the wilds of the country.

But it is not just a case of sitting back and waiting for people to arrive, anxious to be advised. With a missionary zeal which borders on importuning, forays are made into the land of the unconverted. One afternoon I accompanied a group of young women doctors and social workers from the Institute to the police living-quarters. These guardians of public order are so badly paid in India that they belong properly to the proletariat— with the result, it might be added, that they are most unwilling to stick out their necks in defence of the existing order, and, whenever things look unhealthy, prefer to vanish down a side-street. These police lines were anything but luxury quarters : derelict shacks with boarded doors, packed against each other, and behind the door a pitch-dark room with a bedstead and a rusty kitchen-range, the whole populated by a swarming family. We knocked at one door after another. When they were opened—some of them readily and cheerfully, others only after a prelude of sullen questions and curses—the doctor of the team was quick to introduce herself as a helper, since there was hardly a family there that did not suffer from some trouble or other. After a few minutes the conversation invariably worked round to the refrain : " Won't you let me advise you on how further babies can be prevented ? " Throughout this discussion a host of unprevented and unattended children milled around our legs. I must confess that I thought the little brats very well behaved, and I felt that perhaps they deserved after all to have been born.

Contraception ! The reason why, in spite of a vast amount of social work on the one hand and much willingness on the other, no success worth mentioning has so far been achieved lies simply in the magnitude of the problem. How is it to be managed ? The Japanese solution of simply legalizing abortion is impossible because of the respect which Indians have for the sacredness of life. Western-style contraceptives are expensive and difficult to use for primitive people. Just try to imagine their application in some clay hut in a village, with no water, with no lavatory—or in a Calcutta slum, where people live by the dozen in a single fetid room, and where every kind of function is performed in public. The natural cycle method was tried out : the women were given a kind of rosary with different coloured beads on which they might count off the ' safe ' and ' dangerous ' days. But you try to teach an illiterate the necessary accuracy, and then make sure they don't forget ! In addition to all this there is, just as in some regions of Europe, a religious taboo : the religious Hindu feels it improper to interfere with the will of God. If it was to be done, Gandhi had taught, then it should be done not by outwitting but by overcoming Nature : by sexual abstinence. Overcoming of sexual desires was one of the most important, and at the same time most painful, aims which the Mahatma had set himself on his road to self-purification. But are Indian peasants capable of such self-discipline ? " How can you prevent the butter from melting near the fire ? " a simple woman asked the preachers of abstinence. Two states, Madras and Mysore, have chosen a simpler road : voluntary sterilization. Every father of three or more children who submits to a surgical operation—which makes him sterile but not impotent—is given a bonus ! During the first year of the scheme 14,000 men reported for treatment, and the campaign has now been extended to the whole of India. But that is not a satisfactory solution either. What India needs is a pill, to be taken by mouth, and cheap. It is too soon for a definite claim, but unless experiments made in recent months and years are belied in practice, a Calcutta biologist has produced such a pill.

I could not believe my eyes when I stood in front of the Bacteriological Institute of Calcutta, which I have been told was the centre of the research work along those lines. It was one of those dilapidated and depressing buildings with a blackened façade, the kind found by the dozen in every back street. I climbed a narrow, dark staircase, past wooden cages with guinea-pigs and rats, and was eventually admitted to a dark room where Dr Faustus or any other medieval alchemist would have felt at home at once. Its lack of tidiness appeared to be greater even than my own. Test-tubes and flasks had not been washed within human memory, and had taken on a kind of milky opacity. Amid these strange, almost magic, surroundings sat Dr S. N. Sanyal, a Bengali with a permanent smile and lively gestures. He welcomed me with exceptional courtesy, and after a few minutes we were deeply engrossed in scientific conversation.

The venerable Vedic writings contain the advice that Indian widows should eat as many peas as possible. The reason for this was discovered by the Indian university professor N. C. Nag, who in the course of vitamin experiments had fed rats on an exclusive diet of *dhal*, the wild pea of India, which has a high protein content. As a side-effect, he discovered that the male rats fed on these peas produced no ejaculation of semen, evidently because that pea contained an anti-vitamin E, a sexually inhibiting substance. Dr Sanyal pursued this line of research. He injected female rats with an oil extracted from wild peas, and these rats produced no progeny. The wives of several of his friends, whom he boldly enlisted as guinea-pigs, likewise proved upon injection to have a markedly lower capacity of conception. In 1952 he succeeded in isolating the active substance from the oil ; it is called metaxylohydroquinone, and is a substance easily and cheaply synthetized. But Dr Sanyal suffered the fate of so many discoverers : some of his colleagues derided him as a charlatan who believed in contraceptive pills, others denounced him as a dangerous quack who ought to be stopped. Had not an American sociologist, Professor Gamble of Boston University, succeeded in convincing some influential officials of the importance of Dr Sanyal's discovery it would probably have been forgotten. But now the women's hospitals of Calcutta have started on large-scale experiments. Hundreds of women are given a dose of three grammes of the substance on the 16th and 21st days of their cycle. The result has been startling : whereas among a control batch who had been given ineffective pills, 145 women in 1000 became pregnant each year, the rate of conception among the group treated dropped to 59—in other words, a decrease of 60 per cent. Experiments with men proved equally promising ; during treatment the sperm count in the semen dropped markedly, and hence also the probability of fertilization. Metaxylohydro-quinone, therefore, appears to be a substance equally applicable to men and women.

Needless to say, all such apparent miracle drugs must be viewed with great caution, especially as harmful side-effects may not

steel plants at the same time supports this anachronistic form of labour. 'Homespun' is not worn in India for reasons of fashion only, as in Europe. There are State subsidies and impressive State retail shops in all major cities, which make homespun a genuinely competitive article for machine-made textiles. To wear homespun material, from one's shirt to one's overcoat, has been a kind of national duty for many Indians ever since Gandhi's time, in much the same way as rifle-shooting is for the Swiss. Economically speaking, the spinning-wheel by the side of the blast furnace is nonsense : no additional wealth is created, but poverty is shared out by artificial support for antediluvian working methods in competition with modern ones. As so often in life, the middle road between the two extremes, between Lenin and Gandhi, would have been the best solution—in other words, the investment of all the money that has gone into the hastily built steelworks in a highly productive cottage industry, well equipped with small-scale machinery. This is precisely what so experienced an economist as Professor L. Erhard, the man behind the German economic miracle, told the Indians to their faces. I watched the people who visited an American exhibition in Calcutta. True enough, the long queues outside the doors may have been due not only to the exhibited machinery but also to the free pancakes. But I was impressed by the close attention with which the people inside followed all explanations, and by the persistence of the questions as to where these machines might be obtained. All the Americans could tell the disappointed questioners was that so far the Indian Government had found itself unable to release the foreign currency to import them.

A similar smokescreen of Communist recipes has lately appeared in the field of agriculture. Here too independence rapidly brought about an unbloody revolution ; the Zamindars, who had been tax farmers under the colonial administration, and as such had accumulated considerable agricultural property, were dealt with by a land reform. The land shall belong to whoever tills it ! This thesis too had its origin in Communist doctrine, even though it no longer applies there in the age of the commune.

The absentee landlords, who lived in the cities and had their fields farmed by agents and tenant farmers, found themselves stripped of their property in nearly all the states of the Indian Union. True, this land reform was neither violent nor radical, and whenever I spoke to wealthy farmers I always gained the impression that nearly every one had found some legal fiddle— either by cleverly dividing his property among relations or by selling off in good time for a decent price. One of these wide boys had presently invested the proceeds in a cinema, and is to-day raking in a great deal more money than he would have done if he had been allowed to keep all his estates. Judgment on the land reform therefore fluctuates greatly from district to district, and clearly depends on the people behind the official measure. But there is no doubt that making the tenant farmer—who was subject to a moment's notice—into a landowner has greatly increased his social security, and hence also his willingness to work. On the other hand, the disappearance of the patriarchal landlord also has its drawbacks : he was not invariably an exploiter of the peasants, but frequently a paternal protector who supplied them with seed stock, helped them if the harvest failed, and made his contribution to funerals and weddings. To-day the peasants deliver their dues, which used to go to a recognizable person—a villain, maybe, or an angel, but certainly a real person— to some anonymous official and apply for credits to some anonymous commission. Where the Zamindar could have been cruel the official may be corrupt, and the commission unsympathetic. In short, experience has shown in India that a decree cannot of itself bring the solution to a social problem, and that the new system, just like the old one, depends primarily on the moral qualities of the people behind it.

That is also true of the efforts to support the villagers in their first steps toward progress, the so-called Community Development Programme. Government credits help the peasants to build roads, dig wells, set up schools, improve their agricultural methods, and much else on these lines. It is also true of the co-operatives which have already gained some importance in certain states, such as Madras and Bombay—co-operatives for the purchase of seed stock and artificial fertilizer, for the sale of produce, and for the communal procurement of farm machinery. Wherever the official in charge is a hard-working idealist these innovations reveal all their advantages. But frequently he uses his power to line his own pocket. In those cases the old mistrust is born again in the peasants, the paralysing feeling of always being the dupes, and in the end the innovation proves worse than the old state of affairs. A revolution can bring about a genuine change only if it is primarily a moral revolution, bringing with it the birth of a new sense of responsibility. It is this realization that underlies the movement of Vinoba Bhave, which we shall discuss later.

With regard to the future, however, those ill-starred superficial politicians, dazzled by the mirage of progress achieved by externally applied magic—these politicians, though not Communists themselves but good demo-plutocrats with a socialist tinge, have again taken a leaf out of the Communist book. Did not the great Khrushchev himself declare that his Soviet empire would outstrip the United States in agricultural produce in his lifetime ? And are not the Chinese Communists reporting one percentage miracle after another from their collective farms and communes ? Forward, then, let us leap into collectivism ! That, at any rate, was the slogan of the Congress Party meeting at Nagpur in 1959. The time, it was said, had come to expropriate even those landowners who tilled their own fields : no family was to own more than 30 acres. And even that was intended only as the first step in a great co-operative campaign which would culminate in the amalgamation of all agricultural property, in joint work on newly founded village farms, and in a sharing out of the proceeds in accordance with work performed. In short, the classic type of the collective farm. But naturally—the politicians hastened to protest—on a voluntary basis ! And so into the Never Never Land of miraculous production figures !

There are in India some sober economists who have challenged this voluntary-communist wishful thinking. The Russian and

Chinese collective farms, they explain, had their origin in a wartime situation, when it was important to free as many men as possible for the armed forces by mechanizing agricultural operations, and to extort the greatest possible agricultural surplus from a helplessly enslaved peasantry. In other words, the Communist collective farm was conceived, not as a more efficient organization capable of producing greater yields, but as an instrument of internal and external aggression. For India with its millions of unemployed mechanization would be nonsense ; besides, there are no Party cadres to undertake the management and supervision of these collective farms. And what about the voluntary principle ? Considering that the moderate co-operative experiments in the past have so far met with little response from among the conservative peasants, why should it be thought that a large-scale campaign would produce anything but a vastly magnified failure ?

On the other hand, it is perfectly true that there are already a few co-operatives which have gone over to collective management on their own initiative. I visited one of these near Jhansi, in Central India. But this was an experiment undertaken mainly by wealthy peasants with only part of their land—certainly not that complete surrender of individual responsibility that is demanded by true collective management. And that applies to most of the instances which are listed for the visitor as shining examples. Often it is simply a large family which has constituted itself as a co-operative in order to enlist Government subsidies ; after all, the big Indian family, or clan, with 50 to 100 people living under one roof, represents in its patriarchal organization something akin to a collective in itself. In other instances it was the influence of one powerful personality among the farmers, who persuaded his fellow-villagers into adopting the bold solution of collectivization. In all these cases the collective system was not the only reason, but merely one of many reasons, for the visible success. It may be predicted confidently that any officially sponsored all-embracing co-operative movement would eventually be shipwrecked. And what then ?

Would not the system, once its machinery had started to turn, inevitably give rise to coercion, even if to-day it can afford rather grandly to reject it ?

The real problem of rapid progress is the same in India as in other underdeveloped countries : there is no point in achieving the outward forms of progress as long as the people's hearts and minds are not ready for it. Unless, of course, with the contempt for human dignity that is peculiar to Communism, they are forced into these outward forms as into a strait-jacket. The Government in Delhi has correctly reasoned that the key to all further progress lies in the education of the rising generation. In the spring of 1960 the Ministry of Education drew up a record programme, designed to raise the Indian people's educational level at one tremendous swoop : complete implementation of universal schooling. No child born in 1960 is to grow up illiterate. To realize this programme, some twenty million children will attend school for the first time, and half a million new teachers will have to be trained. Not to mention school accommodation ! Already the groups of children huddling in a shady place, without a roof over their heads, and scratching away on their little slates, have become a common sight throughout India. But not only the primary schools are engaged in mass production : the same is true of the universities, and it is obvious that in these circumstances standards cannot be set too high. Especially as the students are in the habit of reacting to over-stiff examinations by protest demonstrations in the streets. While I was in Calcutta a considerable force of police had to be called out to quell an enraged crowd of undergraduates, and save the university building from destruction. It seems that in the development of the human material, as in all other fields of progress, there are certain speed limits which cannot be exceeded with impunity. Education without foundations is apt to do more harm than good : a little knowledge seems to corrode those indispensable rules and obligations which total ignorance used, at least, to respect. In this sphere, too, over-precipitate progress must inevitably lead not to freedom and responsibility but to coercion.

CHAPTER NINE

Cameras and Red Tape

ON MY ARRIVAL IN INDIA AT THE CUSTOMS office when I declared four photo-cameras and one ciné-camera I could see the Indian Customs officer twitch as though he had swallowed a sour lemon. " That's impossible," he said. " According to regulations you are allowed only one camera ! "

I want to say straight away that generally speaking Indian frontier officials are charming people. The officer examining my Swiss passport asked me whether Switzerland was part of the British Empire. Because of India's past associations with the Empire, the average Indian continues to believe that the whole of Europe is ruled from London. Though personally I should have no objection whatever to being the subject of a charming young Queen instead of that of a Federal Council of seven disgruntled old men, I nevertheless decided to give the young female passport officer, who wore her hair in long pigtails, like European schoolgirls, a lesson in elementary geography.

In the Custom-shed I switched over to French lessons. " You are Mr Monsieur," the officer began, studying my passport made out in French. I explained. " Oh, then you are the very man I want ! " he said delightedly. " There is something I've always wanted to know. Do tell me, please, what is the difference between *argent* and *monnaie* ? And what is the difference between *auto* and *voiture* ? " Having explained to him all he wished to know, and thrown in an elucidation of *vis-à-vis* and *rendez-vous*, I had clearly won his heart and his admiration. " You're an educated person," he assured me gratefully.

" About those cameras—why not simply enter them in my

passport ? " I suggested helpfully. In vain. Regulations are regulations. " The cameras must remain here," my French pupil decided almost sadly, after consulting with his boss. " Very well," I suggested, " I'll deposit the Customs duty in full. When I leave the country you return the money to me." But I had not allowed for the snares of Indian bureaucracy. That too was impossible. In fact, everything was impossible. Atari Road was the only crossing from Western Pakistan to India. Through here the entire international traffic passed. But the Custom-office had no authority for anything. They did not even have printed forms for declaring one's foreign currency : I was given a hand-written one to fill in. " If you will pay the air freight we will send the cameras on to Delhi. Then you can settle things there," the officer at last proposed.

When I arrived in Delhi a few days later the air freight from Amritsar had still not arrived. " You'll be lucky if you ever see your cameras again," my colleagues laughed. Why, even the parcels addressed to foreign diplomats in India were more often than not opened and pilfered, especially if their shape suggested their contents to be edible or otherwise useful. I sent off express letters and telegrams. A week later the parcel arrived at Delhi airport and I could go to the central Custom-office to claim it.

All offices in India, Customs or otherwise, look alike. Vast rooms, filled to bursting-point with tables ; only by making yourself as thin as a needle can you sidle through between the desks to reach the official dealing with your problem. On the desks are mountains of paper. And I am not speaking figuratively : they are real mountains, several feet high, skilfully stacked so that they should not collapse and fall on the floor. In point of fact, that would be almost impossible, since the floor too is covered with mountains of papers, with vast glacier-like masses leaning against window-sills and other projections. Paper, paper everywhere. I began to understand how this mass of paper multiplied when my own application for an import permit for my cameras got caught up in this paper maw. Even at the very outset my file contained quite a number of documents : a lengthy account, written by hand—which was why it took a whole week—and adorned with many rubber stamps, explaining ponderously the incredibly complicated business of a stranger conceiving the absurd and totally unprecedented idea of taking four cameras into the country, when surely most normal people were satisfied with one. Having the cameras sent on from the frontier had swelled my file by a number of receipts and other documents, all of which had been punched and were now held together by a kind of shoelace. I was sent from one office to another, and everywhere further receipts, affidavits, and other bits of paper were added ; I signed my name until my fingers ached. Eventually I was informed that some one would have to stand surety for me that I would take the cameras out of the country again. Stand surety ? Who ? It is not so easy to find anyone in India to stand surety for anyone. " Even if you take the things out again they are bound to have lost the report sent by the frontier people to Delhi, or some other piece of paper. One thing is quite certain : there'll be more difficulties," all my friends told me. In the end a diplomat took pity on me. " They can't touch me, anyway," he said. Once more I put my signature to a number of documents, and at last my property was my own again.

Six months later I was leaving the country. The same Custom-office. My French pupil in the meantime had left. " The central Custom-office in Delhi will have informed you that these cameras are being exported again," I said confidently. The officer disappeared into an inner office. He returned. No report. Instead a question : " Where is your receipt showing that some-body has stood surety for you ? " I never had any such receipt. " In that case you can't take the camera out," was the reply, " since you have not proved to us that you really imported it in the first place." As it happened, everything was all right in the end because they managed to find the declaration I had made upon entering the country.

I have related the story of the cameras in such detail because it illustrates an important feature of Indian public life—the red tape which pervades the most trifling aspect of everyday life. True, red tape flourishes abundantly enough in our own countries— what right have we then to see the mote in the Indian's eyes ? There is, however, an important difference : irritating as the red tape back home may be, at least after a tolerable time it will produce some result. In India, on the other hand, every little trifle becomes a titanic duel with the authorities. After a thief had sneaked into my room in Calcutta one night and made off with a few things, it cost the insurance company, the Consulate, and myself many months' hard work to get the police to make an official report about it. " If an Indian Government office wants some information from us," a diplomat complained to me, " everything's got to be done in a hurry. We're expected to produce an answer by the next morning. But we must wait for months, or sometimes years, for decisions which are urgent not only to us but to the Indians themselves. And needless to say, we are invariably blamed for the delay." Here is an example. The Indian Army ordered two Unimog lorries from Mercedes, specially modified to Indian requirements. To be delivered by the end of May. Mercedes worked everything out in order to keep to the delivery date in spite of great organizational difficulties. Both vehicles arrived in Bombay a few days before the expiry of the delivery period. There the Customs got hold of them and the red tape began. It was August when the two vehicles were finally released. Whereupon the Indian Army cancelled the order. The reason ? Failure to keep to the agreed delivery date.

The reason for this particular inertia of Indian bureaucracy is largely a fear of responsibility ; this in turn goes back to the British colonial administration. At that time the lower grades, filled mainly by local staff, were given very little or no authority ; the decisions were invariably made at the top, by the hard-working British chief. This system continues to operate in an independent India. Nowhere else in the world does a Prime

Minister have to concern himself personally with such trifles as does Nehru. At the same time, of course, there is an atmosphere of easy-going relaxation in all administrative offices. I have very pleasant memories of a visit which I paid to a prominent person in the Planning Office. " I am making an exception by receiving you here," the gentleman began. " As a rule my office is strictly closed to all visitors. Otherwise I'd have my colleagues sitting in here all day long, drinking tea, and wasting my valuable time with their silly twaddle. I've got work to do." He had work to do all right. He was working on a novel.

Well, the reader will sigh, perhaps a little enviously, there is the East for you. No doubt in Burma or Indonesia there are offices where things are even more informal. But then the victim does not depend quite so much on their decisions. In Indonesia, for instance, an application is considered to have been granted provided no refusal has been received, and since such a refusal would not be drafted by the office concerned before Judgment Day anyway, life on the whole is very pleasant. But in India— and that too is a survival of British drill—bureaucracy is not only sacred, but it ranks immediately after Shiva and Vishnu. The heavens might fall—but red tape will go on. It is said that remarkable successes can be achieved with baksheesh—but I have no experience of that myself.

Such a state of affairs, naturally, is the more alarming the more power is concentrated in the hands of the State, and hence the bureaucracy. Thus, since civil aviation was nationalized in India, not only has it managed to produce a huge deficit every year, but it has also become well nigh impossible to plan a flight from abroad, since the gentlemen in charge are as a rule too lazy to confirm reservations. The manager of the State-owned machine-tool factory in Bangalore confessed to me that he could use only one-tenth of his time for productive work. The rest was given over to red-tape chicanery and the settling of disputes.

Needless to say, these conditions are reflected in the staffing situation. Whereas a modern European enterprise has one office worker to every three production workers, the machine-tool factory mentioned finds it necessary to have two office workers to every one production floor worker. This might well explain why the steel, the raw material they obtain from a State-owned steelworks, should cost twice as much as it does in the international market—in spite of low wages. In these circumstances it seems highly questionable whether the socialist road which the Government of India has embarked upon is in fact the right one. In view of the small extent of private enterprise it might well appear as the simpler one. But is not India perhaps laying herself open to the diseases of the Communist system without, as a democratic country, enjoying the advantages of that system— totalitarian discipline and totalitarian labour intensity ?

CHAPTER TEN

Vinoba Bhave—a Saint who
wants to regenerate his People

I{T} HAPPENED IN A VILLAGE NEAR AHMEDABAD; I have forgotten the name of it and cannot find it on the map. But that does not matter. Wherever Vinoba Bhave appears the picture is the same. From the distance the scene looked like a village fair. The smell in the air of thousands of human bodies mingled with the dust which their feet had stirred up. Buses and jeeps, filled with the billowing of festive garments, scuttled busily along the roads leading from the bazaar to the school-house on the edge of the village. The meeting had begun by the time I arrived, and I had to force my way through the tightly pressed crouching figures to get to the speaker's dais which rose, pyramid-shaped, from the human sea like Mount Ararat from the Great Flood. At its top was enthroned, behind a fence of microphones, a strange man with a goatee. I should have hesitated even to cough in his presence; so feather-light and wholly demateral-ized did he seem. I was reminded of Mexican mummies which, shrivelled up by the heat, preserve their human likeness but weigh no more than a matchstick. But this man here was alive—very much alive. His voice sounded clear and strong as if it came from a very much more substantial source than the fragile earthly coil upon the dais. The multitude hung on his lips, and he clearly enjoyed his power over them. Not for a moment did he become pompous—pomposity, surely, is the false authority of the in-capable. On the contrary, he captivated his audience by his humour, as their delighted laughter proved time and again. As I was cautiously getting my cameras ready he suddenly turned to

me and spoke in the Gujarati dialect : " If there are four hundred
million Indians," his question was subsequently translated to me,
" how many hands have they got ? " I could feel the crowd
watching me expectantly, but had not understood a single word
of the question, and so just shrugged my shoulders. " Look, the
sahib can't even do a simple sum ! " the old man crowed
delightedly.

I sat down on the steps of the pyramid among Vinoba's
followers, who were all far too busy to be disturbed by a stranger.
Some were fussing about the microphones, others supervised the
turning reels of a tape-recorder. The ladies of the party were
furiously scribbling in copy-books held on their knees. St John
or St Matthew could not have taken down the Sermon on the
Mount with greater devotion, or with greater anxiety lest a
single word of the Master were lost. The meeting was nearing
its end. The old man raised his hand, commanding silence.
Only slowly did the excitement leave the crowd, and only a
jocular word silenced the whispering. And now the silence of
meditation was hovering over the thousand faces in the crowd.
The lined faces of old people, the full vitality of young men, the
graceful features of the girls, and the yet unformed faces of the
children—they all wore the same air of inward reflection, until
unfrozen by a gesture from Vinoba. Five pairs of anxious hands
reached out to help the prophet down the steps, as though he were
a delicate piece of china. His person was surrounded with the
same solicitude as his words. You wish to take off your shoes,
Vinoba ? Please do not trouble yourself. Already a willing
servant has thrown herself at his feet, feeling honoured by the
very act of humility. Even after he has withdrawn to a spacious
classroom, this solicitude for his person does not cease. Vinoba
is no saint in the narrow meaning of the word, and he makes no
more claim than his master and model Gandhi to be regarded as
one. But his picture has grown to such superhuman proportions
in the hearts of his people that he has become the object of
veneration whether he wants it or not.

Night had fallen, and the only light in Vinoba's room was the unsteady flame of a hurricane lamp. It illuminated the modest baggage of the perpetual wanderer—a staff, bast sandals, a few books, and the latest newspapers reporting the public reaction to his wanderings. This is one of the many things, and by no means the least, which differentiate him from the withdrawn Yogis : he reads the papers, for they are an expression of our modern reality on which he hopes to exert his influence. No sooner had I been introduced to him than one of his disciples attached himself to me as a kind of permanent A.D.C.; nowhere in India did I find so much awareness of the value of public relations as here. Besides, a man wielding such far-reaching influence cannot cut himself off : there is an endless stream of visitors at Vinoba's door. They are people whose hearts have been set aflame by his words, people prepared to sacrifice their property or even themselves for his cause. There are also people in search of advice, thinkers who wish to discuss some doubt with him. That evening, for instance, I saw Vinoba—who is anything but a narrow-minded Hindu— bending over the Koran with a Moslem mullah, interpreting to him the universal meaning of its message. But there are also those who give advice to Vinoba, who is not only a dispenser of wisdom but himself eager for modern knowledge. Thus I shared my room for the night with a professor of physics from Ahmedabad. Vinoba had heard of his scientific researches, and, though not acquainted with him, had curtly invited him to accompany him on the next day's march to lecture to him : he was anxious to know more about the effects of atomic radiation on living organisms. And although the professor had some misgivings about our next day's march of 14 miles, he would not have dared to decline such an honour.

What an effort it costs us lazy townsmen to complete a simple day's march such as the saint—we may calmly call him that— does every day, in spite of his physical frailty. Even though my couch consisted of only a few thin blankets on the floor, I sleepily rubbed my eyes when at three in the morning the bell rang to wake us. While the singing of hymns came from Vinoba's room, I surreptitiously shared with the professor the drink in my hip-flask : 14 miles on an empty stomach might be all right for a fakir. But at least these supermen did not carry their own luggage ; a lorry rumbled off with it along dusty, crooked lanes towards the next village, while we—what does a saint care about trespass notices ?—chose the shorter and more comfortable railway embankment.

It was still dark when we set out at four o'clock. A young girl of the party carried the hurricane lamp to light Vinoba's steps ; behind him stumbled about a dozen followers. But the streets were already awake. People were standing outside their front doors ; there were oil-lamps in the windows, and the village looked like a huge Christmas-tree. However, it was not the advent of the Redeemer it was celebrating, but the departure of a man whose step, they believed, sanctified the earth he trod on. Tripurari, my A.D.C. of the previous night, had joined me again unobtrusively, and as we were following in the saint's tracks he began to explain to me the meaning and aims of Vinoba's teaching. Tripurari was one of those young followers of Vinoba such as I was to meet subsequently throughout India. Radiant, almost exultant eyes, hearts full and finding satisfaction only by over-brimming continuously, and the happy laughter of a child. The recipe of Sarvodaya—that is what Vinoba's doctrine of social and spiritual regeneration is called—was quite simple : abolition of private property. That has an almost Communist ring. But in actual fact *gramdan* was the very opposite, conceived as a weapon against Communism. It was no accident that Vinoba had started his work in Telengana, a district in the former state of Hyderabad, where the Communists had incited the landless peasants and set up a terrorist regime. The saint had ventured into the lion's den, visited the peasants, and had seen that basically they were religious and hard-working people who had rebelled only because they owned no land. Vinoba had drawn a simple conclusion : the rich were to give up part of their land so that the hunger of the poorest could be satisfied. In this way he hoped to steal the thunder of the revolution. We have 10,000,000 landless people in India, he calculated ; if each of them is given a minimum of five acres that makes 50,000,000 acres, or a sixth of India's arable acreage. Thus Vinoba began to tour the villages, trying to convert the rich peasants. " If you have five sons," he asked them in his simple way, " accept me as your sixth. Give me one-sixth of your land." The call of this unusual man did not go unheeded. Thousands of landowners joined him, ready to make their sacrifice—their *bhudan*, which is Hindi for ' land gift.' The land thus given was divided by the villagers, at a general meeting, among those who in their opinion needed it most.

But *bhudan* was only a beginning. The idea grew more and more on Vinoba that we humans are not the owners of the land, that the earth belongs to God and is given us only on trust. Why then should only one-sixth be surrendered ; why not all ? Was it enough for the rich to give away part of their lands ? Was not the true community one where the individual ceased asking questions about property, where the village was the owner of all land ? Thus he demanded not merely one-sixth from the rich, but everything from everybody. That was the beginning of a new movement, the *gramdan*, or ' village gift.' It was asking a tremendous lot : give up all you have and start working like brothers, as equals among equals, whether young or old, whether rich or poor. Was such a transformation at all possible on a voluntary basis ?

Not till six months after my meeting with Vinoba did I have a chance of seeing a village, right at the other end of India, in the state of Bihar, where Sarvodaya had become reality. Beraih was not on one of the tourist routes. There were five hours of train journey from Patna, then an hour in an overcrowded bus, and another 30 minutes bumping along dusty farm-tracks in a horse-drawn cart, before the insignificant pile of crumbling clay walls and leaky roofs which bore the name of Beraih appeared among the fields. Beraih is, or rather was, one of the most miserable villages in a sub-continent by no means short of misery. The 83 families, or 400 human beings, who lived here had owned altogether no more than 22 acres of land. A further 30 acres had belonged to some landowners in neighbouring villages, and had been cultivated by the villagers for a daily wage of 8 annas, which is about a shilling. No wonder the village used to have a bad reputation throughout the district—the reputation of a place one ought not to visit without first sewing up one's pockets. Naturally, Vinoba's message has the greatest attraction for the very poor—for what do they have to lose ? But what, on the other hand, have the peasants of Beraih gained ?

Perhaps the most important gain has been an awareness of unity and belonging together, an awareness which induced them, after the surrender of their pitiful property, to make what was perhaps an even greater sacrifice—in future every person must receive the same payment for his work. True, no one would suffer hardship. Rice, milk, and the pulses forming the basis of their modest diet are distributed from the common store. Anyone working in the collective team on the fields of the village community receives one rupee a day. Those who earn more as hired hands working for outside employers keep only one rupee and surrender the rest into the common purse. For many that is not easy. Take Nawal Kishor, for instance, the Sarvodaya worker who acted as a kind of adviser and spiritual guardian angel to the village. He came from a brahmin family of the neighbouring village, and had persuaded his father to give his share in the family property to Vinoba. He was earning 100 rupees a month as organizer of the cottage weaving industry ; of that sum 70 rupees went into the communal purse at Beraih. There were no exceptions, not even for the selfless helper.

But *gramdan* does not confine itself only to levelling ; the awareness of a new start has resulted in more intensive work. After all, what is lethargy if not a form of hopelessness ? Now that the people have a purpose they work for it. Every day each inhabitant does two hours' voluntary work for the village ; thanks to this *sramdan*—which means ' work gift '—Beraih has built a motorable track to the main road within the space of one year. And now they have begun to kiln their own bricks. In a few years time, Kishor told me proudly, only the cattle would be housed in the miserable clay huts ; the people would live in a brand-new village which had already been planned, and which would be built by their own efforts without outside help. No one shirks these tremendous efforts. Kishor took me to a house which at night served as a dormitory for the older boys but during the day was transformed into a textile mill where boys and girls were spinning cotton. The village was already meeting 90 per cent. of its clothing needs from homespun and home-woven materials. In the evening I saw old people in the court-yards polishing rice by means of a primitive pounding device. Elsewhere an ox, blindfolded, was working an oil-mill. Both enterprises were innovations by means of which Kishor hoped to increase the earnings of the village. Already the use of fresh manure and the Japanese method of rice-cultivation had doubled the yield of their fields. Proudly he showed me the savings made by Beraih within a year as a result of this self-help—5000 rupees ! Was this not a confirmation of Gandhi's and Vinoba's doctrine that the Indian village represented a tremendous reservoir of labour and revenue which need merely be mobilized ?

At the same time, many an expense demanded merely by senseless custom might be avoided. I was allowed to be present at a meeting of the village council when a young man's applica-tion for marriage was discussed. A wedding in an Indian village is traditionally an exceedingly costly business, with family prestige demanding such unreasonable expenditure that the father of many a bride has had to pawn or even to sell his land—the basis of his whole future livelihood. To squander the prosperity of a whole family in a single celebration ! It seems incredible, but it is a fact. The peasants of Beraih, of course, have no private property left to consume in this way, since the community is now the only landowner. Our village meeting adopted the obvious solution of combining several weddings.

When the village first decided to adopt *gramdan*, in February 1958, it met with nothing but hostility from its neighbours. Was this not simply disguised Communism, the landowners asked ; and might it not be infectious ? What alarmed them even more was the fact that one of the first measures of the new village co-operative had been the raising of the daily wage to 1 rupee. Very well, said the rich landowners, we must teach them a lesson. We shall simply boycott them. But when the time came for field work they found it more difficult to get agricultural labour from outside than they had thought. And since their peasant pride would not let them surrender to the rebels of Beraih, the fields remained untilled. But was the harvest to be lost because of misplaced stubbornness? That would have been against the spirit of Vinoba. The peasants of Beraih, therefore—no longer agricultural labourers but landowners in their own right—sent a delegation to the neighbouring landowners. " We will cultivate your fields with our own teams of oxen," they began, " without demanding any payment. We shall leave it to you whether, and how much, you want to pay us." And they were as good as their word. The village had yet another opportunity of heaping coals of fire on the heads of their opponents when a terrible storm threatened to ruin the crops. Throughout the long night they worked till their hands bled in order to collect the harvest for the landowners. This double demonstration of an attitude which we Westerners would be tempted to call Christian convinced even the most stubborn among the rich peasants. Not only did they accept the terms of the co-operative, but the example of Beraih was so powerful in publicizing the idea of *gramdan* that 15 villages in the neighbourhood declared themselves prepared to take the same step. Kishor, with the help of a few friends, is going to take them under his wing also, organizing in this way the first continuous area run in the spirit of Sarvodaya.

What is the secret of this almost incomprehensible idealism and altruism which has made human beings, in Beraih and elsewhere among Vinoba's followers, veritable fanatics of self-sacrificing neighbourly love? I got a glimpse of the answer when, to mark my departure, the chairman of the co-operative, who was also a great singer before the Lord, gave a concert for me with a few young men from the village who were beating drums and playing flutes. He sang the same tune time and again, monotonously repeated—to my ears a cheerful melody. Only when his voice rose to a high falsetto was his face distorted in a comical grimace, not unlike that of a keening woman at a funeral. When I asked Kishor to translate the words for me I was unable to conceal my surprise : behind that cheerful and barbaric caterwauling, which I had heard elsewhere in India on various festive occasions, was nothing but a variation on the same macabre theme : Since you must die, O man, do not set your heart on worldly things. Seek to lead a life pleasing to God, since all beauty and all wealth and all happiness are transient. . . . Transience : that is the basic theme of India. The child hears his father sing of it, and the old man hums its message into his grandchildren's ear. Why, then, worry about a few acres ?

However, like all other people, the Indians have their virtues and vices, and one must be careful that a few angels do not make one forget the devils and the ordinary sinners. It is possibly no accident that I had to travel so far before finding the ideal *gramdan*. Another such village, in the neighbourhood of Madurai, in Southern India, left on me a much more equivocal impression. Jari Usilampatti was a settlement of casteless, living in some very nice houses built with Government subsidies. Otherwise there was not much to be seen : *gramdan* had only been introduced a few months before. The biggest landowner, one Subbaya, as a shining example had contributed the lion's share—no fewer than 25 acres. In conversation with him I learned that he had inherited from his father a mere $2\frac{1}{2}$ acres, and had acquired the remaining $22\frac{1}{2}$ by hard work. In this light his sacrifice seemed to me even more remarkable. " Did you never hesitate ? " I asked him. " If I, a Western egotist, had been in your shoes, I should have asked myself : why did my fellow-villagers not work as hard as I ? Why should I be the one to give up the fruits of my sweat ? " But my question was never put to Subbaya. The Sarvodaya worker who acted as my interpreter simply went on strike. " It might give him wrong ideas," he objected. And he confessed to me that the *gramdan*, although accomplished, was as yet far from

consolidated. The peasants, he said, did not yet realize that
Vinoba wanted them to share out the communal harvest not in
accordance with work done but according to need. He feared
that if a lazy person with a big family were thus to come off
better than a hard-working but childless couple this unfair super-
justice might cause a certain amount of trouble. Originally the
surrounding villages too had been carried away by the magic of
the saint's personality into pledging themselves to *gramdan* ; but
when the time came for its realization the wealthy peasants,
frightened by the uncompromising nature of Vinoba's demands,
backed out. "Vinoba applies the yardstick of his own superhuman character to every one," my companion remarked.
"That is his great strength, since enthusiasm alone can produce
results in such an earth-shaking enterprise. But it is also his
weakness. He needs 100,000 workers for the whole of India,
but he has only 2000 because his insistence on absolute poverty
makes only the purest idealists join him. Do you know what
our reward is ? Every *gramdan* peasant keeps a pot, into which
he throws a handful of corn before every meal. From time to
time the contents of these pots are collected and sold. It is from
the proceeds of these gifts that the Sarvodaya workers live. A
fine symbol, isn't it ? But do you know how much hardship it
means ? Vinoba's campaign enjoys the support of the authorities
and of the entire Press—but in spite of all the *gramdan* pledges on
paper, what has in fact been achieved is in no proportion to the
noise that is being made about it. The Kingdom of Heaven on
earth : can one expect ordinary mortals to realize it ? "

But I did not know any of this at the time when, with Tripurari
at my side, I was striding behind Vinoba. Since our start before
dawn the scene had changed. The sun had risen above the
horizon, and had been hailed by the saint with prayer and hymn.
By our side the railway track stretched gleaming into a vibrant
infinity, and the heat began to desiccate our bodies. Along the
railway embankment in the fields the peasants were working—
or, rather, they had been working. For none of them was

surprised by our arrival.   They had all heard of the coming of the
" Father "—as Vinoba is known simply to the people—and as
soon as our little group appeared on the horizon they had hurried
to the railway line to see him pass.   Some of them abandoned
their implements and joined our procession.

In his exposition of Sarvodaya, Tripurari had proceeded from
the social-political aspect to the deeper philosophical ideas behind
it.   Vinoba was an anarchist.   Indeed, it was surprising that
Governors and other worldly potentates should sit at his feet, or
that the police should help to control the crowds at his meetings.
In his opinion the entire State—which could maintain itself only
by a show of force—was an evil thing.   Order could not be
forcibly imposed ;   it must come from within, from the same
spiritual regeneration which also makes the surrender of property
such an easy and almost painless process.   The community,
Tripurari explained, would then be able, by its own means and
without help from the State, to deal with any disturbers of the
peace—provided such disturbers could exist at all in the atmosphere of a moral rebirth.   Peace, non-violent peace, is the re-
current theme of Vinoba's teaching.   He has organized his
followers in ' peace brigades ' and set them the task of ironing out
all the conflicts and divisions at present besetting India by non-
violent means and, if need be, self-sacrifice.   For example, when
serious disturbances broke out at Ahmedabad between different
sections of the population, and when an excited mob was throwing stones at the police in a public square, these ' peace soldiers '
moved in fearlessly between the contending ranks and called on
the ringleaders to stop.   They were answered with jeers and
insults.   The crowd regarded them as undercover agents of the
Government, and pelted them too with stones.   But the police
also mistook the idealists.   When they advanced on the crowd
with tear-gas bombs, striking out with their long bamboo staffs,
the demonstrators melted away, but the ' peace soldiers '
remained, allowing themselves to be beaten and trampled.   It
was the technique used in the past by Gandhi and his followers
in their struggle against the British.   But whereas the aim of the

cal Southern Indian landscape with village pond, gently undulating ground, and women carrying water to their homes.

Straw huts of a primitive tribe in Orissa. The grain is being winnowed by the t

women employed at the Bhilai steelworks take their babies along to the building-site.

Young Indian engineer at the Rourkela steelworks.

icture that is the same throughout the East : *peasants, their backs bent, planting rice.*

d huts, straw roofs, a few buffaloes in the yard : a typical farm in Northern India.
The lady of the house is busy moulding with her hands cow-dung briquettes.

Travelling on foot from village to village, Vinoba Bhave has carried his message social rebirth all over the Indian subcontinent.

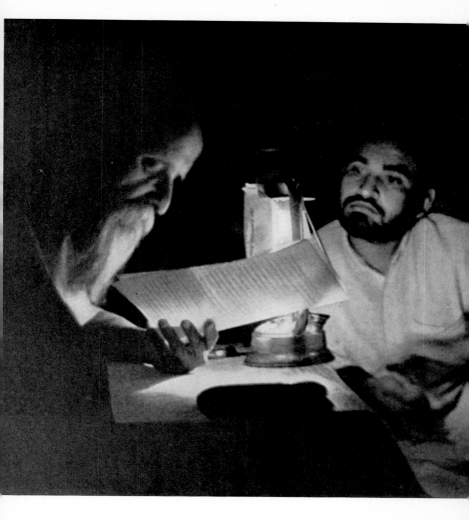

evening with Vinoba Bhave. In a room lit only by a hurricane lamp he studies the questions put to him by disciples and visitors.

Paper-makers in Jaipur : the pulp is kneaded in water and then squeezed dry.

spinning-wheel, a symbol of India's liberation ever since Gandhi, provides an onal income for the impoverished peasant masses. At Beraih the children's work has made the village self-sufficient in textiles.

(above) *The palace of the Maharaja of Mysore now belongs to the Delhi Government.*
It is open to the public on holidays.

(below) *The Maharaja of Mysore on an elephant hunt.*

(Above) " *Children by choice and not by chance* " *is the slogan preached to Indian* *this mobile exhibition.*

(Right) *Birth control is gaining ground : in the bazaar of Amritsar contraceptive* *offered for sale together with wedding cards.*

(Above) *The pavement is my home : this is how rickshaw coolies live in M*

(Right) *A pariah.   To this day the pariahs are for ever bowing and servilely cl
their hands, even when they live in an attractive stone village being built with Go
ment subsidies near Jaipur.*

Brahmin children reciting sacred texts in a Sanskrit school at Madras.

sacrifice then had been the overthrow of foreign rule, it was now something totally different—the overcoming of evil within one's own community. For in the Gandhi sense there is evil on both sides—the disturbers of the peace and those trying to restore it—since both are using violence.

"But tell me, what did the people achieve by allowing themselves to be beaten?" I asked Tripurari. "To me this martyrdom seems somehow contrived, even unreal, since surely nobody compels us to step between two angry beasts." "The peace soldiers," my companion replied, "believe that they achieved their purpose. Afterwards the ringleaders of the mob came to them and apologized. Perhaps they will heed them next time." "Perhaps," I agreed. "But why don't you tell me something about yourself?" I was anxious to learn more about the human side of this extreme, and to my mind almost pathological, idealism. "Oh, you'll be bored," Tripurari laughed. "But if you insist . . ."

Tripurari came from an old family of Zamindars with a turbulent past. In the last century conflict with a maharaja had reduced them to poverty, but hard work and integrity had enabled them to rise to modest wealth again. For surely the ownership of more than 75 acres might be called modest wealth. To judge from Tripurari's account, his had been an almost ideal family, ruled by his eldest uncle; discord had been almost unknown. Tripurari's father had died early of some disease, and his uncle had undertaken the education of Tripurari and his two younger brothers. Had they been treated as stepchildren? Not in the least! The uncle had been so anxious to console the orphans over their loss that in many respects he had treated them better and more generously from his family chest than his own children. When he had reached the necessary age Tripurari had been allowed to attend a commercial college, where he successfully completed his studies with a diploma.

But his altruistic passion, which appeared to be almost a family vice, somewhat upset the plans of the patriarchal uncle. After the family had spent all that money on his education Tripurari ought to have tried to get a post in which, either by wealth or by influence, he could have repaid the family for their sacrifices. Instead he left his family and joined the following of Vinoba. " Even as a child I had always felt an uncontrollable passion for social justice, which I shared with my mother," he told me. " In our family my mother was in charge of supervising and paying the farm-hands, and she used this position for alleviating their poverty from the communal chest without the knowledge of the others. She would give them some grain for their hungry families, or would pass on to them some piece of clothing. At an early age I imitated her selfless actions, but, since nothing was yet entrusted to me, I started to steal things here and there. I was on the right road to becoming a thief from unselfishness when I had a salutary experience. You see, I was caught—and, significantly enough, not in one of my pious acts of thieving but in a perfectly ordinary boyish prank. Outside our school an old man was selling fruit. My schoolmates, wanting a few oranges without wishing to pay for them, instructed me as the best runner to pinch a few and make off with my booty. It was an absurd scheme, and clearly I only agreed to do it because my virtuous thieving had blunted my sense of right and wrong. Everything happened as it was bound to. The old man complained to my teacher, the teacher complained to my uncle, and my uncle gave me such a piece of his mind, so obviously horrified at having nurtured a thief in his family, that I vowed to mend my ways, and henceforward gave up also my virtuous thieving."

But when the young man had completed his commercial college his urge to serve mankind had been too strong to be resisted. First he spent a few months at an Ashram which Jaiaprakash Narayan, the former socialist leader and a friend of Vinoba, maintained near his village. Since then Tripurari had been engaged chiefly on touring the villages of Bihar, enrolling young people as Sarvodaya workers. From time to time he would join Vinoba's entourage for a few weeks or months and accompany him on his wanderings. For his followers this was a kind of retreat, a time of reflection and meditation. And what about his family ?

" My family are angry with me," Tripurari said simply. " My uncle wants me to work and to beget children and to live with them." " You are married ? " I asked. " When I was sixteen I was married to a girl of fourteen whom I had never seen before. I liked her very much, but my call to social work was stronger." " And what does your wife do without a husband ? " " She is living with my family, doing housework." " But is it not considered a misfortune, or indeed a disgrace, for an Indian woman to be childless ? And does she not herself want to have children ? " I asked. " Very much ! " Tripurari confessed. " But I simply can't afford to become a father. If there were a child my family would have to bring it up. It would be a kind of forfeit enabling them to put moral pressure on me to work for its support." " So you have renounced all marital relations, like Gandhi ? " " No," Tripurari laughed. " I am not as strict as that. I like love-making too much to be an ascetic. Every month or so I visit my family, and then I live with my wife." If Tripurari had taken that ultimate step toward asceticism his decision not to have children might have had a certain spiritual logic. But as it was … " Has it never occurred to you," I asked, " that you are being unfair to your wife and ruining her life ? Basically you are still the thief of your boyhood. You are indulging in your social passion without realizing that you are failing in your concrete human responsibility."

Tripurari reacted curiously : he laughed his boyish laughter, whinnying like a horse and showing his teeth, just as if I had made an excellent joke.

In point of fact, this was not the place to argue about such questions. We were evidently nearing our destination. Crowds of people were beginning to meet us on the railway embankment. The stationmaster and some of his assistants had left their posts and had driven up on a rail trolley. Where the road to the village branched off from the railway a vast triumphal arch of green branches had been built. From here onward Vinoba's entry was like the welcome for a popular film star or footballer in the Western world. " Vinoba Bhave, *ki djai*," the crowd shouted along the road. " Vinoba Bhave—victory ! " The shout was repeated from the roof tops and from the trees, to which boys clung like beetles. " Victory to the world ! " the crowd roared in the village square. This slogan ' Victory to the world ! ' Tripurari told me in a whisper, expressed Vinoba's universal striving for uniting the whole world in a spirit of brotherhood, with Communists and capitalists forming part, as it were, of one huge world-wide *gramdan*.

At last it was time for breakfast : shredded corn, a mess of pulses and vegetables, picked up with Indian bread from a plate of dry leaves. The ground served as a table, and every one sat down in long rows. Vinoba disappeared in a house to wash off the dust of the journey. His sinuous body, frail and weightless, showed not the least sign of fatigue. No one would have suspected that he was a sick man. He suffers from a stomach ulcer, and therefore eats only sour milk, honey, and fruit. Never before have I seen physical strength and endurance spring so patently from spiritual resources as in him.

But what is his ' real ' importance—his effect on India ? Is he the yeast which will cause his whole world to ferment—or is he merely a Don Quixote ? Only a few of his critics are worried by his movement. Its effect, they believe, is similar to those resolutions and programmes of the Congress Party which are never, or never entirely, realized in practice : an intoxicating aperitif without a main meal to follow. On his weak feet, through the whole of India, Vinoba carries the revolutionary spark kindling in the peasants hope of a change—and then, more often than not, everything remains as it always has been. Too many people pay homage to him in public who sabotage him in private ; too few people are dedicated enough to do a humdrum job as his lieutenants, as Kishor is doing at Beraih. Disillusionment is inevitable—and who will then take over where Vinoba has failed ? The Communists ; they will not hesitate to use force to deal with a state of affairs which can only be changed by force.

On the previous night, in a short English conversation with Vinoba, I had given voice to these misgivings : with the unquestioning faith of the possessed, he had dismissed them as mere bogeys. There are also optimists who believe that Vinoba's movement, even if it does not realize his ideals, may prepare the ground for the more realistic reforms planned by the Government. " In the past," Donald Groom, a British Quaker now resident in Bangalore, and a whole-hearted supporter of the Sarvodaya movement, told me, " landed property was a social yardstick in India. Peasants were fond of boasting of their possessions and making a display of their wealth. All that has changed : wealth to-day no longer produces pride but only a sense of shame. True, the Inland Revenue Department has done its part in humbling the rich, but the most important reason has been Vinoba's message, that worldly possessions are a theft of God's property. This has brought about a climate in which the State can effect its reforms on a realistic basis. If some progress has already been made with the land reform, without running into opposition, and if further progress seems now feasible, then this is due solely to the fact that Vinoba has prepared the ground for it psychologically."

Small wonder, then, that before the Party Congress at Nagpur, when the collectivization of Indian agriculture was proclaimed as an aim, Premier Nehru called on Vinoba Bhave, the wandering saint. Indian peasants cannot be convinced by economic arguments, but only by an appeal to their deep-rooted emotions. The Premier, therefore, finding himself in intellectual isolation, decided to seek the advice of the sage whose heart was at one with that of his people. It is a great pity that the great man did not, apparently, succeed in becoming a listener. According to eye-witnesses, it was Nehru who spoke incessantly, while Vinoba sat listening patiently and in silence.

CHAPTER ELEVEN

The Steel Battle for India

RED-LEADED STEEL FRAMES, REVOLVING CRANES, the incandescent sparks of welding, the sound of hammering, and the general roar of a steelworks under construction—such is the setting at Rourkela, just as it is at any other steel project. Lorries ploughing through dust knee-deep. A group of workmen with shovels wait on a bank ; as the lorry pulls up they leap on to it and busily begin shovelling out its load of earth on to the road. " Are there no tip-lorries in India ? " I asked the German by my side. " Oh, yes," he replied ; " but this is simpler, more reliable, and, with the wages paid here, no more expensive." Two rupees a day—what, indeed, would one want machines for ? The coolie with his shovel is the machine here. He may not be quite so efficient, but he is a great deal more picturesque. The women especially. They appear at the building-site as if dressed for a feast—in saris of brilliant red, blue, green, or yellow, and with their arms, legs and neck, ears, and even noses adorned with silver rings. They come from the near-by jungle villages, where their fathers still hunt with bow and arrow ; even the Hindus regard them as savages. They do not worship Shiva and Vishnu, but believe in the demons of trees and stones and rivers. And now India's most up-to-date steelworks is rising in the midst of their grass huts. A leap across a gap of thousands of years is performed. But the colourful ladies seem to feel quite happy in this modern jungle of steel and concrete ; at least there are no tigers here. They fill woven cane baskets with earth, and carry them on their heads to wherever they are told. Like ants. I have seen a similar picture before—in China, where thousands of

coolies with scrabbling insect-like legs were moving entire mountains. Yet somehow it had been quite different there : the
conical reed hats, the shoulder-poles, the graceful movement of
the emaciated bodies under their loads—there was something
playful in it all, like the movements of a ballet dancer whose
heavy breathing is not heard in the front rows of the theatre.
But the native ladies at the Indian building-sites are more like
caryatids : they suggest classical drama and blank verse. They
present a splendid spectacle ; tall and erect, moving in single file,
in an endless chain that is continually replenished at the tail, their
saris flowing, solemn and majestic like priestesses. For all we
know, they might be building a temple—a temple of our age.
That, at any rate, is what Nehru in Delhi had called this
steelworks—or something very much like it. By way of
contrast, other parts of the building-site look more like
an open-air nursery : the ladies have brought their families
with them, and while they are hammering stones or mixing
concrete the infants lie on their stomachs on the ground,
watching them. And very practical it is, too : there is no need
to worry if they wet themselves. In fact, it improves the
concrete.

The picture here is the same as at Bhilai, where the Russians
are erecting their steelworks, at Durgapur, where the British
started to build a year later, or even at Jamshedpur, that citadel of
private industry, where Tata has extended and modernized his
steel plant with American money. Only the foremen and words
of command are different. But Germany is represented not only
at Rourkela : some 80 per cent. of the new installations at Tata's
are marked " Made in Germany," and even at Durgapur the
coke ovens have been built by a German firm. The Germans,
much more than the British and Americans, have become the
armourers of India ; the Germans represent the West here in its
great competition with the Russians. Rourkela and Bhilai
are the two concepts which to the Indian public reflect the
dramatic rivalry between the free world and Communism.
Engineers and erectors are playing the part of ambassadors—

even though, as we shall presently see, their behaviour is not very diplomatic.

When Rajendra Prasad, the Indian President, ceremoniously inaugurated the first blast furnace at Rourkela on February 3, 1959, and the first pig iron was tapped at Bhilai on the very next day, Indian commentators could not quite conceal a measure of admiration for the rapid work of the Soviets. Had not the contract with the Germans been concluded six months earlier ? What is usually overlooked is that Rourkela is something entirely different from Bhilai, and not, therefore, a fair object of comparison. Bhilai is a ready-made steel plant—a plant already existing somewhere in the Soviet Union. The Russians merely had to take their blueprints out of their filing cabinets, mobilize their State-owned factories, and at once the project went ahead at full speed. Rourkela, on the other hand, is a unique project, one of the most up-to-date steel plants in the world. Thirty-four private German firms, headed by Krupp and Demag, joined forces under the name of the German India Association, and at a time of full industrial employment at home they nevertheless had to incorporate in their plans the very latest technical achievements and co-ordinate their programmes with one another.

The Soviets, moreover, were fortunate in being allocated the only Indian firm with adequate technical experience, whereas the Germans in their contractors met with many an unpleasant surprise. The Indian engineers who arrived at Rourkela all too frequently turned out to be young boys with no practical experience, only just graduated from technical college, and who had to be laboriously trained first. Many German suppliers were unable to keep to their delivery dates, or else found their consignments held up for months and even years in the overcrowded port of Calcutta. Was that surprising, in view of the presumptuous and impatient attempt to build simultaneously three new steelworks along one railway-line which, for much of the way, is still only single-tracked ? Some of the Germans attributed their difficulties to the Communist-led dockers union, who were said to have sabotaged the German freight and favoured the Soviets. The Soviets, moreover, were able to direct part of their supplies to the small port of Visakhapatnam, on the east coast, which is linked with Bhilai by a double-track railway. In short, while the material for the Russians kept rolling in with breathtaking precision, the Germans got tied up in an awful tangle of mis-calculation and red tape ; for a while it looked as though the Soviets, having started construction later, would outstrip the Germans. " It still seems a miracle to us," a German engineer told me, " that we won the race—if only by a nose. When the Indian President inaugurated our furnace we had been test-running it for ten days ; when the Russians started theirs up on the following day that was really their very first tapping."

The Russians, needless to say, are not slow to exploit their success in terms of propaganda. We are not only faster, they whisper into the Indians' ears ; we are also giving you more up-to-date and cheaper production methods. No worker in the world produces so much or such cheap steel as the Russian worker. These claims, of course, are challenged by German experts. The technical know-how of steel production, they told me, is much the same throughout the world. It was true, they said, that the German plant was costing a great deal more than that at Bhilai ; but that was because it would not only make steel but would include an associated chemical plant to produce the artificial fertilizer which India needs so urgently.

While the technological competition between Germans and Russians may seem to the expert, for the moment at least, to be a draw, I have found all Indians agreed on one point—that in the psychological field the Russians have clearly outclassed the Germans. After a stay of several days at both plants I am able to confirm from my own experience that the atmosphere of human relations at Bhilai is incomparably better than at Rourkela.

Strictly speaking, one would have expected the opposite. Rourkela is situated in a hilly landscape which not only affords interesting diversity to the eye but has also made possible an ideal solution of the town-planning problem. A rocky ridge runs right through the vast building-site. On the one side are the belching chimneys of the steelworks, on the other, screened from soot and gases, lies the vast sea of houses of the residential centre, linked with the industrial district by a pass road over the ridge. The long delays to which the Germans had been subject in the construction of the plant proper had enabled them to devote all the more energy to the residential development, with the result that to-day even a simple steelworker lives in a modest little house, whereas at Bhilai, where the Russians had gone full-tilt at the blast furnaces, the staff must still largely content themselves with primitive mud huts. Real comfort, of course, exists neither at Rourkela nor at Bhilai. The houses still smell of cement. In the naked landscape they look like toys scattered in a vast empty space ; and since the occupants are mostly but temporary, few of them take the trouble of converting the desert into gardens according to their own tastes. At Rourkela the roads at least are lined with trees. But these are still only spindly sticks, protected by low brick walls ; the sun as yet beats down mercilessly, and clouds of dust are raised up by every vehicle. In summer the air-conditioning plant becomes a kind of fortress ; at the end of one's working day one takes cover behind it, without the slightest inclination of putting one's head outside again. This gives the German district at Rourkela a strangely sad air. For a whole afternoon I drove around there, like Diogenes looking for a human being, keeping my eyes open for a small garden or some other sign of German sentiment. At last I found one. Its owner had built a pergola ; white doves cooed on top of it, and a charming little monkey was swinging from it. At last a human being, I thought, and boldly rang the bell. A young lady opened the door and regarded me suspiciously. She did not understand my German salutations. She was an Englishwoman whose husband worked in some Indian enterprise.

What is there to attract a German to Rourkela? True, he earns about twice as much as at home, and many of those to whom I spoke admitted that they were in India only because of the money, so that afterwards they could build a little house of their own in Germany, or enable their children to go to a university. For that they were willing to sacrifice one or two years, lost years with long, empty evenings, and with drink the only consolation. One of the men I spoke to, a father of four, was in despair. While he was raking in money in this wilderness his wife in Germany had left him, and with her lover had spent his savings. While we are on the subject of women—one brief glance at the professionals hanging around Rourkela is enough to make any man an ascetic for life. And if one goes for a woman or girl with a family it only ends in a brawl. That is why the firms have forbidden their staff to engage in any erotic adventures. The Indians are puritans, at least so far as others are concerned.

Which leaves only the cinema at the club—but who wants to go to the films every night? And, as I've said before, drink. But that is frightfully expensive. You drink at the club, glumly, because here too there are no women, not even German ones. The married men do not like to bring their wives, because of the drunk bachelors. You are alone, alone, alone. Loneliness is the basic note of Rourkela.

There is not even any escape into romanticism. The kind of Indian life that has been washed into the new steel towns is comparable to that in the gold-rush towns of the Wild West— not exactly the best public. Old Rourkela, the erstwhile small village, is now over-populated; it is full of spivs who earn a lot of money and sharp practitioners who prise it out of them again— human flotsam in search of easy money. The tigers which, in the reports of fanciful journalists, stalk around the blast furnaces are in reality only mangy dogs. And if a steel erector before his departure dreamed of Mogul palaces, he can now disport himself in crudely and hastily knocked together wooden shacks in front of which the men sleep in the open on their plaited beds.

The worst of it is that not even in their work do they find any satisfaction. I have spoken of the sufferings of the motorist in India, and any foreign expert will confirm the very slight extent to which technical understanding has penetrated the Indian mind.

What is the reason ? Is it innate disposition or is it their education ? " Indian children grow up without those technical
stimulants which almost engulf our boys in Europe," the Swiss
in charge of the training department of the Bangalore machine-
tool factory explained to me. " Hardly any of them play with
building bricks or " Meccano " sets. The adults startle you with
their lack of technical comprehension, a lack which is not miti-
gated by their education, but intensified. In Switzerland you
must have two years' practical workshop experience before you
are admitted to technical training, and throughout your training
you are kept in constant touch with practical work. Indian technical schools, on the other hand, usually content themselves with
demonstrations : you just sit and watch. The student is hardly
ever allowed to touch a piece of equipment. The result is that
young engineers with a very high opinion of their own intelligence
have not a clue to the most elementary characteristics of materials
and how to use them. Here, in our workshop, we first teach
those gentlemen how one uses a lathe for cutting, milling, and
fraizing. It's not as if the people weren't intelligent. Their skill,
once they have been trained, is in no way inferior to that of a
European—although their perseverance may be."

As a result, the performance of a Swiss factory floor worker is
about 50 per cent. higher than that of his Indian colleague, and that
of an erector about double. Naturally, he also earns about five
times as much—a fact which continually horrifies all foreigners
in India. " Machines costing hundreds of thousands of dollars
are entrusted to a man who earns 100 rupees a month, who may
be undernourished, and whose attention may be distracted by
worries. Just think of the tremendous values which are being
risked here ! " The situation at the big industrial projects being
built by the Indian Government is much the same as that of the
motor-cars in the streets—it is surprising that they should exist
at all, and that they should function at all, in the face of red tape
and Indian technicians. There must be a special providence
watching over India.

From a foreigner employment in India demands first of all

patience, and then again patience. And that is a virtue which the Germans have long since surrendered in exchange for the more profitable haste of the economic miracle. " You can show an Indian how to do something five times over, and the moment your back is turned he'll do it wrong for the sixth time ! " This lament has become the theme song of Rourkela. " And even in the end, when they have learnt their job, the moment you transfer them to another operation they forget their old skill." The conclusion is : " It will take generations before they can keep a steelworks going." And this contemptuous judgment is uttered so undisguisedly and so loudly that, of course, it does not remain hidden from the Indians. And Indians are proud and touchy people. They do not show their offence ; but they are offended for all that. As a result, there has been a strange harden-ing of the mood at Rourkela : bitterness and impatience on the part of the Germans and provocative truculence on that of the Indians. There is no love lost between them, and no love feigned. " We'd do a lot better if instead of blast furnaces we built gas chambers for four hundred million Indians," I heard a particularly ' tactful ' foreman cursing. To such rudeness the non-violent Indian replies with a smile. But in his soul he commits sabotage. Whenever I saw workmen at Rourkela talking to their German foremen there was something about the look in their eyes that I did not like. And the Germans, sensing this hostility, look down on the Indians, treat them offhand, or even like importunate insects. At the building-site this means in practice : ' Go to hell ; I'd rather do the job myself.'

The Russians owe the better start in their relations with the Indians to an organizational difference. At Bhilai the State Steel Corporation is in charge of the building, and the Soviets, at least in theory, are only there in an advisory capacity. Every one of the 700 Russians has at his side an Indian engineer or worker who performs his task under his supervision. At Rourkela, on the other hand, German workmen tackle all the jobs of any importance themselves. At the British building-site of Durgapur the share of the work done by Europeans is even greater. The Indians, who are already dreaming of building a fourth steel plant entirely on their own, naturally learn most at Bhilai, and the Russians, who pass on to them this knowledge, are doing their best to publicize this aspect of their work with phrases of ' brotherly co-operation.' " The Germans won't teach us anything " is the general opinion in India to-day. " They are here to make money—they are efficient, but with an eye to the main chance. The Russians, on the other hand, are helping us along. . . ."

As a result, there is not only a different organization at Bhilai, but also a different spirit. The irritation which hangs in the air at Rourkela is totally absent here. The simple reason is that the Russians in India are happier than are the Germans. They are allowed to bring their wives and children with them, and from the ground floor of one of their hotels I could hear the voices of schoolchildren chanting in unison. There is nothing here of the loneliness of the Germans. On the contrary : in the evenings groups of women sit around in garden chairs, outside their houses, chatting, and keeping an eye on the children who are playing together. The men flop down behind chessboards as soon as they have a free minute. Wherever four Germans are gathered to-gether they curse the Indians. Wherever four Russians are gathered together they make up two boards of chess and forget the troubles of their working day. If there is anything they complain about it is the heat. They simply have better nerves than the Germans. Probably they are also slower themselves, and not so terrifyingly efficient ; hence the Indian temperament does not irritate them so much. As a result, the atmosphere of Bhilai is more peaceful, without the shaking of fists and furious scowls. After all, the Russians have their own *Nichevo*. They are not easily put out, and are good-natured like bears.

There is only one thing that makes them angry—a camera. They either beat a hasty retreat or else they come for you aggres-sively. At first they thought I was an American who was going to publish their picture with some sneering caption. When I revealed myself as a neutral Swiss several of them patted my

back in a friendly manner. But they would not let me photograph them all the same. "Maybe you're working for an
American paper," they suggested. Or perhaps the women,
whom I snapped buying clothes in the local store, got so angry
because they were afraid Big Brother in Moscow might see the
picture. That the young lady whom I caught engrossed in an
American thriller should have escaped the moment she saw my
camera seemed understandable. Generally speaking, there was
little of a Communist atmosphere to be noticed in the hotels
where most of the Russians lived. No pictures of Stalin, no
pictures of Lenin, no flags with hammer and sickle. The Indian
management of the project had firmly asked them to avoid such
displays, and the only things to be seen in the hotel lobby were
the familiar production graphs, illustrating the superiority of the
Communist system over the American. Nor did I get the impression that the Russian Government had sent to Bhilai only
hand-picked Party members. I had a lot of conversations with
several young engineers who spoke English, and who talked to
me more freely than would have been possible in Russia. Most
of them, for instance, admitted frankly that the crushing of the
Hungarian rebellion had been a piece of folly and a crime, and
merely made the excuse that any other great Power would have
acted likewise. When I asked one of them— the husband of the
young lady interested in detective fiction—whether they had
political meetings at Bhilai he burst out laughing. " No, no ; we
don't have those here, thank goodness ! "

But then it is not surprising that the Russians should be happy
in India. Whereas for the Germans Rourkela is a kind of exile
from the pleasures of civilization, India for the Russians is a kind
of holiday from tyranny and a consumer paradise. Their children
are dressed so smartly in imperialist nylon as though every day
were a feast day, and the men indulge themselves in a luxury
confined back home to the very highest of Party functionaries—
suits made to measure. The shops of Bhilai have all put up
notices in Cyrillic letters, and every evening are invaded by
Russian customers. The Russians, it is true, are not as well off

as their German colleagues. Their pay, 60 per cent. of which
they receive in Russia and 40 per cent. in Indian rupees, is only
half as big again as it would be back home. But since the rupee
buys considerably more than the rouble, the Russians are nevertheless better off. Some of them, I was told, were saving up
their Indian money in order to buy a motor-car when they got
back to Moscow ; in this way, by paying in foreign currency,
they could cut out years of waiting.

The one thing the poor devils lack is vodka. Bhilai is situated
in a dry zone, with total prohibition. And the project management—no doubt wisely—had declined to make a special application for an alcohol licence. Thirsty people therefore must
travel some 20 miles by rail in order to leave the dry zone and
enter a wet one, where they can stock up with the frightful hooch
that is distilled in India. They must do their drinking in the
privacy of their rooms so as not to spoil the good impression of
the temperate Russian. And if one of them is seen swaying a
little on his way home, then that is merely the heat affecting his
sense of balance, and he should be in hospital.

The hospital is a chapter by itself. The Germans in Rourkela
have their own splendidly equipped hospital, with two-bed
wards, air conditioning, and the most modern operating theatre.
" We couldn't possibly have our people share the place with the
Indians," the German doctor explained to me. " We should be
swamped by native patients, since white doctors command a
higher prestige than native ones. And then, think of the traffic !
You know the Indians : a patient's entire family comes along to
hospital with him, they sleep by the side of his bed, sometimes
even in it, look after him, and maybe cook for him. Share the
same hospital ? Impossible ! " Well, the impossible has been
achieved by the Russians. The Russian doctor shares with his
Indian colleagues his work of looking after his patients, regardless
of the colour of their skin ; just as he treats Indian patients, so the
Russian patients allow themselves to be treated by the Indian
doctors. And apparently to everybody's satisfaction.

I have mentioned the club which the German firms have built

to give their employees at least a fraction of the amenities they would have back home. After having gone without baths for about 18 months, they can now have a dip in the swimming-pool after the day's work. The Russians merely have a minute pond in the yard of their hotel, and the solitary billiard table in the hotel lounge cannot compare even remotely with the elegance of the German club. But these amenities are bought dearly by the Germans. As they did not wish to expose the women in the swimming-pool to the lascivious stares of the natives, membership was restricted, if not to Europeans, then at least to Europeans plus a very small, exclusive group of Indians—a camouflaged colour bar which was eased only following intervention by the German Ambassador. In recent years the Indians have become very colour-conscious. They react with growing irritability to anything that might be interpreted as colonialist haughtiness. In Calcutta all clubs which refused admission to coloured people had their drink licence withdrawn. In Bombay the Breach Candy bathing-beach, which used to be reserved for Europeans only, was compelled by street demonstrations to waive its exclusiveness. "For the Germans to build a separate hospital and an exclusive club at this moment was a tremendous mistake," one of the leading journalists told me. "Even if the firms claim they have built it all with their own money, and they will hand over everything to the Indians as a generous gift once the steelworks is built, this cannot appease the bitterness in our hearts."

I do not think that the different attitude of the Russians springs from deliberate political intention. It just seems perfectly natural for the Indians to eat in the Russian canteens, and for Indians and Russians to sit among each other in the buses on their way to work. After all, the Russians are half Orientals themselves. There is a comradeship between them, cutting across race barriers.

There is, however a different kind of barrier. No matter how charming the Russians are to work with, an Indian engineer told me, there is no such thing as close social contact. Even though they move more freely in India than at home, the eye of Big

Brother is on them all the same.   Opposite the porter's lodge in their hotel a loudspeaker blares away all day long, relaying Moscow Radio.   On the first evening, when I strolled about the hotel lawn among the Russians enjoying their leisure, a tall man approached me. " What are you doing here ? " he asked me in perfect English, casting a disapproving glance at my shorts.   The Russians regard such imperialist nakedness as undignified ;   even in the worst heat they wear long trousers.   I introduced myself as a neutral journalist, and tried to involve the haughty gentleman in conversation.   " And who, if I may ask, are you ?   Your English is excellent."   " Thank you," he barked.   " Are you an engineer ? "   I persisted.   Without a word, he turned his back on me.   But throughout the evening, whenever I managed to get into conversation with a Russian, the tall man appeared in the background ' by accident.'   I was not born yesterday.   Nor, for that matter, were the more intelligent Indians.

The efficiency of the Russian housewife eliminates yet another source of continual friction—servants.   At Rourkela a cook and a nursemaid are *de rigueur* for any reasonably respectable household.   They cost about 60 to 80 rupees a month—twice as much as in Calcutta or Bombay—and rob their masters right and left. In the end, when the infuriated master has shown them the door, there is not a grain of salt left in the larder, and the successor must first be given a good sum of money for stocking up with the most fundamental supplies again.   The wise employer will keep out of his kitchen.   The sight of the fly-blown goat carcasses which the cook has bought in the market for roast lamb, or the sight of him chopping up the meat on the floor, might ruin his appetite for ever.   In this respect the Russians show a very sensible national reserve.   They do not want to get dysentery.   In the works canteens there are Russian cooks.   And at home the Russian housewife does the cooking, and, what is more, she also does the shopping in the market.   Thus the whole crowd of thieving parasites that infest the houses at Rourkela do not exist at Bhilai. Likewise, there is no sign at Bhilai of the rickshaw boys who exploit their German victims so ingeniously at Rourkela ;   the

Russians regard it as a degrading form of exploitation to be propelled by the muscular force of another human being. What the coolies think of this view I do not know. It is hardly likely that it will convert them to Communism.

That brings us to an important point—propaganda. Not even the most naïve Indian will believe that the Russians are building a steelworks at a rate of interest of only 2·5 per cent.—compared with the 6·3 per cent. charged by the Germans—merely for the sake of Nehru's *beaux yeux*. Where then is the rub ? Well, for the time being, plain achievement is the best and the only propaganda made by the Russians. Ironically enough, the conciliatory spirit of Bhilai seems to awaken in the Indian work-man a much greater sense of responsibility than the German efficiency in Rourkela. Whereas there the Communist trade-union is busy subverting, and the threat of a strike is continually in the air, the workers of Bhilai, in spite of their Red friends, are firmly in the ranks of an organization supporting the Govern-ment. And the same drivers who at Rourkela turn their Mercedes buses into battered scrap-metal maintain their vehicles in exem-plary condition at Bhilai.

And what about the 700 engineers who are returning from being trained in Russia ? I do not believe there is a serious risk of infection. Most of those I talked to combined admiration and liking for the Russian people with considerable doubts about their political system. A few, of course, may succumb to Com-munist influence, especially if it is combined with feminine charms. Among all the pleasant and cordial encounters I had in Bhilai there was only one, with a mixed couple, which ended on a jarring note. Mrs Alla Garga, the daughter of a high Communist functionary, who had met her Indian husband at a steelworks on the Sea of Azov, was certainly no beauty—in either appearance or disposition. I visited her home together with a Russian companion, and had an exceedingly stimulating discussion along highly unorthodox lines. Throughout it she sat in almost sulky silence. Not till she saw us to the door did she suddenly open her mouth. " The Americans are idiots," she crowed. " We Russians are intelligent. If war comes we shall smash them. And then all of you will be on your knees before us—all of you ! " We looked at each other in embarrassment—my Russian companion, an Indian colleague, and I. Only her husband nodded agreement. " In that case I fear we shall not be on our knees but we shall all be under the ground," I contradicted softly. I had suddenly realized with a shiver that somewhere behind that courteous mask of Bhilai was the diabolic grimace of a claim to world domination. And suddenly I preferred the cursing, colonialist, tactless Germans.

CHAPTER TWELVE

Hurrah, we are off to Prison!

THE MAIN SQUARE OF THE TOWN OF BELGAUM, in the border area between the states of Bombay and Mysore, near the Portuguese colony of Goa, was filled with an expectant crowd, which thronged the steps, windows, verandas, and even the roofs of the surrounding buildings. Had I arrived on a feast day? In the centre of the square the portrait of a seventeenth-century maharaja had been fixed to a lamp-post. The text accompanying it was in Indian script, and I had to appeal to a stranger to explain to me what was going on. The old gentleman in the picture, he explained to me, was Sivaji, the great ruler of the Mahrattas, who, together with the Sikhs and the Rajputs farther north, make up India's great warrior races. Sivaji and his successors had carved out for themselves vast areas from the crumbling empire of the Moguls, and in chaotic wars over the centuries succeeded in holding them against other claimants—until friend and foe alike came under British rule. At any rate, the Mahratta name has ever since been indissolubly linked with Indian heroic history, and even under British rule they had continued, in the Indian Army, to play a glorious and important part.

But there was quite a different story behind Sivaji's portrait in the town square of Belgaum. A group of police officers were standing near by, and all round the crowd was kept under control by a number of constables. Suddenly from a side-street, there appeared a strange procession. It consisted of about seven men, old peasants with yellow and red lines painted on their foreheads, and youths who seemed scarcely out of school. Round their necks they wore garlands of flowers, as the Hindus do on festive

occasions.   As they advanced towards the town square in single
file they chanted slogans which were received by the population,
and especially by a group of boys on the roof-tops, with stormy
applause.

The moment the demonstrators hove into view the police
came to life : they moved in to meet them, halting the procession with imperious gestures.   One of the officers placed himself in front of the leader of the garlanded group and for a few
moments spoke to him.   The old man shook his head, and the
officer motioned to a near-by policeman.   Thereupon the line
of demonstrators moved off again, but now behind the policeman, towards a police van with barred windows, and calmly
boarded it as if setting out on a sight-seeing tour.   " What's
going on here ? " I asked my neighbour in the crowd.   " These
people are being arrested," he replied, " because they wanted to
garland Sivaji's portrait."   " And that's forbidden ?   And why
did they want to garland it ? "   " Public demonstrations are
subject to a police permit," the man explained.   " Besides, gar-
landing the portrait is only a pretext ;   the people do it simply
because they want to infringe some regulation or other in order
to be jailed.   It happens every day at this hour, at half-past five,
and so as to make things easier for the police they are given
advance notice of the place of venue and of the names of the
offenders.   Look, here's another lot coming."

The same process was repeated :   the police officer rattled off
his caution with an air of revulsion, like an actor who is sick and
tired of his part ;   and again, patiently like sheep, the second
party of demonstrators climbed into the Black Maria.

The following morning, at nine o'clock, I witnessed the
process in reverse.   Outside the prison gates a group of men with
garlands of flowers was waiting for some fifteen women, who
like ordinary convicts were now coming out by a door carrying
their few possessions in suitcases.   I drove with them to the offices
of the local paper, where the ladies were to be interviewed over
a cup of tea.   They belonged to the same strange militant
Satyagraha groups as the men of the night before—fighters who

want to achieve their aim not by violence but by non-violent means, not by giving but by suffering pain.

Satyagraha is an invention of Gandhi's, and it was this method he chose for his fight against British colonial rule. *Satya* is an elastic concept, meaning anything from ' truth ' to ' love ' and ' soul.' *Graha* means ' firmness ' or ' strength.' *Satyagraha* therefore means ' spiritual strength ' or ' steadfastness through love.' " Satyagraha," Gandhi had explained, " means to make truth heard in a way that causes pain not to one's opponent but to oneself." While violence only breeds counter-violence, embittering the atmosphere beyond all hope of conciliation—Algeria is a case in point—the Indian method has the advantage of shaming rather than inflaming one's opponent. Gandhi believed that such an opponent would end up by feeling his rights to be unjust and by laying down his arms—and history, in the struggle against British overlordship in India, has proved him right. The history of the Indian struggle for independence is full of such strange feats of heroism, when hundreds and thousands of people deliberately broke the law, mostly in a symbolical way—such as infringing the British salt monopoly by getting salt from the sea—even if that meant police truncheons and several months or even years of imprisonment. The sheer number of willing victims must paralyse the arm of even the wildest and most enraged hitter, and overcrowd even the most spacious prisons. Satyagraha thus became a method of struggle hallowed by Gandhi's name, and it enjoys an almost mystical prestige in India to this day.

Now, the cause of the citizens of Belgaum, who have been regularly sending their victims to prison each day for several months, is certainly not so earth-shaking as India's struggle for independence. In recent years the Indian Government has started to rearrange the former British provinces, which had frequently been drawn in accordance with strategic or administrative whims, and to redelineate them in accordance with linguistic considerations. India, as is generally known, is not so much a nation as a continent, inhabited by peoples and races differing from one another no less than those of Europe. There are 14 officially recognized languages in India, which in turn are subdivided into 720 dialects. While the northern group of languages go back to Sanskrit as their common root, and hence show the kind of similarity that French shows to Spanish, the southern (Dravidian) languages are totally different from them—as, for instance, Hungarian is from German—and that difference can no longer be bridged by the speakers. For this reason English has remained the official language of India to this day, even though every effort has been made to replace it by Hindi, which is the most widespread of the northern languages. The attempt at redrawing the boundaries of the administrative provinces in accordance with linguistic principles provoked a totally unexpected provincial patriotism which has in many cases caused a lot of headaches to the Central Government in Delhi. In the north the Sikhs want to carve out their own Sikhistan from the Punjab, which is already divided between India and Pakistan. In Bombay, which embraces two groups, the Gujarati, who are clever businessmen, and the Mahrattas, the warrior race mentioned above, as a bilingual country, the conflict between them has grown into such bitter hostility that a reluctant Central Government finally has found itself compelled to divide the state. But to return to our Satyagraha fighters of Belgaum. This town, although predominantly inhabited by Mahrattas, as is also the surrounding countryside, has been incomprehensibly assigned to the South Indian state of Mysore—which almost amounts to foreign rule for the population. Not only do the people of Mysore differ totally from their northern neighbours in race and customs, but their language, Kannad, is as strange and incomprehensible to them as Arabic is to us. It is hardly surprising that this has led to trouble.

Naturally, in a democracy this ought not to be an insoluble problem. Canvassing for signatures, elections, and other means of public opinion polling ought to make it possible to solve the problem to everybody's satisfaction—either by redrawing the frontiers or by safeguarding the interests of the minority in a state with a different language. However, all these means had been tried by the citizens of Belgaum, without eliciting any response whatever from the cumbersome administrative machinery in Delhi. The Indian Press publishes articles full of sympathy. The Ministers make fine promises. And that is all. In the end, to lend emphasis to their demands, the people had resorted to Gandhi's well-proven method.

Yet it would be a mistake to be overawed by these citizens who are prepared to go to jail for their convictions. When I asked the leading lady of the group which had just come out of prison to tell me about her sufferings I got a somewhat unexpected reply. "It was a lovely holiday for us all," she said. "You know how a housewife is always in harness, with hardly a free minute from her daily domestic chores. In prison we had a splendid time : we sat together in one large cell, chatting, playing games, and singing, and those who could not read or write were taught by the rest of us." But among the men, too, there are a lot of cheerful Satyagrahas. "A considerable proportion of the demonstrators," the police officer told me, "are, as you can see, aged people no longer capable of work. The political organization gives them a few rupees, and in return they are only too willing to be housed and fed at the public expense for a few weeks." For that reason the police have lately adopted a new method. They charge only those demonstrators who have a regular means of livelihood, and to whom imprisonment really constitutes a sacrifice. The others arrested—hired good-for-nothings—are at about midnight driven by police van some 15 or 20 miles out into the country and set down in small groups. A long walk in the dark is far less enjoyable than a few weeks' holiday in prison.

"Men's actions are ennobled by their aim," says the poet. That is also true of Satyagraha, which within the framework of the struggle for independence had a certain grandeur, but which in trifling matters only too easily becomes a caricature of itself. While the citizens of Belgaum are at least engaged in a just struggle, there are also a lot of eccentrics in India who use

Satyagraha as a means of imposing their particular unreasonable demands upon the community. People fast or go to prison for any reason you can think of, and for a lot that you cannot. For instance, in order to compel the Government to give up English as the official language. Some men in Madras did not like the name of the radio-station—reason enough for them to lie down in front of it and fast. And why, indeed, should these semi-lunatics not resort to this means of political pressure, when Nehru himself allowed the hunger strike of a fanatic to induce him to set up the new state of Andhra Pradesh, although at first violently opposed to it ? And was it not this decision that triggered off the whole dispute about linguistic boundaries ? A lot of pressure can be brought to bear on a Government which is not sure of its own mind !

If the idea of non-violence is to-day being reduced *ad absurdum* it may well be asked whether this absurdity has not in fact always been inherent in it, and had only been temporarily eclipsed by the outstanding personality of Gandhi. In the final analysis, was not the Mahatma's obsession to torture himself to near death on every suitable or unsuitable occasion terrifying rather than impressive ? Louis Fischer relates that the amorous adventure of an American woman, a visitor at his Ashram, with one of his disciples had occasioned such a ' penance.' You can interpret it as a secret communion with everything that exists, when the guilt of one part can be punished or atoned for by the suffering of another part ; but you can also call it plain masochism, which again is nothing but repressed and inverted aggression. The most irritating thing about this curiously equivocal attitude, which uses violence the more effectively by its non-violent persistence—like a fly which returns to the same spot on your face no matter how often you brush it off—is the element of hypocrisy in it. Everybody applauds non-violence as a great moral feat, whereas in fact it is nothing but thick-skinned perseverence, terror practised by the weak. But even hypocrisy has its limits. Many an action committed in India gives the lie to the spirit of Ahimsa. Even Gandhi was forced to admit that the non-violence campaigns, translated to the level of the masses, were apt to result in furious outbreaks of violence. And the hecatombs of victims butchered on both sides of the demarcation line during the partition of India differs from Auschwitz only in that in Germany horror wore official uniforms, whereas here the human beast acted collectively and beyond comprehension. I do not know which is worse.

CHAPTER THIRTEEN

Fortunes and Misfortunes of a Maharaja

TO BE A MAHARAJA TO-DAY IS BY NO MEANS ALL pleasure. I visited two of the noblest representatives of this category, and I would think twice before exchanging my humble existence with theirs. The more illustrious of the two, in terms of descent, was the Maharaja of Udaipur, whose family has its equal only in that of the Emperor of Japan—both of them trace their origin back to the Sun.

No, it certainly is no pleasure to be a maharaja, at least if the laments of this deposed ruler are to be believed. Strictly speaking, ' deposed ' is not quite correct. In 1947, when Sardar Patel, the energetic Minister of the Interior of independent India, persuaded or compelled the major and the minor princes to surrender their power ' voluntarily,' and to allow their countries to be incorporated in the great new mother country of them all, Udaipur was still being ruled by the Maharaja's father. Again, strictly speaking, ' father ' is not quite right. The last direct scion of the old line of warriors was so degenerate and paralysed that, although he had tried his luck with three wives, he had not managed to produce an heir to the throne, and had therefore adopted the most handsome and cleverest boy from a collateral line. Certainly the young maharaja with whom I spent an evening chatting in his palace is handsome, clever, and pleasant. His palace is everything the exacting tourist expects a fairy-tale palace to be : it is mirrored in the famous Pichola lake. The situation did not lack a certain comical element : I had put on a formal dark suit for my visit, but his Highness came in from playing cricket, in white trousers and an open-necked shirt. Now that his little country had been incorporated in the new state of Rajasthan, cricket was about all that was left to him. And he did not seem bored in the least. His worries were of a different nature : we spent all evening talking about taxes. The Indian Government, it appeared, had thought up such an iniquitous system of tax laws that sooner or later every citizen who has money at all must get caught in its mesh. If he hangs on to his property he pays property tax ; if he gives it away he pays donation tax. If he decides to have a good time with it he risks having to pay luxury tax. Not to mention the excise tax which every article bought or sold carries. If he dies a rich man his heirs will have to pay death duty. In short, money in India is like butter in the sun : whichever way you turn it, it melts away in the end. That, it appears, is true also of the property of the maharajas whose privilege of tax exemption was withdrawn in 1957. Moreover, further disasters are in the air : land reforms, which will reduce to a fraction those lands from which they have in the past derived their income.

And for how much longer is the Government of India going to pay the annuities which, in order to sweeten the bitter pill, it undertook to pay their Highnesses at the time of their abdication ? 56,000,000 rupees a year for the 158 deposed princes is a tidy sum of money for such a poor country, especially if every penny is needed for its industrial development. Will some more radical Government not simply declare one day : Enough ! we aren't paying those parasites another penny ? " I thought it wise to send my son to technical college," the Maharaja of Udaipur said wistfully. " At least he will be able to make himself useful as an engineer." He himself, for the time being, still received the agreed one million rupees. " Not a sum to be sneezed at," I suggested. But his Highness shook his head sadly. " Before independence my father's income was three million a year," he sighed. " Not by any means for personal luxury only. This money paid for the entire administration of our little country. There were three thousand people on my father's payroll, and there are fifteen hundred left on mine." After all, just because the capital has been moved to Jaipur, one could not let the people starve. Oh, yes, if their Highnesses could use their annuities for themselves they might rub along very nicely. But no self-respecting maharaja would do that—certainly not a Maharaja of Udaipur, where chivalry and the obligations of rank have always been held in high esteem. But even that does not exhaust the patriarchal expenditure of a maharaja. " Unfortunately, the people have yet to understand that we are deposed," the prince complained. " Whenever a child is born in the town, whenever anybody gets married, and whenever anybody dies, the people still knock at our door and expect us to contribute a present. And I just can't refuse them—even if I have only one million instead of three. I've got to keep up the family honour, at any price, even that of my own fortune. We have been almost entirely stripped of our privileges, but the duties that went with them seem to cling to us tenaciously. And not only financial duties. For instance, I can't shop in the market and I can't enter a cinema. The eyes of my whole country are still on me, and the moment I do anything which the people consider not befitting a ruler they start muttering ! "

Being a maharaja really is no pleasure. Unless, of course, he manages to perform the leap into the present century, unless he uses his traditional prestige for acquiring, by way of democratic elections, a new form of power—if, in fact, he takes the step from ruler to member of parliament. Many of these noble gentle-men—and also one lady—have accomplished this successfully. But the Maharaja of Udaipur was held back from attempting this step by his high sense of honour. " India is rotten," he explained to me. " The next few years are bound to bring tremendous changes. And I'd rather not tarnish my name by association with unscrupulous politicians." Thus nothing much is left to him except playing cricket.

But this is not the universal recipe. A different solution has been found by the Maharaja of Mysore, the only one of these exalted gentlemen still to reign. True, he is no longer a star of first magnitude, but merely a planet of the central sun in Delhi, from which he derives his light. In other words, he is a Governor who enjoys all the colourful trappings of a constitutional monarch. And just as a constitutional monarch can, by the force of his personality, exert decisive influence on Government business though himself remaining in the background, so the Maharaja of Mysore enjoys a similar prestige—so much so that some people are even suggesting that one day he might occupy one of the top posts in Delhi. He enjoys this prestige without seeking it, and without descending into the market-place of politics—indeed, probably, because he does not do so. Even before independence, Mysore used to be India's model state. Its rulers, in particular the uncle of the present maharaja, not only disdained exploiting their people, but on the contrary incessantly worked for their welfare. Even the hurried tourist can gain a clear impression of this as his car glides along the magnificent concrete-surfaced roads under a vaulting of banyan-trees. Because the dynasty was rooted so deeply in the hearts of the people, the Central Government simply could not avoid taking the maharaja, the last sovereign ruler, into their service ; and he in turn considered it an honourable duty to accept in spite of the unattractive political conditions to which ' democracy ' had given rise in his little country.

Jaya Chamaraya Wadiyar—that is his name—comes as a shock to the visitor. A gland operation has caused the still young man to grow to shapeless obesity, which almost conceals his mental agility and sensibility. His Highness, in fact, is one of the best educated and most widely read men in India. When I was introduced to him as an author I could hardly believe my ears when, while shaking hands with me, he enumerated the complete titles of those books of mine which have been published in English. Again I thought I must be dreaming when, in the evening in his jungle hunting-lodge near Bandipur, I suddenly heard the entire third act of Wagner's *Valkyrie* coming from his room. He always took a whole stack of L.P. records with him on his hunting expeditions, and would play classical music in the mornings and evenings, before and after the business of hunting, while he was writing his books.

As we were bumping along in his car over uneven jungle paths, looking for tigers and elephants, his Highness talked to me about the most profound philosophical questions. He appeared entirely immersed in his thoughts, but the sureness with which, in the middle of the conversation, he would spot our quarry among the bushes at very great distance showed that one part of his mind remained firmly on the ground. He was just explaining to me the different degrees of consciousness, arguing that we Westerners were wrong to confine awareness to the conscious state of our brain ; according to the Hindu view the dream and the state of dreamless sleep are an equally profound source of wisdom to the truly wise—when abruptly this seemingly clumsy fat man leapt up from his seat, snatched up the heaviest rifle in the car, and brought it to his shoulder in a flash. In the bush on our side, a dozen yards from us, stood a huge elephant. Or, more precisely, he was standing no longer, but had just begun to trot threateningly in our direction. Suddenly he changed his mind, and with a kind of reluctant gesture vanished in the bush. The maharaja put down his rifle, relieved. " That might have been unpleasant," he said calmly, as though discussing again the mysteries of the universe. " If that bull had really attacked us he would have been on top of us in two seconds, and the most massive coachwork would have been no protection against his colossal strength. Even his death would not have saved us, because the huge mass of his charging body would have crushed us. Our only hope would have been the very heaviest ammunition, which would have thrown him back, but which would almost certainly have meant a cracked collar-bone or a dislocated shoulder for me."

Indeed, it was no unmitigated pleasure to be the maharaja and to be hunting big game at Bundipur. For it also meant that he *had* to hunt whenever the safety of the surrounding villages demanded it. The elephant which nearly attacked us was a dangerous fellow, and the following day we decided to have a

closer look at him. The whole enterprise had about it something of the tense secrecy of a military operation. Again we
started by bumping along the jungle tracks in the powerful car,
until we reached a group of men who were awaiting us in a
clearing with two tame working elephants. Lithe young lads
swung themselves on to their necks, with their toes scratched
them behind their ears, and in this manner commanded them to
get down on their knees. The rest was almost as at an airport :
a little stairway was wheeled up, we ascended it and climbed on to
the back of the grey colossus, where a wooden platform provided
accommodation for four. The elephant getting up on his feet
again was like an earthquake ; following in the wake of his
comrade, he now left the familiar track and plunged into the deep
jungle grass, like an ocean steamer breasting the waves. The tall
grass reached up nearly to our feet, and from above the branches
reached down towards our heads. The elephant pushed his vast
mass through everything that would overpower and swallow
up a small human being—calmly, good-natured, obedient, a
servant and a friend. Now and again a brown figure appeared
from the grass, gesticulating and whispering—the scouts of the
tracker-party, reporting their observations. None of us on top
of the elephant uttered a word. For already we were near the
herd. Provided we succeeded in getting close without their
hearing us, the elephants would not be greatly put out by our
presence. If, on the other hand, they were to hear us we should
be at the mercy of their mood. One of them might be in a bad
temper, and the adventure might end in a mass charge. In that
case even the loyalty of our tame elephants would not be much
help, since under their load they cannot gallop as freely as the
wild ones. The only way to save ourselves in that contingency,
his Highness explained to me, would be to jump out into the
thick bamboo undergrowth, which would screen us from the
eyes and the fury of the elephants.

It may even happen that suddenly a tame elephant rediscovers
its wild elephant soul. On one occasion when his Highness,
enthroned on an elephant cow, was approaching a male elephant

in order to kill it the lady fell in love with the doomed gentleman at sight, and made straight for him, anxious to make his acquaintance.   It would, of course, have been most unfair for the hunting-party to mar this flirtation by any shooting.   Besides, the amorous elephant cow had come up so close to the male animal that, if he were to collapse, he would bury her complete with rider.   In the end the huntsmen succeeded, after much effort, in regaining enough distance to risk the shot.   But they had not counted on the vengeance of a broken female heart.   When the elephant cow saw her beloved collapsing, and the blood spurting from his black body, she went furious.   With one movement, as if flicking away a midge, she threw off the Maharaja and his party and, deeply hurt, vanished in the jungle.   One might be tempted to say that she was suffering from a broken heart had the party not succeeded in recapturing her a few days later, when she seemed to have forgotten the whole adventure.   Thus brief is woman's love.

Love altogether seems to give the elephants a lot of trouble. For even the great state elephant of Mysore, a sixty-year-old bull who heads the procession of his fellow-elephants at all great festivities, owed his captivity to excessive infatuation.   A passionate elephant is as though drunk—intoxicated with a self-produced liquor which trickles down into his mouth from a minute hole above his eye, and makes him entirely unaccountable. The state elephant in question had been so hopelessly intoxicated that he did not even notice the human beings approaching him and chaining him to a tree.   When he came round again eventually he struggled violently for three whole days to get free. After that he calmed down and made friends with his jailers, and nowadays he is led through the streets every morning so that he should get used to big crowds.   The people feed him bananas and other delicacies, and he allows his attendants to give him a bath with visible pleasure.   A life of luxury, in fact—all at the expense of his Highness.

The bull we were after was likewise an elderly gentleman. That was proved by his long tusks, which were worth a good 2500 rupees.   In India, unlike Africa, the tusks are a male privilege.

The female elephants are denied this adornment. The reason is a deficiency of chalk : the African elephants swallow a great deal of volcanic ash, which the Indian elephants lack. But there are also some male animals in India which remain without tusks— miserable animals, you might think, whom no elephant cow will ever notice. Far from it ! The tuskless elephants are in fact much more feared than their tusked colleagues. His Highness told me that he had once made friends with a tuskless elephant by wooing him with occasional presents. One day, as he was feeding him with bananas, another bull with powerful tusks appeared from the jungle and challenged the tuskless animal. There is nothing to compare with the sight of two of these mountainous masses charging at each other. The challenger seemed to be certain of victory ; he aimed his tusks at the chest of his opponent, and at the moment of impact would undoubtedly have sunk them into his heart if Nature had not compensated the tuskless animal with a particularly powerfully developed trunk. The friend of the maharaja swiftly flung its trunk round his opponent's tusks—a jerk, a frightful cracking and splintering sound, and off they came. It was now an easy matter to knock down the disarmed elephant and trample him to death.

We succeeded in sneaking up quite close to the herd, which was grazing cheerfully in the deep grass among the trees. Their merry trumpeting showed that they had not observed our approach, or else had no objections to it. But we never saw our bull that day. He seemed to be an individualist, an outsider, who did not seek the company of his kind. We learnt of his misanthropic nature from our scouts, who came racing up breathless to tell his Highness that they had encountered the animal in a different part of the forest, and it had tried to charge them. That news sealed his death sentence. As a result of the unrestricted hunting of elephants by past generations, their number in the state of Mysore has now shrunk to 6000, and that of tigers to a mere 200, so that a kill is performed only in case of necessity—almost like a surgical operation, although no doubt there are among the hunters, just as among surgeons, a few

whose diagnosis may be coloured by their inclination. The end
of the bull elephant, after he had rejoined the herd on the following day, was as undramatic as can be imagined. Together with
the master of his household and some friends, his Highness again
climbed on his elephant and, as on the previous day, rode through
the tall grass. The rifles of the four of them went up in unison :
their quarry was not too far away, and for once, when attack
might have saved his life, he seemed to take no notice of the
human beings. He was fitfully pulling up clumps of grass with
his trunk, and with a swinging motion shoved them into his
mouth, as though to demonstrate what a peaceful, harmless little
elephant he was. The shots rang out—I counted 14 reports—and
the herd retreated in cowardly fashion. The colossus alone
remained, evidently unable to comprehend the pains which raced
through his vast body, and suddenly, without even an attempt
at fight or flight, he collapsed ingloriously where he stood.
There was little triumph on the side of the hunters. This, no
doubt, is what executioners or witnesses to an execution look
like afterwards. " I really know more about elephants than
about people," his Highness said softly. Perhaps he liked them
better too.

" And why do you kill animals at all ? " I asked the Maharaja
when we were back in the car. " Aren't you forbidden to do that
as a religious Hindu ? " " No," he protested. " Like most
people from the West, you are confusing the Hindus with the
Buddhists and with the Jains, who even wear a mask over their
mouth so that they should not inadvertantly kill an insect by
inhaling it. Only the brahmins are vegetarians. But all other
Hindus are allowed to eat meat, and hence also to kill it." " Even
for pleasure ? " I asked doubtfully.

I found it difficult to see what pleasure a philosophically minded
person could find in this kind of hunting. To stroll through the
forest with a gun and a faithful dog, to listen in the dark stillness
of the woods to the secret of life and death—that is wonderful.
But here the forest, at least during the dry season, was neither
green nor fresh nor dark—but quite simply dusty. And totally

bare of secrets. And we rode, as I have said, in an open car, a Dodge, bumping along over ruts and boulders. The antelope, our most frequent quarry, listens out only for the rustling step of the tiger, for the snap of a twig, for the warning cry of the birds. It allows the noisy vehicle to approach it quite close without a thought of flight, because to its instinct this vulgar form of threat is unfamiliar. And even when the first wide shots sing past its ears it still does not realize that its doom has come.

The tiger which we hunted another day together with a whole army of scouts was considerably shrewder. That animal had made heavy inroads on the livestock of a neighbouring village, and the hunt had been staged, as it were, in its honour. It was that tiger we were after when, driving out at night, we turned our spotlight on every corner of the jungle, only to meet the frightened, blinded eyes of harmless animals. At last, when the trackers had sighted the beast and the beaters had surrounded the area, I climbed up, together with his Highness, the master of his household, and a couple of American diplomats, into the tree-top box from where we had an unobstructed view and line of fire into a clearing. Several paths intersected below us. Again silence and the suspense of waiting. We did not have to wait long. In the distance we could hear a noise—shouting and clashing of metal, as though knights in armour were locked in battle. Below us there was no movement. A ring of beaters was to drive the tiger in front of our guns. From which direction he would come was uncertain—he might come from the left, he might come from the right, or he might come through the middle. The only thing that was certain was that it would all happen like lightning, and that it would be over within a few seconds. During those few seconds we must get him. The louder the noise around us grew the more tensely did we rivet our eyes on the empty scene. By now we could clearly make out the voices of several men. And there : a movement, a white shirt appearing in a gap between the trees, a brown face, a long stick, white shirts everywhere, more faces, an army of hundreds—

but no tiger. Evidently it had ducked into some hollow of the ground and, with nerves of iron, had allowed the noisy beaters to move past, without feeling fear or appetite, and had subsequently made good his escape behind their backs. Somehow I felt that he deserved to have got away.

After all, were there not enough tiger-skins in the palaces of his Highness ? Tigers and elephants are ever present, and the heads of gaurs stare down from the walls. Tigers bare their teeth on the floors of reception rooms and corridors, as if snapping at the feet of the visitors ; they leer from under beds—terrifying cats, perpetuated for generations by the furriers' skill. Elephants are a little more useful. Their feet, hollowed out, make wonderful waste-paper baskets. The trunk can serve as an ash-tray, and the tail—God help us—as a frame for a family portrait. The furnishings of a maharaja's palace are not exactly tasteful. The combination of *deuxième empire* and traditional Indian Mogul ornament results in a pretentious ostentation among which the truly beautiful, if it exists at all, is smothered in a jungle of meretriciousness. The old palace of Mysore was burnt down about the turn of the century and rebuilt in an imitative manner. It positively swarms with colonnades, vaultings, oriel windows, gilt ornaments, crystal chandeliers, and marble floors. Indian art always tends towards over-abundance, and in this pseudo-art it becomes a positive nightmare. Nowhere an empty space which would allow one to breathe. Even his Highness's grandfather, father, and uncle are present as wax figures under huge glass covers. These torture chambers of taste are to-day empty and deserted. The palace no longer belongs to the ruling family, but to the Central Government in Delhi. The Maharaja, as it were, is only a tenant in his own house, and that only while he is Governor. He was not even authorized to allow me to take photographs inside the palace, since that would have required a special permit from Delhi ! I cannot say that I was sorry. Perhaps, if the to and fro of the former Court had filled the rooms, some life might have been breathed into the æsthetic barrenness of the building. But as it was, the vast halls, with only a few old servants shuffling about like ghosts, seemed like an abandoned film set whose seeming preciousness conceals only plaster. The master of the household, who receives the visitor in a silken turban, trips away over the polished marble floors to take his name to his Highness ; although I was the Maharaja's guest, it took me several days to work my way through the jungle of ceremonial. The term Governor means nothing to the people. To the truncated court staff his Highness is still invested with all the glory of princeliness, just as to his uneducated subjects he continues to be a personified deity.

This petrified ceremonial in a world that has changed so fundamentally might contain a comical element if the post were occupied by a more worldly person, such as the cricket-playing Maharaja of Udaipur. But in Jaya Chamaraya Wadiyar there is a philosophical and mystical disposition which imparts real meaning to the concept of the divine right of kings. Only his intimates are told by the Maharaja about the secret of his illumination. As a young man, after his father's death, he had been in his palace in the mountains, engrossed in sacred writings, when suddenly the unexplained and inexplicable was revealed to him. Ever since, all his thoughts and dreams have been of religious things. He gets up at four every morning, to prepare himself for his day's work by meditation and sacrifice in the palace temple.

As soon as he has signed the documents prepared for him, sitting behind his desk beneath a picture of Ganesh, the elephant-headed god of wisdom, and, robed in a long white garment with ruby- and emerald-studded buttons, has received a number of visitors, a picturesque old man in embroidered uniform shuffles into his study. This is his teacher and spiritual adviser, Pandit Venkatsa Shastri, a great authority on Sanskrit literature. From then onward the doors are closed against all visitors. Together with the sage, the Maharaja pores over books and manuscripts, asking questions, discussing, writing—for two or three hours a day. His forehead is smeared with white ash, the symbol of the transience of all things earthly, a token that its bejewelled wearer stands above all earthly ties. It is in these conversations

that his Highness's books are born ;   the manuscript whose
growth I witnessed to the strains of the *Ride of the Valkyries* deals
with Indian æsthetics.   Certainly this maharaja has little time for
cricket.   As a rule he spends his evenings, unphilosophically, at
the house of his mother, in the circle of his wife and five children.

" Kings are slaves of their station," laments Queen Elizabeth
in Schiller's *Mary Stuart*.   And that is true also of the maharajas—
at least, if they take their job seriously.   Whether I accompanied
his Highness to the foundation-stone laying ceremony of a
temple, or whether I tried to catch a breath of a natural human
relationship when I saw him in the circle of his family—there
was always in his features the same ceremonial withdrawnness.
I do not know whether this man can rave, laugh, or cry.   Even
his wife and children appeared scarcely able to bring him, whose
duty was to the Absolute only, back to earth.   True rulers—I
realized in my contact with this prince—remain lonely because
the symbolic character of their office swamps their humanity.
Only as public figures are they fully themselves.   When I saw
Jaya Chamaraya enthroned amid a devotedly attendant crowd,
and when afterwards I saw that crowd almost frantically straining
against the line of policemen in order to touch the hem of his
garment as he strode past—for such physical contact with his
divinely inspired Highness brings blessings—his obesity suddenly
did not seem to matter.   On the contrary :   it gave him something
of the helpless and yet awe-inspiring immobility of an idol.   To
that kind of rôle a man must be born.   And, as I have said before,
to be a maharaja is no unmitigated pleasure.

CHAPTER FOURTEEN

The War of the Castes

KSHATRIYA," REPLIED THE YOUNG PROFESSOR whom I had offered a lift in my car, when I asked him about his caste. I had assumed him to be a brahmin. But there you are : in the hurly-burly of modern life, when pariahs are raised to universities and Ministerial chairs, what use are the old yard-sticks ? My friend certainly did not look like a warrior, as his caste, the second highest in the scale, would have required. " Besides, I attach very little importance to it," he told me ; " all that's a thing of the past." " In that case you will probably marry a girl of your own choice ? " I questioned him. " Yes . . ." he replied. But it did not sound very convincing. " Are you en-gaged already ? " I persisted. His ' No ' sounded equally am-biguous as his ' Yes ' of a minute before. "Surely you're old enough, aren't you—I should put you at twenty-two ? Now come clean : you've got a girl friend already." The young professor laughed embarrassedly. " You've guessed it," he said. And now he continued of his own free will and quite frankly, almost as if my shrewd guess had earned his confidence. " No-body knows about it," he confessed. " She is a pupil of mine— only eighteen. We should like to get married, but my girl friend is a brahmin : her parents would never allow her to choose a husband from the warrior caste. Nor would it help me to have a wife from a higher caste than my own. My own caste would expel me. The whole network of social relations through which our families are interconnected would be torn up. Our relations and our friends would no longer know us. We should be totally cut off, and our children would not belong anywhere. They would be casteless, pariahs. . . . The parents of my girl friend know nothing of our love. Their house is open to me as their daughter's tutor. They believe that my interest is for her as a pupil, and they like to see me give her my full attention. They trust us ; they frequently leave us alone in the house, believing us to be talking of Disraeli and Napoleon. My father is a doctor, a generous man—I've told him all about it. Personally, he would have no objection to my marrying. But why, he asks, make complications in marrying across caste barriers ? Is being a social outcast worth while for the sake of love ? Sometimes I ask myself the same question. And even more frequently my girl friend asks herself it. She has several sisters. If a man climbs over the caste hurdle it is his own affair. But if a young girl does so she disgraces not only herself but her whole family. No suitor would regard the hand of her sister as desirable any longer. Sometimes, when our love lends us the courage of despair, when we are prepared to champion the rights of the heart against an absurd tradition—for, after all, the trend of our age is on our side, and I hardly think that I would lose my post—this realization descends on us like a load of lead. For we are responsible not only to our-selves but also to our families. You will say that others have taken the same step, that Gandhi's son, though belonging only to the third caste, the merchant caste of the Vaisya, married the daughter of the brahmin Rajagopalachari, and that many other couples in Bombay, Calcutta, and Delhi have done likewise without suffering for it. That is all very well in the big cities. If I could only find a job there . . . But that is impossible. I am doomed to living in this provincial dump, and here the old cruel caste system is still intact. Tell me, what am I to do ? "

I did not know how to advise the rebellious lover, and remained silent. Once again I had found confirmed what I had seen time and again throughout India—legislation on paper and reality are two different things. The Indian Constitution, which tries to scrap untouchability with a bold stroke of the pen, and hence to sweep the whole old caste system into the waste-paper basket of history, is not much more than a façade. Customs which have shaped a people's way of thinking through hundreds and thousands of years are surviving stubbornly, like a resistant strain of germs, against all injections of progressive reason.

But not all young Indians are cast in the same rebellious mould as our professor. At the steelworks of Jamshedpur I asked an engineer, likewise a Kshatriya by birth, the same question about his choice of a wife, and received a totally different reply. " My elder brother is the head of the family," he told me. " He is a very tolerant, I would almost say irreligious, man—as, for that matter, I am myself. When I reached marriageable age he put it to me that I was free to choose my future wife, without any caste restrictions, according to my own taste. I was not at the time in love, and did not have my eye on any particular girl. ' I am grateful to you for your generosity,' I said to my brother ; ' but I really do not see why in making my choice I should leap the barrier of our caste. Even if you attach no importance to it, there are plenty of people who do—so why offend them ? Therefore I shall be glad if you would choose me a suitable partner, and I am quite prepared to accept any girl you like.' Why are you looking at me so oddly ? "

Really, this was the limit : a man voluntarily renouncing the freedom he had been given, and submitting to the chains which others were trying so hard to cast off ! "We Europeans just don't understand it," I said to him. " To us the choice of a partner is something so personal, something we would not surrender to anybody else, that such arranged marriages exist now only among a few communities of backwoodsmen. Do you love your wife ? " " I am content," he replied. " She is orderly and obedient. As for love—why, that comes by itself as you get used to each other and as the children come." " How strange," I said ; " in Europe it very often ends with that."

But my engineer was not an isolated instance. Many girl students, who mix freely enough with young men at the university, gave me the same answer : that they would leave the choice of their husbands to their parents, and that love would come of itself in the course of married life. A sense of personal

fate exists only in a very rudimentary form in the young generation of India to-day. People deal with one another as though
they were interchangeable units, and in such a situation the strait-
jacket of castes is not found to be excessively irksome.

Take a third example. A student from Kashmir who was
being trained in Bihar told me with a smile that he did not know
to what caste his girl friend belonged. True enough, among the
Hindus of Kashmir caste consciousness is less strongly developed
than in the Indian plains—no doubt because of Moslem influence.
" We don't discuss these things," he confessed, " because we feel
that they might lead to complications. I even suspect my fiancée
of being a Christian. I'm not certain of it : we never discuss
religion or politics." " But surely these things come out by
themselves, in conversation on almost any major problem," I
objected. " Not with us," he replied. " Besides, I probably
shan't be able to marry her anyway. My studies will take another
two years, and her father wants to see her married this year. I
don't know if the girl will be willing or able to wait another two
years . . ." " Surely yes, if she loves you ! " I exclaimed. " She
is a dutiful daughter," the student remarked uncertainly. " So
she will jilt the man she loves and marry some fool that's been
picked for her merely because she doesn't want to wait two
years," I added sarcastically. After what I had heard I did not
think it at all impossible.

No, we do not need to pity the Indians because of their castes.
Most of them are no happier without these fetters, either because
they don't know what to do with their freedom—instance
number two—or because the relationship resulting from an
absence of caste—instance number three—is irrelevant anyway.
No, it is a great mistake to do like so many Western rationalists
and dismiss the caste system as a detestable institution. Strictly
speaking, is not the thesis that all men are equal, that article of
faith of modern individualism, every bit as questionable as the
thesis that man is merely a link in an unassailable and immutable
order ? Just consider how wonderfully in this structure of ranks

and values the conflicts which beset our Western ethics are solved!
For instance, a priest, a representative of Christ's religion of love,
blessing the arms destined for the murder of other human beings !
In the caste system the warrior is subject to a different moral law
from the brahmin. He is allowed, and indeed obliged, to do
what would be sin to the other. Morality is relative. How
wonderful that the highest caste, the brahmins, was originally
condemned to poverty and impotence, whereas the mighty of
this world, the maharajas, belonged merely to the second caste !
How wonderful also that the brahmin is nearly stifled in a jungle
of duties, taboos, and ritual ceremonies, while the pariah enjoys
a moral freedom to do anything his heart desires—at least, within
his own sphere. The highest man is also the one that is most
bound, and the freest is he who has least worth. The casteless, I
was assured by an expert, do not by any means envy the brahmins,
who are not allowed even to brush their teeth without ritual
ceremony : one of the curses of the casteless is " May you be
reborn a brahmin in your next life ! "

After all, the caste to which a man belongs is not determined
by chance ; it is Karma, reward or punishment for merit or guilt
in an earlier existence. And if fate has condemned a man to bear
burdens, then it also gives him the shoulders to do so. That is
also the reason why, at least until quite recently, there was no
caste struggle in India comparable to our Western class struggle.
Class struggle has a meaning only in an open society, where a
newspaper boy can rise to millionaire. But what use is a struggle
of castes if promotion, even if worked for, can be achieved only
by death and rebirth ? If you live out your fate patiently as a
pariah who knows whether the future may not grant you an
existence as a maharaja ? If, however, a man does not believe in
reincarnation—well, such unbelievers, reduced to the pitiful span
of a man's life, must rebel against the strait-jacket of a seemingly
ineluctable fate.

Even though the Indians have on the whole remained a deeply
religious nation, our modern age, as everywhere else, has robbed
a good many of the educated—and, even more, the semi-educated

—classes of their instinct for the eternal. To these people the castes are meaningless ; worse, they have become an evil. They are ashamed to speak about them to a European. Even men like Gandhi, who was too much of an Indian to challenge the caste system as such and instead tried to ease the lot of the casteless. He no longer called them pariahs, but harijans, which means ' God's children.' And although a good many other things proposed by Gandhi's idealism have gradually been forgotten under his successors, this loving care for the lowliest of the lowly continues to be the official policy of the Indian Government. God's children who were in the past prohibited from entering a temple, may now approach their god with impunity. Anybody chasing them away as untouchables risks finding himself in court. At all higher schools and in all branches of the Civil Service a number of posts, proportionate to their numerical strength, is reserved for the harijans. I have seen many villages that seemed like a world strangely turned topsy-turvy. The harijans receive gifts of money from the Government to enable them to build new homes for themselves—350 rupees, not a princely sum, but adequate for Indian conditions. They move from their hovels into new stone houses, while the brahmins continue to live in their mud huts. It pays to-day to be a pariah, for these children of God are now being pampered because of a guilty public conscience—that, at least is what certain Hindus of caste whisper enviously. Injustice has been replaced by privilege. In many respects, however, the harijans are hardly worthy of their privileged position. Centuries of contempt have made them genuinely contemptible. The ablutions performed by brahmins to meet their exacting demands of cleanliness and hygiene were not required from the untouchables, with the result that a great many of them are covered in filth, the more so as they are largely engaged in unappetizing occupations. They look as if uncleanliness had penetrated their skin and their character ; you do not have to be a psychologist to recognize the timid doglike and cringing attitude of the untouchables as an awareness of their low position. Even if you address them in a

friendly manner they will keep their distance by an almost
repulsive servility : their instinct is not yet able to make anything
of the equality guaranteed them by law.

By way of contrast, how different is the atmosphere in a
brahmin home ! I want to introduce here Mr W. K. Narasimhan,
editor of the famous Madras paper *The Hindu* which, written by
brahmins from the first page to the last, may claim to print the
best English of all the numerous Indian dailies.   There is a kind
of select language among the brahmins, a kind of indefinable
distinction which surrounds even the unorthodox.   Narasimhan
is an enlightened but loyal supporter of his caste ; a modern
brahmin, as it were, who sees salvation no longer in the slavish
observance of all the absurd rules, but in their intelligent inter-
pretation.   " Nowhere is strict brahmin practice followed more
rigidly than here in Madras," he told me.   " Not only do we
haughtily draw a line between ourselves and all other castes, but
even within our own community we are divided into various
groups, each of them with its own taboos differentiating it from
any other, just as though they were different castes.   For instance,
there is a caste subdivision whose rules say that food must be
brought into the room only after the eaters are all seated.   In
another group it is a strict rule that you must not sit down until
the food has been placed on the table.   And all that is not just a
matter of custom which you are free to observe or to change :
no, to the end of your days you are in duty bound to observe it—
anything else is sin.   It is this rigorous observance of traditional
laws which keeps alive the divisions in our society, far more
than social snobbery.   Modern conditions have not brought
much change to this fanatical belief in possessing the only true
faith : only its content has changed.   We Indians are zealots—
ready to kill for the sake of a letter, or to allow ourselves to be
killed."   Narasimhan himself had cleared these hurdles by his
brilliant intellect.   He had invited me to his home one morning
for half-past nine.   Without ceremony I was taken straight to
the room where, sitting on the floor by himself, he was about to
eat his breakfast with his fingers from a tray covered with many

small bowls.   His wife who, in accordance with Indian custom,
had her meals after he had finished, was standing by his side
watching him.   She had opened the door to me with a little
embarrassment, but from inside I had heard her husband's
sonorous command to bring me in.   Strictly speaking, brahmins
do not consider it proper to be watched by anyone while engaged
in so dangerous an occupation, fraught with every possible risk
of defilement, as the taking of food.   When he had finished he
showed me over the house and, with a triumphant sideways
glance at his wife, took me into the kitchen.   It looked like most
other kitchens in India :   the customary earthenware stove at
floor-level, no refrigerator or any other sign of modern comfort—
indeed, nothing worth seeing.   And yet this visit to the kitchen
was a gesture of exceptional friendliness on the part of my host,
or perhaps a deliberate demonstration of his lack of prejudice.
No orthodox brahmin would allow a stranger to enter his
kitchen.

Narasimhan then accompanied me to the Sanskrit school,
which was near by.   As we stepped into the court we found
ourselves surrounded by a strange crowd of laughing boys.   The
front part of their heads had been shaved, and the rest of the hair
allowed to grow long till it could be tied up in a knot ; this lent
their unformed faces a curious air of poetic intellectuality on the
one hand, and feminine softness on the other.   Their foreheads
were marked either with horizontal lines, showing them to
belong to the sect of Shiva worshippers, or with the sign of a
bird's foot, the symbol of Vishnu's followers.   The only other
place where I have seen a similar picture was the orthodox
quarter of Jerusalem :   young boys prematurely arrayed as adults,
nature forced mercilessly into the surrealist mask of sectarians.
Altogether there is a strange similarity between brahmin and
Jewish orthodoxy in their predilection for the bizarre.

But boys will be boys :   they were busy tormenting a donkey
which had been left standing in a corner, when a teacher drove
them back into the classroom.   There we saw them again later,
a picture of pious scholarship, reciting sacred texts.   The school

...cal dancing, formerly the exclusive domain of semi-prostitute dancing girls, has become socially acceptable. This young girl is the daughter of a doctor from Udaipur; she wants to train as a professional dancer.

Hindu architecture in a Moslem mosque : the famous mosque at Aj

Outside the mosque at Delhi.

The Taj Mahal at sunset : " . . . the dome floated high up under the departing sun fragile against the pale silk of the sky . . . like the breast of a delicate woman

The famous " House of the Winds " at Jaipur.

The ghats at Banaras (Varanasi).

Meditation beside the Ganges.

An itinerant flower-vendor in Srinagar, Kashmir. " Simply gorgeous," he coos English.

Floating homes in Srinagar, Kashmir.

Festival at the Mogul Gardens near Srinagar, Kashmir.

Young girl and boats on Lake Dal, Srinagar, Kashmir.

Idgah prayer in Srinagar, Kashmir.

*y prayers in Lahore.   Only a solitary sleeper is left in the fore-court of the mosque.
Religious zeal, evidently, is not over-strong.*

A temple festival in Kerala.

certainly did not look like an antheap—unlike most secular schools. The upper forms likewise consisted of no more than half a dozen boys, sitting around their teacher, their noses buried in Sanskrit writings. After all, in the new India which holds out great opportunities to engineers and doctors, why overload a good young mind with the memorizing of the Vedas? Where a command of logarithms is more profitable, even the most pious of brahmins gives in. In fact, I have been told that many Sanskrit schools, far from charging school fees, are now forced to pay out quite considerable sums of money to the parents of their pupils in order to fill up their classes at all. We subsequently visited an old professor who lived in a little house in the school grounds. The wall of his room was adorned with a number of pictures of venerable saints in the lotus position, and while the two men were talking together I walked up to inspect them. As I was about to lift down one of these portraits, which was hanging over the door, in order to get a closer look at it the old professor jumped up with a cry of dismay. "What are you doing?" he exclaimed. "You have touched the picture with your hands, with which you took off your shoes a little while ago. It is desecrated. For heaven's sake, please don't touch anything else." No doubt my thoughtlessness caused the poor man no end of cumbersome purification ceremonies, or perhaps he even had to throw out the valuable picture.

Apart from this I got on famously with these long-haired old gentlemen, in spite of their old-fashioned manners, or possibly because of them. It is a great mistake to think that faith must be logical : if you want to be logical you do not need faith. These brahmins, for the most part highly educated people and well acquainted with European thought, have not allowed their outlook to be coloured by cosmopolitanism. They know that prayer enriches human life, no matter to whom or what such prayer is addressed—indeed, the enrichment may be the greater the more absurd the form of prayer appears to reason. " He prays to idols," a man once said to me of a colleague, almost with an air of reverence, as though imparting to me a truly exquisite secret. I liked sitting with these eccentrics, watching them, or seeing them in the evenings in the streets, as they hurried home from a ritual dip in a sacred pond, clad only in a light cloth, carrying water in a brass pot. Many of them had nobly moulded features, betraying many centuries of breeding from a pedigree stud of spirituality. In their eyes was an unfathomable depth which defied human sounding. Now and again I was tempted to call it haughty arrogance : there is no doubt that the brahmins of Southern India are not free from that vice.

For down here in the South brahmin society had outgrown its intellectual and spiritual confines and had become a kind of exclusive aristocracy occupying all the key positions of power—positions where brahmins, strictly speaking, do not belong. They occupied all Civil Service posts, for the simple reason that their higher intellectual training enabled them to outshine competitors from lower castes in the entrance examinations for these highly coveted careers. Excessive intelligence, especially if it lacks the seasoning of humility, can be more dangerous than stupidity. The superciliousness of the brahmins not only earned them the hatred of the despised pariahs, but forced all other lower castes into an unnatural—and, according to strict Hindu principles, sinful—alliance with the pariahs. Paradoxically enough, in the democratic India of to-day the brilliant brahmins of Madras have become outcasts. For with decisions depending on simple majority, and not on nobility, they find themselves hopelessly outnumbered, and are being increasingly squeezed out of those Civil Service posts which used to be their personal prerogative. Naturally, they do not easily accept defeat, but are trying instead to repeat their success at a higher level, in the Central Government in Delhi. This in turn causes much grumbling in the North about the influx of the Madras intelligentsia. These are the curses of excessive intellect !

As a result, a caste struggle has broken out in the South—a struggle entirely or almost entirely unknown in the rest of India. The leader of the anti-brahmins is an eighty-year-old fanatic with a white beard and a black shirt— the uniform of his Dravida

Khazarham movement. No one would suspect a dangerous demagogue in the form of a helpless old man who can move only with the aid of a stick, and leans on other people : but it is not for the first time that the voice of hatred speaks more shrilly from a handicapped body than from a healthy one. For what this choleric mouth utters is embittered, impassioned aggressiveness, which to German ears must sound like tragi-comical retribution. All the evil in the world, this old man raves, is due to the Aryans—the Aryans who many centuries ago burst into India from the mountains of Afghanistan and imposed upon a classless Dravidian population their own religion with its infamous caste system. The equality which the Indian Constitution guarantees to all citizens, Ramaswami argues, is only a scrap of paper. Are not all leading figures in Delhi brahmins—the President, the Vice-President, the Prime Minister, the Deputy Prime Minister, the woman President of the Congress, and so on ? It is all a brahmin conspiracy ! There is no other way out but radical extermination, a kind of ' night of the long knives '—nothing less than the extinction of the Vedic religion which perpetuates the caste system as opium for the people, nothing less than the secession of the South from the accursed North, the foundation of an independent Tamil State, where true brotherly equality and equal opportunity for all shall reign. Just as in Russia, the old man adds, assuring his listeners in the same breath that he is no Communist. One is reminded of Nietzsche's saying : " Not only the reason but also the insanity of past centuries bursts out from us."

I was reminded of this saying every time I accompanied some of his helpers to see how they worked among the people. A great man cannot hate, only despise. But he who bears within him the vileness of generations becomes vicious like a much-kicked dog. Take, for instance, Jeevarathnam, a former town councillor of Madras. He suffered from what one might call a fisherman's complex. He came from one of those fishing colonies which are strung out all along the seashore—simple, poor, reed-covered huts. " Fishing is one of the oldest and

noblest occupations," he used to assure me whenever we met.
" But look what the brahmins have made of us : casteless ! Just
because they regard it as reprehensible to kill living things ! "
Jeevarathnam has organized the fishermen politically.   In the
Dravidian secession movement they constitute a group of their
own, with their own flag, and with blue shirts as their uniform.
Their leader has a face like a boxer dog that is roused to aggressiveness by the evil intentions it believes it scents each time it
draws breath.   At our first meeting he invited me to a restaurant
and there ate meat, smacking his lips, as a kind of political
demonstration against the vegetarian brahmins.   My other pariah
friend was a meeker character, and did not belong to the blue-
shirts.   He had organized the casteless rickshaw coolies into a
trade-union, and tried to ease the lot of his brethren, about whom
he was continually kept informed by collaborators throughout
the country, by submitting petitions to the authorities.   One
morning he drove out with me into the country at dawn, when
the women were still collecting at the wells to draw water.   Out
there, in the villages, the decrees of the Government had as yet
had little effect : the harijans were still confined to their own
well, or else went there from force of habit.   In such places
where they ventured to a communal well one of the ' pure '
women would haul up the bucket from the well and pour the
water into the vessels of the ' impure.'   This symbolic and
essentially noble gesture implied that the casteless, the untouchable, even while conforming with the old laws, was nevertheless
acknowledged as a neighbour in a higher sense.   And that,
surely, is what matters.   Government decrees cannot work any
changes, but can merely ratify what takes place anyway.

And this spontaneous change does in fact proceed at a fairly
rapid pace.   The strict brahmin would regard himself defiled,
not only by physical contact with a casteless, but even by contact
with his shadow ; but how can such taboos be kept up in the
hustle and bustle of the modern city or on the railways ?   In the
public schools brahmin boys and harijans share the same desks.
And where would a factory be if an engineer tried to avoid all

contact with a casteless worker ?   Or, for that matter, a brahmin
worker—even that exists—who refused to clean his machine ?
No, this order was born in the remote atmosphere and the slow
pace of village life ; in the environment of an industrial society
it must shrivel like a plant in the desert air.   What remains are
outward forms, forms which are crumbling.   The casteless when
he receives money still cups his hands so that his social superior can
drop his coin in ; but he scarcely knows any longer why he is
doing so.   The sons of my brahmin eccentrics were not greatly
put out by the sweeper's venturing into the living-room after
cleaning out their bathroom ; the only thing from which they
still shrank, in spite of all their liberal-mindedness, was marriage
with a casteless.   That was where they drew the line.   In a
similar way it is this irrational fear of race mixture which, more
than any other bar, keeps racialism alive in the southern states of
the U.S.A.   I was told of a highly respected and well-to-do
senior civil servant in Madras who had tried to find a wife by
advertising and had received dozens of replies ; all applicants,
however, had hastily melted away the moment he revealed his
casteless origin.   The poor man—but maybe he needs no pitying
—is still a bachelor.

And what bearing has skin colour on caste prejudice ?   If our
Western beauties tan their white skin with various bronze-tan
chemicals, or stubbornly expose themselves to the martyrdom of
sun-bathing, so that those with a deep tan can treat the miserable
new arrival with snobbish contempt, then all this seems no less
absurd to the Indian than his caste system does to us.   For in this
country, where skin colour ranges from the ivory white of the
North-west to the pitch-black of the Tamils, a light skin is considered aristocratic, and a person's business and matrimonial
prospects depend on it.   " I shouldn't trust that black fellow,"
some one warned me once, as though his black skin was a sign of
general depravity.   "My daughter-in-law to be," a worried father
confessed to me, " is very dark—unfortunately—but she has a lot
of money."   The seductive women in the advertisements invariably display a flowery white skin, and Indian film stars are

powdered as pale as though they had just crept out of a bag of flour. This predilection for rosy cheeks would not matter very much were it not for its possible political consequences. Might it not damage the spirit of Bandung ? Might not this contempt for a dark skin be transferred to the Negroes, now labelled the Indians' allies in the struggle against colonialism ? An African student, in Delhi at the invitation of the Indian Government, responded to my question with unexpected violence. This black man from Africa found himself systematically ostracized by his Indian fellow-students ; he was being cut on all sides, and was himself miserable and lonely. In four years he had not been asked to a single Indian home, he had made not one friend ; in his social relations he was restricted to his African colleagues, a minority hemmed in by invisible bars. When a public opinion poll was organized at the University of Madras about the students' sympathy for other races the Negroes came out bottom. Merely because their skin is black.

CHAPTER FIFTEEN

Kerala, the Red Paradise

THE MAN WAVING TO ME FROM THE UPSTAIRS
window might have been old Spinoza himself. For the first time
since my arrival in this country I had the impression of being not
in India, but in some old European township. Holland, perhaps.
Yes, that was it : the angular little streets with their whitewashed
walls and the tall gabled roofs, the archways and the little turrets
—they all suggested Holland. Only the sun was not northern ;
hard and brilliant, it beat down into this medieval scene, causing
the snippets of paper which had been strung across the street to
celebrate India's National Day to flash so brightly that—a strange
contradiction—it looked as though it was snowing. The
previous day Cochin had observed the occasion by a gymnastic
display in the big field below the ancient grey church walls which,
with the Gothic flying-buttresses, looked down strangely upon
the hustling dark-skinned bodies. The sports had finished as was
to be expected : the Sikhs and Punjabis of the Navy and the
coastal fortress, huge hulks of men, had snatched all the prizes
from the small, wiry Southern Indians. The tug-of-war between
them looked like a contest between elephants and ants. It was
during those festivities that I had met Selim, and it was he, of
course, who now was waving to me from his window, motioning
me to come in. I had had a most enjoyable conversation with
him the night before, and was only too willing to accept his
invitation. Selim was an Indian of a rare kind : he was a member
of that Jewish community which had survived at Cochin since
the days of King Solomon, and although his long line of ancestors
had remained faithful to their Indian native soil, there was in him

something that suggested ties with an entirely different sphere. He had that wisdom seasoned by irony which is found so often in cultured old Jews, paired with a love of lecturing which made him pounce eagerly upon any stranger who seemed a potential listener. Needless to say, I did not have to ask him twice to tell me the story of the Jews within the ancient walls of Cochin.

As I have said, it was at the time of King Solomon that Jewish traders from Palestine crossed the Arabian Sea to reach the southern point of India, where they bought various exotic treasures. After all, did not the great King, as Selim told me with a merry wink, make love to his 150 wives and concubines on a bed of ivory ? That ivory had found its way to Jerusalem from Cochin. But whereas the wealthy merchants married only the daughters of Israel, and thus kept their race pure throughout thousands of years, and their skin white, their servants, warriors, and attendants were not so fussy. While still on their voyage across the Arabian Sea, they had amused themselves with Arab girls, and when they reached the Malabar coast they did not despise the local dark-skinned women either. Thus the white skin of the Chosen People gradually turned chocolate-brown, and eventually black. Their number was, moreover, swelled by slaves who rejected their Hindu faith, with its strict caste system, to embrace Judaism because, under Judaic law, they had to be given their freedom after seven years. But this step did not save them from discrimination ; on the contrary, the Hindu spirit spread to the white Jews, who presently fenced themselves off from their black co-religionists. Eventually there were two Jewish quarters in Cochin, and two separate synagogues, and intermarriage between the two communities was as impossible as marriage between a brahmin and a pariah. And whereas the white children of Israel earned high respect and a social position as merchants and intellectuals—Selim himself was a lawyer—the black ones, like all the other low strata of the population, led a miserable life as an undernourished proletariat.

When the State of Israel was founded in 1948, and called upon all oppressed Jews throughout the world to return to their new-old homeland, the black Jews, of whom only a very few can have carried even a single chromosome of Abraham, decided to follow the call, whereas the racially pure white Jews discovered that their hearts—and possibly also their purses—were in their native India, and were therefore reluctant to exchange their comfortable life there for an uncertain future in Israel.

At first the Israelis were anything but pleased about this Indian immigration. They had quite enough social and hygienic problems on their hands with their co-religionists from North Africa. Above all, the doctors were against it : on the Malabar coast elephantiasis is endemic, a disease which causes the limbs to swell to inhuman size. The beggars suffering from it support themselves on crutches and drag their excrescences, which no longer show human form, behind them like a strange burden which they cannot shake off. It was not surprising that the Israelis should oppose the importation of so questionable a gift.

But they had made their calculations without Selim : though a white Jew, he was liberal-minded enough to feel a sense of responsibility for his black brethren. However, even with all his liberalism, he is orthodox to the marrow. He never shows himself with his head uncovered, and every morning as he rises his left hand first washes his right hand, and then his right his left, as the law prescribes. It was a dramatic struggle which he had to fight for his compatriots when he travelled to Tel Aviv to argue with the Israeli immigration authorities. " Do you know what decided the issue in the end ? " he asked me. " My knowledge of the Bible. I was able to quote to the gentlemen two passages— two prophecies to the effect that some unspecified disease would leave those returning home and pass on to their enemies. That convinced them. The black Jews were allowed in."

I was able to tell Selim about the village near Beersheba, in the Negev desert, and about Galilee, where I had met the black Jews of Cochin as hard-working farmers. And were they able to bring themselves to love the hard, dry earth ? Did they not at times feel homesick for the sea, for the palms, for the tropical

magic of their birthplace ?   Only ten black Jewish families had
stayed behind at Cochin, which was also exactly the number of
the white ones which still lived there.   For they too appeared to
be threatened with extinction.   Their problem was inbreeding,
and consequent degeneration.   It was no longer easy to find a
suitable white Jewish girl of marriageable age in India—except
perhaps in Bombay or Calcutta, where some refugees from
Hitler had settled.   But who wants to bury herself in a forgotten
little port like Cochin ?   Even the children of the local inhabitants,
especially if they have been to college, do not wish to stay there.
One of Selim's sons is a lawyer in Delhi, and the other an engineer
in Bombay.   One of his daughters is married to a Christian,
another to a brahmin who had been courageous enough to leap
the barriers of caste and race.   The orthodox father, very wisely,
had not opposed these unions.   Loyal as he was to his faith, he was
tolerant enough to allow his children to work out their own
lives.   " I am greater than you," he would tease his son-in-law.
" You are only a brahmin of India ;   I am a brahmin of the
world ! "   A remarkable and strange person !   " I have written
a letter to Eisenhower," he told me.   " I told him that the only
way of preserving world peace was to hand over the Jewish holy
places to Israel.   That's in the Bible too."   Tolerant and intolerant at the same time—in spite of his Judaism, was not Selim a
typical Indian ?

   This mixture of tolerance and fanaticism is typical not only of
the Jews but of the spirit of the Malabar coast as a whole.   Indeed,
it is a kind of religious nature preserve.   On my drive down from
Mysore I had seen a crescent on a green ground flying from
numerous houses, in a kind of flag war against hammer and sickle,
whose red was only just able to maintain its position among so
much Islamic zeal.   In these villages live nearly 3,000,000 Moslems,
who can look back to a line of ancestors no less long than that of
their Jewish fellow-citizens :   their Arab ancestors had likewise
come over in the grey and distant past as merchants from the
Persian Gulf.   Islam had had enough time to adjust itself to the
tropical conditions :   I saw Moslem women harvesting rice,

half-naked, like the girls of Bali—a far cry from the jealously
veiled harem ladies of the desert.

One Sunday morning I drove with the Archbishop of Trivandrum to Gothuruth, a village near Cochin, which was celebrating
the feast of its patron saint. The Christians of the Malabar coast
likewise pride themselves on their ancient traditions. Surely it
was the Apostle Thomas himself who in A.D. 52 carried the
message of his Master into this area of mixed races, and paid for
his militant faith with a martyr's death ? Later, in the second and
third centuries, Nestorians from Syria followed his route, and
much later still came Jesuit and Franciscan missionaries, accompanying Vasco da Gama. Later still the British imported the
Anglican religion, together with every conceivable variety of
Protestantism. All these rival churches and sects embrace some
3,500,000 Christians—a quarter of the entire population of Kerala.
At Ernakulam, which is divided from Cochin by a picturesque
lake, there is the portal of a church or an episcopal palace at every
other street corner. This is the Christian capital of the Malabar
coast, and if Cochin is cast in the Dutch mould Ernakulam bears
all the traits of Portugal. One might feel transported to Bahia, or
any other old Brazilian town. The high, vaulted whitewashed
rooms of the archiepiscopal palace, where I met the prelate of
Trivandrum, were clearly Latin in conception. After a short
drive in a Mercedes car, which the Archbishop had received from
a German colleague and which still proudly displayed the letter D
on its international plate, we arrived at a landing-stage where the
road ended and we had to transfer to boats. And then, abruptly,
we found ourselves in a totally different world from that of the
mainland. We were gliding along narrow canals, above which
the tops of coconut-palms, separated by the water and leaning
longingly towards one another, were secretly kissing. All other
vegetation seemed to have receded from the presence of these
royal trees. There was a long vista between the slim stems, a
space filled with the flicker of moving shadows, a vast basilica of
grey tree-trunks, with now and again a little hut covered with
palm straw. " The palms are the source of life for everything,"

the young police lieutenant, in whose boat I was following that of
the Archbishop, said enthusiastically.   " It's the most wonderful
life you can imagine.   One single palm yields hundreds of nuts,
all the year round, and four palms are enough to support a family.
The outer husk is processed into coconut fibre—that's one of our
chief industries—the white substance inside yields coconut fat.
Most people also tap their palm-trees—you know how that's
done ?   You make a cut near the top, and the sap flows out by the
bucketful.   A splendid drink, raw or fermented—our toddy.   Or
you distil it and you get palm brandy.   It's forbidden, of course—
it's a Government monopoly—but I'd like to know all the illegal
stills hereabout !   On this issue there's no difference between
Christians and Hindus.   And all the black distillers make pots of
money !   I can tell you, Kerala is a paradise."

The canals had led us into a bigger waterway, something like
a giant river, whose banks, lined with coconut-palms, seemed to
recede into infinity.   You can follow these waterways in a boat
for hour after hour, over distances of a hundred miles, right down
to Quilon, where they connect with the railway.   This is the
romantic South Sea world—no longer India.   Brown bodies
paddling canoes with picturesque birds' beaks at the prow, or
poling along barges carrying neatly stacked loads of coconut
husks.   " And this paradise—if I may believe you, almost a Never
Never Land "—I turned to the police lieutenant—" why did its
inhabitants elect a Communist Government ? "   " Ssh," he
replied in mock-serious warning, " we mustn't discuss politics.
Still, you are quite right : why are the people in Never Never
Land starving ?   It's a good question, but it's very easy to answer.
There are too many of them.   We've got 14 million people
here, crowded so close together that along this fertile coast we get
nearly 2600 people to a square mile.   In no other Indian state are
the people treading so painfully on each other's toes.   Don't you
sometimes feel that you can't even pass water without a crowd
watching you ? "

Gothuruth, which I was told had 2500 inhabitants, seemed no
more than a village :   barely a dozen huts huddling around the

ancient colonial church, with its thick walls and dank grey vaultings. Five years ago a new, very much bigger church had begun to spring up next to it—so big, in fact, that the money ran out long before its completion. Thus the Archbishop broke the Host and raised the Chalice among the bare walls and buttresses, with the palm tops and the blue sky looking in strangely through the pointed Gothic arches. But even this vast unfinished shell was too small for the crowds which had arrived to meet their prelate. Small boys were kneeling all the way up to the altar steps, and outside the doors the throng listened in the open. Clearly this was only the centre of a community which in small isolated settlements was spread out far and wide over the lagoons.

Only among the Indian tribes of South America have I seen processions comparable in brilliance of colour and impressive spectacle to the celebrations at Gothuruth. Crimson and yellow canopies swaying above magnificent pictures of saints moved through the pale green foliage down to the river and back again. In front went a group of half-naked musicians, of anything but Christian appearance. The drummers were beating their instruments like men possessed, and the pipers produced from their picturesquely curved horns truly marrow-piercing shrieks— primeval orgiastic sounds which bore no relation to a hymn or any other religious tune. They were the same instruments and the same frantic ecstasy which I was to see a few days later at a Hindu temple ceremony. As the procession returned to the square before the church it suddenly seemed to have come under heavy fire from an enemy machine-gun company. I had been wondering about the small packages which I had observed, tied to one another by mysterious threads, hanging among the tree-tops. Now I knew : gunpowder. With an alarming crack, the first of them exploded, and the flame spread with lightning speed along the fuse cables to the next one and the one beyond that. There was a deafening banging and cracking, as though the whole world was about to explode.

Again I encountered the young police lieutenant, who was clearly enjoying the spectacle. " Well," he said, when I had told him of my impression, " what difference is there really between us Hindus and you Christians ? We get on famously with one another. Here we have co-existence of all gods. After all, your Christ does not differ all that much from our god Khrishna, and your Mother of God fits exceedingly well into our Indian heaven. And if by any chance you think that there are no castes any longer among your brothers in Christ, why don't you go and ask those people why they attended Mass outside the church walls ! They are pariahs—Christian pariahs ! "

I had lunch with the village priest around whose richly furnished table all the visiting clergy and the local elders met. I tried to question him—a jovial, potbellied, elderly gentleman— about the political situation, but received only evasive replies. " This Christian district has elected a Communist deputy," the lieutenant whispered to me, with a malicious glance at the priest. " The people were not properly informed," the priest objected, having overheard the remark. " It will be different next time, quite different."   Another guest, who revealed himself as a rich landowner with 3000 coconut-palms, to my surprise declared himself a friend of the Communist Government, without explaining his reasons. " He does good business with them," the lieutenant again whispered to me, " and he also contributes to the Party funds. Not only the religious boundaries, but the political ones as well, are fluid here. The Communists are human, and with human beings you can always come to some arrangements."

When the meal was over a young priest took me by the arm and drew me into a back room, where an intimate circle of men, including the village priest, were surreptitiously downing little glasses of arrack, the palm brandy. " Why the secrecy ? " I asked the lieutenant, who was standing by without taking part in the drinking. " I can't tell just by looking at it whether this arrack was distilled legally or illegally," he said with a smile. " We'll assume the former. I've told you, without arrack the people here would be much poorer—in fact, they wouldn't have been able to build such a fine new church."

I was in Kerala at the end of January, and at that time the entire country seemed to be swept by a fever of festivities. On the road to Trivandrum I overtook several festively caparisoned elephants, with golden ornaments on their foreheads, accompanied by masses of canopies, drums, and trumpets, as if they too were archbishops. The villagers calmly organized their ceremonies in the middle of the main street, and if it meant holding up a motor-car for several hours—well, that was just too bad. Certainly no one would have cleared the road for it. And to run over an elephant is even less advisable than running down a cow.

At Quilon they had three of these elephants. They moved along in a procession, one behind the other, accompanied by lath-and-cardboard horses glittering with gold and silver, and, mounted on wheels, tall carved images of deities with a bewildering profusion of arms and heads. Towers, 20 to 25 feet high, made of wood and coloured paper in several tiers one upon another, swayed along on the shoulders of about a dozen young people, whose distorted features betrayed the pain and the discomfort which the pressure of the carrying poles caused to their bare shoulders. Yet the delight of helping to carry one of these heavy, monstrous structures seemed to outweigh the suffering. Youths were elbowing their way forward to relieve the carriers, pushing in among them and relieving them whether they wanted to be relieved or not, or at least touching the carrying poles with their hands. The towers looked like a cross between giraffes and centipedes. I do not know whether the young people were drunk with toddy or whether the excitement of the celebration, the noise, and the proximity of the divine pictures had put them into a trance. In any event, the turmoil around the carrying poles got steadily wilder, and the swaying and the gyrations of the towers increasingly alarming. What would happen if one of them . . . ? And there it happened. The first tower had leant over too far to regain its balance. For an instant it seemed to be hovering in the air under the frantic efforts of the centipede, and presently collapsed, as if exhausted, right in the middle of the dense crowd. I gasped. Was there no scream? No; no one was injured. It seemed a miracle. But when the other two towers followed the bad example of the first I realized that these disasters had been intended. What had not been intended was that one of the elephants, evidently annoyed by the crowd, got restless and suddenly broke loose. All of a sudden the delirious crowd seemed transformed : like leaves before the wind, they scattered in all directions, seeking cover behind fences, and a moment later continuing their flight, for neither fence nor wall offer protection against an enraged elephant. Some were facing the panicking people, trying to calm them. " Don't lose your head," some one in the crowd said to me. " Better stay near your car. Sometimes a stampede like this is deliberately organized by shady characters as a cover for stealing and looting." But things did not get that far on this occasion. A moment later news reached us that the elephant had been got under control again, and fettered with iron chains. Relieved, the crowd returned.

On the edge of the festive square a small shed had been transformed into a bookstall. A loudspeaker was blaring above a picture showing Stalin and Lenin in intimate conversation. A red flag bore the hammer-and-sickle emblem. Propaganda brochures, Russian classics in English translation, and children's books were piled on a table around which a curious crowd had collected. Purpose and political conviction were beyond doubt here. But what was I to think of the proprietor of the tea-house who had opened his stall opposite ? Above the entrance was a large picture of Stalin—the Indian Communists are a few years behindhand with their personality cult, and to the simple and slow mind Stalin is several cuts above the much too intellectual Lenin anyway. Hanging amicably by his side were Gandhi, Nehru, and the god Khrishna—the latter even in duplicate. I was reminded of the words of the police lieutenant about the coexistence of gods. Quilon, with its numerous industrial enterprises, was considered a stronghold of trade-unionism. The young lads who were now so eager to act as bearers for their gods were employed at the brickworks, and presumably were

Communists. But that did not in the least damp their religious fervour.

Altogether a great many things in Kerala are different from how they are pictured in the West—and, for that matter, different from the rest of India. It is not only the landscape that suggests the South Seas : the people too, unlike the humourless and almost sad people of the ' mainland,' have something of the gaiety of those happier latitudes. Where had I seen these swaying towers before ? In Bali, to be sure, at the cremation of a dead body— the very same towers, down to the ornaments. No doubt the people of Kerala, boldly sailing the seas, had carried their political and cultural influence to Indo-China, Java, and Bali. Somehow one feels that these people have a wider horizon. Wherever I stopped a curious crowd collected at once : lively young boys, ready for fun and games. And this livelier intelligence does not mean a lessened religiosity—on the contrary. Kerala, like Bali, is a country of miracles. I shall not forget in a hurry the Indian Government information officer—a Mr Menon—on whom I called to get some political briefing, and who for several hours treated me to supernatural stories. About how, as a boy, he had seen a man walking on the sea at Calicut : Yoga, he explained to me, made it possible for a man to make himself light—lighter than water, lighter even than air. True, Mr Menon admitted, he had never actually witnessed a levitation—the floating in the air of a Yogi thus transformed into a balloon. But he remembers all the details of the man who had walked on the water, down to the splashing of the waves around his feet. And then there was the man who sat in the middle of a roaring fire, too hot for those around it even to approach it, and who had rubbed his body with incandescent coals, just as if he were sitting in his bath. And then there are the mediums which must arouse the envy of every policeman engaged in criminal investigation : as soon as a murder has been committed anywhere a child under six is put in a trance. He thereupon begins to talk with the voice of the dead, demanding the dead person's favourite dishes, and devouring them hungrily. And what is most important from a practical point of view—he then relates in detail the circumstances of his death. Finally, there are those strange places, also in Kerala, where a man finds himself flung out of his bed in the middle of the night by some mysterious force. Menon himself had woken up one night and felt himself floating some six inches above his bed. As he reached out towards his mattress, unbelieving, he dropped back on to it, but had been unable to sleep for the rest of the night. Now, all these things, as I have said, were related to me by an information officer of the Government from whom I really wanted information about the Communists. Certainly it was much more entertaining, but I myself have not had any preternatural experience in Kerala. In Trivandrum I was glad to find a perfectly ordinary bed without spirit forces in it.

I do not know whether the chronic overcrowding of the capital of Kerala has anything to do with the Communist regime. Arthur Koestler, at any rate, who tried to find a hotel room there at the same time as I, attributes it to some secret political sabotage. He had booked a room in the best hotel by telegram, and was most annoyed when upon his arrival nobody admitted any knowledge of his cable. Nevertheless, he was most obligingly put up in a kind of emergency quarters in a sitting-room, through the glass door of which some uninvited eyes would now and again look at the famous writer. Koestler believed that he knew the Communist system too well not to suspect behind these proceedings a kind of psychological torture, or even police surveillance. After two nights of suffering he left this Indian Moscow, and his protest that the Red Government had shamefully betrayed its duties as a host was carried by the entire Indian Press. Poor fellow ! With a little less persecution mania he might have enjoyed the same truly princely reception that was given me after I had called on the Director of Tourism, a former master of the household of the Maharaja. I found myself installed at once in the Government's guest-house, a former British Residency magnificently situated on a hill, where normally only Ministers and diplomats are put up, and where a vast number of servants were hovering about me all day long, permanently at my beck and call. No ; the Communists of Kerala certainly were no Bolsheviks in the classical mould, with torture, secret police, or slave-labour camps.

I found this opinion confirmed by the American who lives at Trivandrum as the representative of the U.S. Information Service. " The authorities," he confessed to me, " treat me with downright touching friendliness. My every wish is fulfilled before I even utter it, and on all public occasions I am assured of a place of honour." The local population, for its part, regards the U.S.I.S. less as a centre of subversion than as a kind of credit bank. If a man needs money he sits himself down in the U.S.I.S. library or its office, and does not budge. A kind of Satyagraha with a positive purpose ! One of the regular visitors is a loyal old Indian who has still not got used to independence. He spends his time running after Westerners, throwing them a military salute on every suitable or unsuitable occasion. Another regular caller wears a pullover with the inscription " You are my brother. Jesus saves you." The temptation to enter into the closest possible relations with the representatives of so wealthy a country as America is extraordinarily strong. Thus a young man appeared in the office one day, thrusting his hand out to the American. " Let's be friends," he proposed, and for several hours his host could not get rid of him. The same performance was repeated on the following day. Not till the third day did the ulterior motive behind this exuberant wooing of American friendship emerge : the young man wanted to borrow the U.S.I.S. jeep for his sister's wedding.

Certainly life in Kerala was most enjoyable, in spite of the Red Government. One reason may be that, as I have said before, these Communists were anything but uneducated proletarians ; nearly all of them came from the leading families of the country. The Prime Minister, E. M. S. Namburipad, for instance, belonged to the wealthy tribe of the Nambudiri, the most aristocratic and the wealthiest brahmins, who trace their descent back to the Aryan invasion. K. P. Govindam, the Secretary-General, belonged to the Nairs, a powerful group of Hindus whose influence is based chiefly on the intellectual training of their children. I could not suppress a smile when I asked Mrs Thomas, the only woman Minister, which of her colleagues were of proletarian origin, and she replied, almost offended : " We are all rich ! "

In judging Communists one can lay down the almost certain formula that their qualities are in inverse proportion to the economic and social development of their country. In Britain or in Switzerland no Party member is likely to be entirely sound intellectually or morally. In China, however, or in India, where the body politic really needs an urgent major operation, or is in process of undergoing one, where the issue under discussion is not revolution as such but merely its means, it happens frequently that very brilliant and high-minded individuals, genuine idealists, are attracted to the idea of Communism.

No doubt the political good manners of the Red rulers in Kerala were not due entirely to their good breeding. In April 1957, when they came to power as the first Communist Government in the world to be elected by ballot, they had scored a very narrow victory. Only 35 per cent. of the votes, just over a third of those cast, had been for them, and since they secured only 60 out of 126 seats they were obliged to buy the support of five independent coalition partners by appointing them to Ministerial posts. Besides, an Indian state enjoys fewer rights than a state in the U.S.A. or a canton in federal Switzerland. Its Governor is appointed by Delhi, and so are the top officials in the police and administration. Laws are subject to the approval of the president of the state and, if he considers it necessary, the Supreme Court. If the democratic Constitution is infringed, or if law and order are no longer maintained in the country, Delhi is empowered to expel the state Government and to assume direct control. The Communist rulers of Kerala were thus compelled by the democratic law under which they had come to power to display a democratic behaviour—and who knows whether they were happy in that rôle ?

There is no doubt that these well-bred Communists, if they had felt like it, could have played a different tune. The meek Indian Reds had shown their viciousness in the state of Hyderabad towards the end of the forties, when their gangs in Telangana committed murder and manslaughter, and shed innocent blood by senseless attacks on railway trains—all to spread terror. Only the rifles of the Indian Army and the gentle persuasive power of Vinoba Bhave had then restored order. But these acts of violence had almost entirely wrecked the popularity of the Communists among the Indian public. It was to be regained only by sub-scribing to new tactics, the non-violent tactics of parliamentarian legality, by a non-revolutionary effort to improve the welfare of the common people. The victory at the poll in Kerala and 12,000,000 votes throughout India were the result of the new tactics. I repeat, tactics—not a change of heart. Kerala was to play the part of a base, of an Indian Yenan—that Chinese province to which Mao Tse-tung withdrew with the remnants of his Red Army after his Long March to practise peaceful admin-istration until the time was ripe for a revolutionary seizure of power throughout the country.

In Kerala, at any rate, the predecessors of the Communists had not made it difficult for them to act as the benefactors and loving fathers of the people. Kerala used to be one of the worst-governed states in India, with haughty, incompetent Ministers who made wonderful speeches but did nothing except line their own pockets. All that was now changed. Throughout the rest of India an exceedingly anti-social pay scale is in operation, which allows a top civil servant to earn nearly 100 times as much as a bottom-grade civil servant. Unbelievable as it may seem, the Communist Ministers started by making sacrifices themselves, by reducing their own salaries to less than half and instead raising those of the office servants. The land reform, perpetually post-poned in the past, was suddenly given teeth. The Panchayats, the councils of village elders which are again being set up throughout India in accordance with ancient tradition, as a kind of local self-government, were given extended powers. Bolshevik legis-lation ? Not a bit of it, the Communists declared triumphantly.

All these fine things had been promised by others, but never realized. We, they said, are the men of action. And that was nothing more than the truth. Even wealthy citizens of Kerala, and indeed some foreign businessmen, told me quite frankly that the Communist Government was the best Kerala had ever had. " In the past, if I wanted to see my Minister," a senior civil servant told me, " I had to wait for days, and then hang about in his ante-room for hours, before at last being able to state my business. Nowadays the same process takes about ten minutes. And if necessary I can even buttonhole him in the street, outside office hours."

While I was in Kerala an 'irrigation week' was in progress, the purpose of which was to clear out installations which had silted up through the negligence of the villagers. The Government contributed 80 per cent. of the costs, as well as the co-operation of the Public Works Department, provided a village community undertook to give up its Sundays for voluntary work. The Communist Party mobilized its local cadres to inspire the peasants to co-operate. Once the village pond was full of water again, and the fields bore richer crops, they could stand up and say : " And to whom do you owe all this ? To us, the Communists." Party propaganda, subsidized by the State to the tune of 80 per cent. No revolutionary jargon, no inflammatory speeches— simply work by brain and brawn. One Sunday morning I visited a village near Trivandrum and found the work there in full swing. A police detachment were digging away for all they were worth, and schoolboys carried the dirt away in their hands. A short, bullet-headed man, the Panchayat chairman, was supervising the operations. His round face was reminiscent of Gandhi's : it showed the same simple and honest dedication. But this man was a Party member, and had been one since 1942. As I found out in conversation with him, he knew his Lenin inside out.

Help for the common people ! There was, for instance, an old law, that had never been put into effect, authorizing the Government to give financial support and advice for the setting-up of co-operatives. In the past most attempts of this kind had miscarried. But now the Communists were creating co-operatives of working people everywhere, and these received not only state credits but also orders. In the past the palm-tappers, who risked their necks getting the toddy from the tops of the palm-trees, had received a mere pittance for their dangerous work, while the farmers who bought their drink-selling licence from the state by auction had made huge profits. These licences were now being granted to tapping co-operatives, and the money thus went into the pockets of the common people. Private printers discovered with a shock that Government orders were now being given to co-operatives of their former employees. At state building-sites bricklayers' co-operatives were employed. Needless to say, the Communists saw to it that these organizations were in the hands of loyal Party men, and presumably a portion of the profits from the attractive state orders eventually found their way into the Party coffers. One day I visited a coconut-fibre-mat factory which had been allowed to decline by its private owner, and had since been taken over by a newly founded co-operative of workers. A trade-union secretary was its business manager, and an experienced old workman was its technical director. If they were to be believed the works now paid wages 15 per cent. higher than its competitors. The coconut-fibre mats which I saw being manufactured by machines ready for the scrap-heap were all destined for Moscow. The coconut-fibre industry of Kerala, which had been in the throes of a serious recession—the prosperous citizens of Europe to-day prefer Persian carpets—had been rewarded immediately after the Red election victory with a huge order, worth several millions, from the Soviet Union. Who can blame the Russians for placing their orders not with well-equipped modern British firms, but with a number of small and obscure factories for which they felt political sympathy ? One of the European managers disclosed to me the background of this transaction. His own firm was working all out for the Russians—on contract to that trade-union secretary who had accepted a mammoth order vastly in excess of his own capacity. The only condition was that a substantial proportion of the proceeds would go not through the books but to the trade-union secretary in person—in other words, into the Party coffers. The leopard does not change his spots. The good the Communists are doing on a small scale nevertheless serves their evil ends. But their opponents are not idle either.

Outside the entrance to the Government building in Trivandrum sat a small girl about five years old, under a huge poster in Malayalam script, and gazed cheerfully at the unending procession of cars and pedestrians which flowed past her. At mealtimes her food was brought to her to eat on the pavement, and late in the evening she was collected and then brought back again the following morning. For that little girl, as the poster by her side explained, served as a political demonstration. Her home had been torn down by the landlord while her parents were dying in hospital, and now she sat in front of the Government building, day after day, as a protest against it. She wanted to have her home back—a little girl of five alone in the world. " We wanted to put her in an orphanage—that's where she ought to be," the police officer on duty explained to me. " But her uncles are members of an opposition party and have sat her down there in order to put the Communist Government under pressure. We can't remove her since she is not obstructing the traffic. And if we did one of her uncles would be sitting there to-morrow morning, to protest against an infringement of civic liberties. Will you excuse me for a moment, please ? " A group of men had approached the gateway and had quietly lain down on the ground, blocking the entrance. The police officer bent down and courteously asked them to get up again. When they refused a few constables put them on their feet and marched them away. " They are Socialists protesting in this manner against the high food prices," the police officer continued his explanations. " But do they lower the price of rice by lying down in the street in front of the Government building ? " I stammered, somewhat confused by the strange logic which was here being put into

effect. " Of course not," laughed the officer. " But they want
to discredit the Communist Government. You've got to
understand that everything in this country is politics. More than
half the population of Kerala can read and write—in fact, almost
the entire younger generation. We are by far the most intelligent
state in the whole of India. We have thirty-four daily papers,
and every one of them is printing lies for all it's worth. These
lies are being read by eager readers from dawn to dusk, and
equally eagerly believed. And then they go and protest against
the Government. To-day it's the Communists, yesterday it was
the Congress Party and the Socialists. The procedure and the
principle have always been the same : whoever is not in power
does everything he can, by way of obstruction, defamation, and
incitement, in order to overthrow the Government. That is why
Kerala has the least stable conditions of the whole of India :
we've had eight different Governments in ten years of independence. As I've said, we are the most intelligent state in India,
maybe too intelligent. And the most dangerous occupation here
is that of a policeman."

The anti-Communists at last scored their victory when the
Communist Government had its new education Act approved
by the President of the Republic. If the people of Kerala can
boast of the highest educational standards in India, then this is
due largely to the Christian churches and to the wealthy Nairs,
who used to run and finance three-quarters of all schools. The
school reform was to give the state increased control over
expenditure, selection of teachers, and the curriculum in those
private schools. It was not a particularly ' Bolshevik ' law ;
any modern state must try to have some control over its educational apparatus. But because it was the Communists who
introduced the law the Christians were afraid that atheistic
teachers and textbooks would be foisted upon them, and the
Nairs feared that their caste schools would be swamped by
casteless pupils. As a result, something was achieved which
it had not been possible to achieve until then—a united front

against the troublesome innovators.   School strikes, demonstrations, Satyagraha, with the police opening fire—the whole
gamut of an excited, insubordinate populace, or perhaps only
its conservative groups, was played out in front of the public
buildings of the unfortunate country.   ' Freedom fighters '
against ' Communist terror.'   In the end Nehru decided to
depose the Red Ministers and to put Kerala under emergency
administration by the President of the Republic.

Was this performance, half tragic and half comic, half sincere
and half hypocritical, a victory for democracy ?   It is difficult to
say.   The Communists had been raised to power, not by ideologi-
cal sympathy, but by public desperation over the incompetent
and corrupt politicians of the old school.   The Communists were
in turn swept away because, rational social technicians that they
are, they had underestimated the irrational religious passions of
this people, and had too clumsily laid hands on traditions which
had deep roots in the hearts of the people.   Would one be
justified in regarding the action that was possible in Kerala
against their mild and good Government as an omen for the
whole of India ?   Is it true, as some traditionalists confidently
predict, that, in a nation so indissolubly linked with the Deity
as is the Indian, dialectical materialism can seduce at most a few
intellectuals but can never capture the masses ?   Perhaps.   But
the revolutionary spark is still alive among the cinders.

CHAPTER SIXTEEN

Lions with Blue Turbans

A DEALER IN RAZORS IN AMRITSAR, THE CAPITAL of the Sikhs, would go bankrupt in no time. The most conspicuous feature about a genuine Sikh is that he does not cut a hair of his body, either with scissors or with knife. As a result, a Sikh in *déshabillé* looks exceedingly strange : he has his hair tied up in a knot on top of his head, and unless he wants his beard to hang down to his navel he forces it up towards his temples by means of a net. Hair, hair, and more hair. For the sake of a tidier appearance in ordinary everyday contact this hirsute glory is packed up throughout the day, during meals and office hours, in that famous turban which, tied tightly in two halves, forms a smart angle on the forehead. It is this turban which marks out the Sikh at a hundred yards ; other characteristics are a comb in this mountain of hair, an iron ring worn on the arm, and a dagger or sword in the belt.

A real Sikh is tall and broad-shouldered—in short, a martial figure. They rightly call themselves ' lions '—that is what the name Singh means, which invariably indicates a Sikh. The religion of these ' lions ' starts with their mane. One of their ten Gurus—that is what the founders and early rulers of their community are called—issued that strange ban on cutting their hair. When I questioned the High Priest of the golden temple at Amritsar, the Vatican of the Sikhs, as to the meaning of this prohibition he unfolded to me an entire philosophy of hair. Because hair consisted of pigment-carrying cells with a special affinity for the ultra-violet rays of the sun, their rôle, surely, was evident: to store the solar energy as a perpetual source of power, in much the same way as does the chlorophyll in plants. For that reason it was exceedingly dangerous to one's health to cut one's hair, as was also excessive use of soap, which removed the grease in the hair, that represented a kind of natural humus for a healthy growth. I was even given statistical proof of this theory. Whereas the rest of mankind suffered from the scourge of tuberculosis, the Sikhs, thanks to their refusal to cut their hair, suffered from this disease to a very much smaller degree. The best thing altogether, I was told in conclusion, would be for people to walk about entirely naked, like the beasts of the forests and fields, but unfortunately this ideal state of affairs could not be realized because of social and moral considerations.

It would be a great mistake to think that, just because of these theories, the Sikhs are a lot of crazy eccentrics. Amritsar, their holy city, has a strange poetic atmosphere like no other Indian town. Oriental hospitality is practised here to an excessive degree. Instead of staying at an hotel, for instance, you may ask to be put up in a temple, and you will get four days' free food and accommodation. That is, unless you have previously been captured by one of those pious Sikhs who go out into the streets of their own accord in order to find guests. The dentist who invited me in this manner owned only a small, modest house and had to share his bedroom with his guests. It was not a very comfortable night, as a dreadful dog slept by my feet, and whenever it was not snoring it was noisily exploring the darkened room. Still, it was a gift bed, I consoled myself. The visitors' book, where I entered my name on the following morning, reflected a truly universal neutralism : even members of the Soviet Embassy had perpetuated their names in it. To the Sikhs hospitality is not merely a nice custom but an expression of their universal article of faith : whatever your religion may be, or your caste, or the colour of your skin, it makes no difference to us, because we are all brothers. The guide who takes the visitor round the temple, free of charge, ceaselessly repeats this principle of unconditional brotherhood, and this emphasis makes it clear that on this point the Sikhs differ most from the Hindus. Altogether, the Sikhs are not all that far removed from Christianity, and many of their customs and ceremonies are reminiscent of the practices dear to us.

I shall never forget the observance of the birthday of Guru Nanak, the founder of their religion in the fifteenth century. It may not be fortuitous that this anniversary is observed on December 26, one day after Christmas, and somehow the glitter of lights which met me inside the Golden Temple reminded me of our Christmas-trees. The sacred lake, in the middle of which the temple stands, was surrounded by countless oil-lamps whose little flames painted innumerable flickering semicolons on the nocturnal surface of the water. Everything was steeped in light ; everything was live, wind-animated flame. The gilt walls of the temple, which at sunset shimmered with an unearthly radiance, now glowed mysteriously like a dying fire. On the bridge leading to the temple was a dense mass of people, advancing slowly step by step, towards the entrance from which came a strange, monotonous music, an uncertain fluid melody of strings and human voices above the discordant notes of a harmonium. " Persons of non-Hindu faith not admitted " is an intolerant and exclusive notice frequently found outside Indian temples. But when I tried here to slip away from the crowd I found myself held by one of the people and pulled along, carried by the stream of humanity flowing towards the temple gateway at the far end of the bridge. " We are all brothers," my companion whispered into my ear. At the temple threshold he knelt down, touching it with his forehead, as did all the others, and a moment later the golden interior received us. In the centre sat the musicians with their instruments and singing priests ; a large cushion was covered by the coins given by believers as if with strange flowers. And was not the next rite just like Christian Communion ? There was a fragrant brown paste on a silver tray, and as the believers shuffled past him a priest pushed a small bit of it into everybody's mouth. It tasted sweet, and its constituents were readily identified as butter, honey, and flour. My companion stooped down quickly to pick up a small crumb I had dropped, and reverently put it in his mouth : not a grain of the precious substance must be lost. I was carried farther by the current, towards a side entrance and out into the dark night, down the steps towards the water of the lake from which the believers scooped up the purifying liquid in their cupped hands to drink it noisily. I did likewise, without hesitation : I felt as if this strange communion had made me one of them.

The Sikh religion was in fact an attempt at reforming Hinduism which by the fifteenth century had not only degenerated spiritually into superstition but was also rocking politically under the victorious advance of Islam, by transferring to it the idea which accounted for the force of the Semitic religions—monotheism, the belief in one single invisible God, the creator of all things, a God that can no longer be served by magic ritual, but only by a moral, good life of purity and love. And, above all, an *active* life. All that which characterizes Hinduism to this day—its abnegation of the world, its withdrawal from the wickedness of finite reality into the contemplation of the infinite—was one of the main reasons why the active Moslems succeeded in subjugating the country so easily. Guru Nanak realized that the enemy would have to be fought with his own weapons, that it would be necessary for his people to harden their spirit by discipline and a positive philosophy of life. His efforts were crowned with success : Sikhs became the vanguard in the struggle against the advance of Islam, and under successive Gurus assumed ever more martial character. Eventually, when the fifth Guru had been tortured to death by the Mogul Emperor Jahangir, his son, Guru Hargobind, took the decisive step of transforming his religious community into a regular warrior caste, which for a long time ruled powerful empires in the north of India, until they were defeated by the British. Subsequently, in the Indian Army, they became one of the most loyal pillars of British rule. This military tradition has survived to this day. Some 15 per cent. of all Indian soldiers, and more than 20 per cent. of their officers, are Sikhs, although they account for no more than 2 per cent. of the Indian population. They have been equally success-ful in business : throughout India they are found as entre-preneurs, and have a reputation for technical skill. Most of the taxis, even in Bombay and Calcutta, have a turbaned Sikh behind the steering-wheel.

India's independence has demanded the greatest sacrifice from the Sikhs. Having halted the advance of Islam in the past, they had achieved peaceful coexistence with their former enemies, the Moslems, in the Punjab, when the creation of Pakistan and the resultant partition of the Punjab, together with the disturbances which followed, compelled millions of them to emigrate from the area assigned to Pakistan. In the bloodshed which took place in consequence the old warriors played a quite considerable part. Many of the refugees went to Bombay, to Calcutta, or even to Singapore to build up a new existence. 6,000,000 of them remained in the truncated East Punjab as a minority among 14,000,000 Hindus.

My meeting with Master Tara Singh, the aged Sikh leader, was surrounded by an atmosphere of tragedy. The night was pitch-black, and the old man received me in the courtyard of his house, warming his hands by a fire which in turn died down to a dull red and then flared up again whenever his daughter, a charming young student, put on new firewood. The uncertain light played over the lined features of the old man and the friend with whom he was consulting, and the long white beards of the two seemed alive like waterfalls. This was how I pictured King Lear fleeing from his ungrateful daughters. Ingratitude, blackest ingratitude, was also Tara Singh's lot. He, the worthy successor of the ancient Gurus, who had united in his hands the religious and political leadership of the Sikhs, had been squeezed out from the board of the religious council by a treacherous election manœuvre of collaborators whom he had thought to be his friends ; that religious council administered not only the temples

of the Sikh community but, more important, its finances. " They
are a miserable lot of careerists," Tara's friend hissed, while Tara
himself sat brooding dully. " Tara Singh is the prototype of the
selfless man of the people, the type dreamed of by Gandhi. Just
look how modestly he lives : his house only has three rooms, and
his own daughter does the work of a servant. The politicians
live a parasitic life of luxury, acquiring vast personal wealth.
These traitors have now allied themselves with Nehru in order to
get rid of Tara, who had become troublesome to them. But
there'll be a bad end . . . a bad end. . . ." the old man whispered.

Betrayal ? Only if one can so describe a well-justified change
of opinion. The simple truth was that Tara Singh, the patriarch,
had become a little old-fashioned. Pakistan, the Moslem state,
tempted him. Why should it not also be possible to set up a
Sikhistan, a Sikh state with its own capital, its own Ministers,
its own Embassies, and with Tara Singh as its President ? True,
it would be a small state, and, since Hindus and Sikhs live
scattered among one another, the demarcation of frontiers and
the solution of minority problems would cause a lot of headaches.
Nevertheless, there are always eccentrics in India, prepared to
foist their phantasms on a real world. Admittedly, when I talked
to Tara Singh he firmly denied such separatist aims. He had
scaled down his demands : Sikhistan was no longer to be an
independent state but merely a province of India, carved out
from the Punjab, with its troublesome Hindu majority, with a
recognized language of its own—Punjabi—and with its own
script, the Gurmukhi invented by the second Guru. But that
wicked man Nehru had refused even these modest demands.
Carve up even further the little Punjab which had already been
partitioned ? Certainly not. Somewhere a line must be drawn
against that separatist parcelling up of India, unless the state of
Bombay was to be split as well, unless the South was to secede
from Delhi, and unless Assam too were to demand autonomy.
Besides, the Sikh doctrine, quite apart from its limited extent,
was a sect of Hinduism rather than a separate religion. Evidence
for this surely was the ease with which the dividing-line could be

crossed between the two : there are Hindu families which bring up the first-born as a Sikh, and there are Sikhs who cut their hair and regard the Hindu way of life as more sensible. A separate Sikh state, or even a separate province, would be absurd. Presently the blue-turbaned nationalist Sikhs streamed out into the streets, demonstrating. Delhi gave in as far as was possible ; it instructed the schools to teach Punjabi, and in every possible way poured oil on the troubled waters. And a miracle came to pass : for once the day was won not by unreasonable fanaticism but by good sense. On the day following my night encounter with Tara Singh I was driving through the countryside when a pleasant sight at the little village of Kohara induced me to stop. In a fenced-in square, by the side of gymnastic apparatus, hundreds of little Sikhs were sitting on the ground in rows. Even these little ones had their turbans, a sea of colourful dots, tied as tightly and neatly as their fathers'. Tablets, covered with strange letters, books, and copy-books were stacked up beside them. This was the village school ; for throughout India it is much more enjoyable and better for the children to have their lessons in the open, during the dry season, rather than inside those grey prisons which most schools are. When I introduced myself as a foreign reporter a young teacher showed me round the classes, pleased and proud. From the first form, where little boys with wooden pens were applying ink as generously to their faces and clothes as to the paper before them, up to the tenth form, where mustachioed young men of eighteen nearly broke the benches by their vitality. All this had been built up by the villagers' own efforts during the past six years. When I told the teacher about my interview with Tara Singh he openly declared himself as an opponent of his. " We must not allow our people to be torn by religious and separatist conflicts at this moment. We Sikhs are a small community ; our road must be that of compromise, of collaboration with the Hindus. Besides, look what the old man has been spending our community's money on ! Huge sums every year on building new temples and maintaining old ones ! I am a good Sikh myself, but this school gives me greater pleasure.   The people who have squeezed Tara Singh out of the religious council are no traitors : they simply hold more modern views."

Poor Master Tara Singh !   He was a splendid patriarch, and bore the attribute Singh—' lion '—by right.   He was certainly a more picturesque and stronger personality than the teacher.   But he had been left behind by history.   Time and again one meets in India Europeans who overrate the strength of traditionalism in the clash between progressive rationalism and Indian tradition, and whose forecasts are coloured correspondingly.   To them the black shirts in the South are agents of a future division into North and South, and the Sikhs to them are something similar. And yet the issue there has now been decided in the opposite sense.   Tara Singh is an old, sick man not only physically ; the young people no longer follow him.   It is true that communalism —that is the name in India for the traditionally and religiously rooted separatism—still represents a force that can stage spectacular demonstrations.   Because of their romantic character, they strike the foreign observer more forcefully than the less spectacular, sober, modern transformation.   My personal inclination is not towards hailing this progress or hoping that it will gain momentum : too much that is beautiful and great is engulfed by it.   But it would be futile to try to maintain something that history has passed by.   One can regard it only with wistful sympathy, as I did the old lion whom I faced that night across a fire at which he tried in vain to warm his ageing paws.

CHAPTER SEVENTEEN

Three Faces of Pakistan

PAKISTAN : A NAME CONJURING UP A VARIETY OF different pictures ! This state has sprung up, not through race or geography, but through a common religion—Islam. The faith of the Prophet holds sway in many parts of the world. Around Mecca, his holy city, lies the desert. Among the bare mountains of Persia his faith blossoms forth in delightful mosques, and in Indonesia his followers lie down to pray underneath the palm-trees. In Pakistan all these facets are united. My most beautiful memories are of the mountains near the Afghan frontier : naked, rocky humps, inhabited by the wild, white, never entirely tamed tribes of the north-west. Peshawar, at the entrance to the Khyber Pass, has all the picturesque magic of a frontier town. It is an entrepôt on the edge of the forbidden land : one of the few sur-viving spots on earth which have successfully resisted the advance of civilization. Though citizens, in theory, of a modern state, the Pathans of the north-west province have preserved their own customs. No tax-collector, no policeman, no judge, and no soldier ever penetrates to their villages, where justice is still being administered by tribal councils in accordance with ancient law. Even the British preferred to send gifts of money rather than bloody punitive expeditions into this wilderness, and to tame these insubordinate people not by force but by generosity. In vain did I try to get an entry permit to their territory. In Karachi —I was told by Osman Shah Afridi at the Office for Tribal Affairs—such visits were not encouraged. It was not that the stranger was suspected of evil intentions—on the contrary, it was feared that for some reason or other the tribes might perhaps misinterpret some gesture of the inexperienced visitor and, in accordance with ancient custom, finish him off. There would be trouble with the Embassy, and besides, it would not even be possible to investigate the affair. Much better to keep everybody out. Strangers are only allowed as far as Darah, in the tribal territory of the Kohat ; a visit to this part of the country at least conveys an idea of this strange world. Darah is the centre of the Krupps and Schneider-Creusots of the north-west province. Or perhaps a better comparison would be the Greek god Hephaistos. Over an open fire, nourished by bellows, weapons are hammered and rifle barrels turned on strange drilling machines, in smoke-blackened holes, by smoke-blackened, savage-looking men. Quite small boys, barely able to walk, help with the work. The armourer's shop is at the end of the street. You can buy there rifles and pistols of any nationality—British, German, Spanish, even Russian models—all of them made in Kohat, by means of a bellows and an antediluvian rifling machine. It seems hardly believable : in the twentieth century ! Any weapon, even the most up-to-date type, can be copied here at the customer's request, a local craftsman told me, exact to within a tenth of a millimetre, provided it is not an atomic gun. Perhaps, as you negotiate, a dignified old man will enter the room, a wide cartridge belt across his chest and a pistol in the belt over his baggy breeches. He embraces the shopkeeper and presses him to his chest : this is the greeting of Homeric heroes. Everything here is still martial : human beings, homes, landscape. As far as you can see there are no separate individual houses—only fortresses, built of stone and topped by towers. Every man is either the ally or the enemy of another : even from a mile away entire generations can be wiped out by blood feuds.

Osman Shah Afridi, the young man in the Office for Tribal Affairs, does not in his external appearance betray his wild lineage. He has studied anthropology in England, and is now an official. He wears Western clothes and acts in an enlightened way. In the afternoon he invited me out to his property, a little over a mile outside Peshawar. It was a village of over 80 inhabitants, with clay walls. I was welcomed by his father, a retired captain in the old Indian Army of the British. To his great regret, he did not speak English. Feeling that his inadequate education had cut short his career—so Osman told me—the old man had sent all his sons, four of them, to the university. He had bought the village cheaply, together with two other officers, upon his retirement from active service. In the past because of the robbers one could not venture out of doors except heavily armed. But things have changed now. The family are to-day building a big guest-house. The old captain is counted among the local nobility, up there in the mountains, and that entails the obligation of providing free food and shelter for any member of the Afridi tribe. This means, in effect, being something like an hôtelier, just outside Peshawar, except that he cannot charge anything. But even to this family, which has escaped into civilization, the old tribal rules continue to apply : whenever Osman rides up into the mountains he leaves Cambridge behind. Somehow his Western manners are a veneer : you do not have to scratch very deep before the fierce warrior with the cartridge belt round his chest shows through even with him. " What are you going to do with your wife when you marry ? " I asked him. That is the acid test for every modern Moslem. Osman's wife will have to lead the life demanded by the community, even if she is an emancipated woman and has studied abroad. No Afridi revolts against the laws of his tribe. Throughout my visit I never saw a female being.

The desert stretches right down to the sea, all round Karachi. It is a strange capital, cut off on all sides : on the one side by water and on the other by sand. It is, as it were, a symbol : the geographically impossible capital of a geographically impossible country. Lahore in the north, which in point of status would have had a prior claim, is in too exposed a position but a few miles from the Indian Customs post. Plans have been worked out for a radical solution of the dilemma—the construction of a new capital, as in Australia or Brazil, somewhere near the mountains, near the white tribes, where the real heart of Pakistan lies. Then

Karachi can once more relapse into the unpretentious hustle and bustle of a harbour, with its import and export businesses and the almost painful colourlessness of its crowded streets.[1]

The historical disaster which raised Karachi to the rank of capital continued to disfigure it even more afterwards. Of the eight and a half million Moslems who streamed into the new country of their faith after the partition of India, more than seven million went to the West, and hundreds of thousands of these came to Karachi, where work and money were beckoning. As a result, the population of the city was trebled within a few years. To this day you can see the same accommodation that I found there in 1949 : clay walls, inadequately covered with tarpaulins or corrugated iron, with doors made of old crates, with rusty oil-drums as water-containers—the same picture of destitution and hardship. While I was being driven to the outskirts in one of those motor rickshaws which crowd the streets of the city we were overtaken by a screaming fire-engine. Smoke was rising from the slums : a fire had broken out and swept like lightning through the whole neighbourhood. Once again the familiar picture : people dejectedly slumped on a wooden bench, with only a few salvaged possessions around them, a woman crying, the men dully fatalistic. I questioned one of them as to where the fire had started, in the dry grass or the reeds—but no one knew anything. Nothing covered by insurance. Probably the Government would help, but these things took a long time. Besides, the people were not quite so miserable as they looked. The husband was earning a decent wage as a carpenter in a building firm—and 125 rupees here is a decent wage. Most of the occupants of these mud huts, he told me, were employed in textile mills at a mere 100 rupees a month.

One day they hope they will leave these mud huts, and then bulldozers will come and sweep them away. The Government is building housing estates out in the desert—simple white cubes dotted over the sand-dunes. They are not particularly

[1] In October 1959 Rawalpindi became the new interim capital of Pakistan, pending the building of a new city near by that should be the eventual capital—*Translator's Note*.

comfortable homes—but who asks about comfort here ? At any rate, the people will have a roof over their heads. Somewhere in the sand, among the straggling shrubs, stands a notice-board : " Site Reserved for School." So far hardly a blade of grass grows out here. The water needed for this metropolis *malgré lui* is brought over a distance of hundreds of miles, and is in short supply. A little nearer the city centre you breathe more freely again : lawns, and here and there even a tree. Man has been victorious.

All around there is a thirst for water—not only in the desert of Karachi, but also near Multan, farther inland, where the fields bear cotton and wheat. The fertility of the Indus plain is man-made, forcibly brought about by irrigation. And, if human wickedness decides, just as easily wrecked. The religious frontiers have done a disservice to the believers : they have cut across a system of canals which had been built by the British for a united India, and now the headwaters and flow-control sluices are in the hands of the hostile brother nation. India wants the water for herself, for the deserts of Rajasthan—oh, yes, every one has enough deserts of his own—and West Pakistan, if it does not want to dry up, must build huge new installations to divert the precious fluid from its own rivers. An impossible partition ; an impossible state ! [1]

And what is one to say about East Bengal, the other half of this state based on religion ? West Pakistan is an amputated limb, severed painfully yet healing up in the end. But East Pakistan is a piece of flesh cut from an organism carved out of the body of Bengal as by some Shylock : a pound of your liver belongs to me. On either side lies India, across a frontier drawn by a reeling drunkard across the plain—haphazardly, in accord-ance with the accidents of religious belief. On both sides of the line live the same people and stand the same villages : it is one nation. If the Creator had set out deliberately to produce the very antithesis of West Pakistan : a country without mountains

---

[1] In October 1960 India and Pakistan concluded an agreement on the use of the waters of the Indus and its tributaries.

and deserts but with water, with water without end, with the dry land no more than islands among the rivers, he would have created East Pakistan. Neither railways nor roads are any use in this primeval landscape, or at least not much. East Pakistan's means of transport are ship and aircraft. Ships making their unhurried way along the meandering waterways, through palm forests like the ones in Kerala, from village to village, surrounded by crowds of little boats at each landing-stage, with electric fans whirring in the hot cabins at night. Aircraft flying to Calcutta, the old natural capital, to whose loss the country has never quite reconciled itself, or right across to far-off Karachi, 1800 miles away, the new capital, scarcely real and yet all too real.

But what have these Bengalis, these lovable and yet impossible characters, in common with the people over there, in West Pakistan ? Those Punjabis are huge hulks of men, powerful, slow both physically and mentally, well-nourished on mutton and bread. The Bengalis, on the other hand, are short, with their finely moulded faces suggesting regions farther East— perhaps Malaya. Just as Western Pakistan has some of the elements of Persia, so the royal calm of Bengal hints at Siam, or even China. Perhaps this affinity with the East is due to the rice, to the reflections in the paddies which lend the landscape its poetry. Rice is the food of the Bengalis—rice and fish. They cannot even share a cook with the Punjabis. In mental make-up they are intellectual, sensitive, proud and touchy, almost pathologically unstable, and given to excesses. Bengal is the classical country of revolutions. The British, who have had much unfortunate experience with them, accuse the people of being intriguers and treacherous. Politics are their passion, as they are of the people of Kerala, but here politics are written in blood. Subhas Chandra Bose, the violent ally and opponent of the non-violent Gandhi, tried in the last War to liberate India with Japanese bayonets : he was a Bengali. What kind of fate was it that chained these mercurial types of the East to the phlegmatic people of the West ? These Bengalis, who are numerically superior, and whose jute provides the exchequer with the greatest part of its foreign currency, who can look back on a glorious literary tradition—are these people now to accept Karachi as their capital ? Even their intellectual and artistic heritage has somehow degenerated as a result of partition. The spirit of Bengal was neither Hindu nor Moslem : it was Bengali. Culture needs a metropolis, and Dacca is merely trying to be one. In losing Calcutta, East Bengal lost its head and declined into provincialism. The civil servants who are transferred to East Bengal from Lahore or Karachi will assure you with a sigh that things are not really too bad, and that anyone can bear this exile for two or three years. But it remains an exile nevertheless, an exile to an unloved country. " But what have you really in common ? " I asked a bank manager from the West. " How are you ever going to understand each other ? " " We shall do so," he replied, " the moment that common sufferings and blood jointly shed have forged us together into a community." A wonderful prospect.

Certainly, the fish-eaters of Dacca have not always been a source of pleasure to the carnivores of Karachi. Repeatedly they have staged successful revolts, by ballot and with paving-stones, in an attempt to ensure their individuality and equality. In the administrative offices of Karachi half the chairs are occupied by Bengalis, expatriates in their own state. Bengali is, after Urdu, recognized as the second official language. Certainly there are still some Bengali hotheads who would like to cut adrift from the West, and there are a considerable number of well-organized Communists. However, during my visit to Dacca I found it difficult to discover anyone who did not watch his tongue. For the past few months an energetic officer from the north-west, Ayub Khan, had been reigning in Karachi—a man who would have liked best to shut that favourite organ of every politician, his mouth. But we shall speak of that presently.

CHAPTER EIGHTEEN

" *Why do You exist at all ?* "

I ADMIT THAT THIS IS A SOMEWHAT UNUSUAL question to ask a Foreign Minister—worthy, perhaps, of an existentialist author like Sartre. But the Foreign Minister of Pakistan was such a charming person that one could put the question to him without embarrassment, especially as it was meant not so much in a philosophical as a political sense. We were having breakfast at his villa in Karachi. I had been introduced to him the day before, at a reception, and the informal conversation which I then began with him was now being continued. His welcome had an almost Japanese ring. " Please excuse the unpleasant smell," he began. " It rises at low tide from the brackish inlet down there. I've got the worst house of all the Ministers. I was in no hurry at the time to pick one of the official residences, and so I had to take what was left." " But you, as the Foreign Minister ? " I expressed surprise. " Just because of it," he said. " And in a way I am quite pleased. If a member of the Cabinet must make the sacrifice, why not one of the senior members ? " " That has quite a Christian ring," I retorted. " But surely you're a Moslem ? " He smiled. " Even Gandhi might have acted in this way." It was a moment of acute irritation and tension between India and Pakistan. " Does this principle apply also to your politics ? " I asked. He smiled. " I believe so," he said, " at least, as far as I am concerned."

Manzur Qadir, a man with the face of a bird and with shrewd, questioning, penetrating eyes, was no politician. He was a professor of constitutional law, who, almost against his will, had been snatched from his post at Lahore University when amid a

general sigh of relief a corrupt democracy ended in military
dictatorship. He had begun his career in the capital by dismissing
two of the four servants who welcomed him at his residence.
" The Government's got to economize," he said. He was
anything but a fanatic. His best friend, a Sikh, told me in Delhi
that at the time when India was still undivided and under British
rule they had organized alternate meals with beef and pork to
prove to each other their indifference to religious taboos. I also
knew that Manzur Qadir had been an avowed opponent of that
unfortunate partition which divided the continent into India and
Pakistan in 1947.

" Why do you exist at all ? "—meaning Pakistan. Who
could be more qualified to answer this question than this man,
who from being an opponent of Islamic separatism rose to be the
Foreign Minister of its state ? Had the setting up of Pakistan not
been a misfortune and a piece of folly ? Misfortune, because a
political organism which the British had welded into a well-
functioning economic and political unit had been arbitrarily torn
asunder. Folly, because the driving force behind this partition,
different religions, had ceased to be a force of importance. I told
Manzur Qadir of the strange impression I had had in the great
Mosque of Lahore at the time of the Friday prayers. A short
while before I had witnessed such prayers in Communist Tash-
kent, when a deeply stirred multitude of thousands had filled the
court of the Mosque and overflowed into the street. In Lahore
the small space under the domes was enough to hold all the
believers, and the vast open space of the courtyard had been
empty like a desert—except for a few boys chasing each other.
Was the religious fervour on both sides of the partition line, in
Pakistan and in India, so great that it would not have been
possible to find some other solution to the problem of coexistence ? What justification was there for a state founded on
religion in an age in which unbelief and secularization had
become the fashion, at least among the younger intelligentsia ?
Were not economics and geopolitics dislodging abstract ideals as
the driving force in world affairs ?

The Foreign Minister had listened to me with a thoughtful smile. " Why," he asked, " must it be religion in the narrowest meaning that gives our state its justification ? Have you never known any unbelievers in Europe who, whether they were aware of it or not, nevertheless had a Christian outlook, quite simply because they had grown up in a society moulded by Christian ideas ? Exactly the same thing applies to us. One does not have to attend Friday prayers to be a Moslem. The Hindus pray to idols, whereas we are monotheists. Not only the religion of the Hindus but their entire irrational mentality is alien to us, and suspect. Fundamentally, we feel closer to the Christians. And, of course, closest of all to the other Moslems. You are probably aware that in the First World War the Indian Moslems could only be persuaded into refusing obedience to the British because the British were at war with the Sultan of Turkey. What was the Sultan of distant Constantinople to us ? Well, he was the Caliph, the spiritual head of all Moslems." " But surely you have sprung from this Indian soil, you are of Indian race, and you speak an Indian language. Is there no affinity in you to the Indian world ? And, when all is said and done, is not this affinity stronger ?" Manzur Qadir shook his head. " When I hear an Indian heroic epic," he told me, " it leaves me unmoved. But when I hear the name of a great Arabian hero of the faith my heart starts vibrating even though—let me make that clear—I am not a religious person. And it is these most intimate strings which are made to vibrate, or else not to vibrate, which determine our choice. Do you know that in spite of his anti-Western policy Nasser enjoys much sympathy among us ? "

" Yes, but what advantages has Pakistan so far got from its Moslem brothers ? Where is this friendship of the Arabs ? And do you really get on so well with your allies the Turks and the Persians ? Is your tune of Islamic solidarity not really a case of sour grapes—the grapes, of course, being the natural association with India to which, when all is said and done, you belong? Your respect for Gandhi, your contentment with a smelly home— are not these typically Indian attitudes ? No Arab would act like this—never ! I believe myself that a different policy on the part of India could still change the whole situation. The things that divide you—Kashmir or your quarrel over the canals—are nothing permanent. Surely India, the much more powerful country and the genuine heir of the British raj, must desire as its neighbour a friendly, weak Pakistan. It ought to try, by wise concessions, to pacify Pakistan's furious opposition, and eventually its greater weight must surely bring the smaller brother under its influence. Sometimes I think of a future in which an India organized on decentralized federal lines and a Pakistan that has become friendly and trusting again would redress the disaster of partition and restore the unity of the continent——"

" Never," the Foreign Minister firmly interrupted me. " Even if India were to treat us with yielding love to-morrow, we should only regard it as a trap. Our mistrust springs from an incompatible mentality, as I've told you. Pakistan was born because we did not wish to be crushed as a minority among four hundred million Hindus. Don't tell me India is a secular State where the rights of the Moslems too are respected. Only on paper, in the Constitution ! In actual fact, Moslem officials who have stayed behind after the setting up of our country are finding themselves at a disadvantage with regard to promotion, and for young people the prospects of a Civil Service career are slight."

I shrugged my shoulders. If only the creation of Pakistan had provided a clear solution ! But 35,000,000 Moslems—in other words, nearly half the population of Pakistan—are still living in India. How do these 35,000,000 Moslems of Indian nationality feel now ? If religion becomes a national criterion must they not feel a secret allegiance to the hostile brother state ? And must not the Indians, for their part, suspect the dubious loyalty of these Moslems ? Especially as their caste system favours the fanaticism of small groups ? I remember an almost eerie interview which I had ten years earlier, on my first visit to India, with Maulana Azad, the Minister of Education, a great theologian who had nevertheless adopted India as his country. Throughout the time I was questioning him on these matters the old man sat in silence, and at times I thought I could hear him sigh. But he avoided an answer. Not till I left him and had a few words with his private secretary in his outer office did I find my misgivings confirmed. The Moslems in India are not happy : the more sincerely they try to be good Indians the deeper is their dichotomy.

Naturally, as soon as one touches on these problems in conversation with a Hindu all the arguments of the Moslems are swept aside with a smile. How can there be discrimination against their advancement ? Surely in India all these posts are competed for by a written examination ? To ensure complete impartiality this examination is strictly anonymous: only the candidate's performance decides. If the young Moslems come out less well than the young brahmins we are very sorry—then they are simply less intelligent, or they work less hard. For one reason or another they are less suitable. Had it not always been like this, even under the British, who surely did everything in their power to protect and even to favour the Moslem minority ? Why was it that even then the Civil Service, the higher educational institutions, and the offices of the big business firms were staffed almost exclusively with Hindus ? Presumably because the Moslems lack that intellectual agility and a sense for modern progress. They have remained frozen rigid in the traditional outlook of their ancestors : they are peasants, or artisans, or else rich men defending the feudal order for all they are worth. True, Hinduism is likewise a social system with great conservative inertia. But this inertia has not been elevated into a rigid dogma as was the case, at least until quite recently, in most Moslem countries. India is swarming with deities to suit all tastes—not just Allah triumphant as sole tyrant. And the same applies to the representatives of the deity : India had no organized priest class to wave a stick over the believers, and in the Hindu teaching there is room for many truths, including modern Western progress. The Hindu world is open, non-militant, and seemingly unprotected : that was why the Islamic conquerors found it so easy to impose their rule upon this amorphous mass. They had found it more difficult in matters of faith : it was mainly the casteless who embraced the new religion in the hope of finding liberation from their under-privileged position.   Otherwise the Hindu builders and stone-masons imprinted upon the mosques and palaces of their masters the stamp of their own native country.   There is an exuberance, a tangled, unchecked growth : geometry comes alive with jungle vegetation.   What is left of Allah, the arid despot of the desert ? The great and wise Mogul emperors, in particular Akbar, realized this trend very well.   Tolerant, they strove for synthesis rather than imposed domination, and in doing so they acted, almost unwittingly, in the Hindu spirit.   For Hinduism, as I have said, does not reject foreign elements.   It makes no claim to being the exclusive truth.   I have been told the story of a Christian missionary who was received with open arms by the brahmins. " If you know of yet another way to God," they said, " that's wonderful !   You can't ever know enough of them."   In this atmosphere of universalism any proselytizing religion, which claims to be the exclusive truth, must run short of breath.   Jungle-like, as its ornaments, Hinduism will twine around anything that penetrates into its sphere.   It had coped with both religions that have sprung up in its midst, the Jains and the Buddhists ; it was similarly about to digest Islam.

Consider all the things that the Indian Moslems have learned from their Hindu neighbours—or perhaps have remembered from the time when they too were Hindus !   For example, their feasts.   A wedding, to whichever faith the young people belong, is a superb spectacle : the celebrations continue through-out several evenings and nights in a specially built fairy-tale palace under the magic light of hundreds of Chinese lanterns. The bridal procession moves through the nocturnal streets, accompanied by ear-splitting music, and with the wedding presents, lit up by torches, carried by servants on their heads so the whole town can admire them.   Or take the sweeper who crept into my bathroom every morning : in Lahore, and even in the cosmopolitan Karachi, he was avoided as an untouchable every bit as much as are his colleagues in caste-conscious India !

The Moslems are reluctant to admit it, but the passion which enforced the setting up of Pakistan was not so much religious fervour, bursting from an over-full heart and convinced of the justice of its own cause, as the sense of insecurity of a religion which found itself spiritually forced on to the defensive by the jungle-like, silently operating superiority of Hinduism, which infiltrated unnoticed and without struggle assimilated the Indian Islam. To this must be added a perfectly matter-of-fact economic defensive : the Moslems did not wish to be squeezed out by the more efficient Hindus from all the Government posts in an independent India, but if possible to conquer new ones ; to this end new ones had to be created in a new state. Thus Pakistan, the 'land of the pure,' is a creation of the Islamic inferiority complex.

Its practical beginnings were correspondingly primitive. When I first visited Karachi ten years ago Ministries, editorial offices, and the radio were still housed in ancient wooden buildings with dark, windowless rooms—because of the heat—or simply in hastily knocked-up wooden shacks. There was a shortage of everything, from furniture to manpower. There were offices without desks and chairs, without telephones, without—I almost said without a cup of tea, but that was always available, served by some lazy servant. This most important requisite of an Indian office was simply indispensable : how else was a baboo to employ his time ? There was, as I have said, a manpower shortage. The Hindus who were streaming across the frontier into India, as refugees, represented the élite of the country—a loss which could not be offset by the stream of refugees in the opposite direction. But in the land of the blind the one-eyed man is king. Those who, as Moslems in India, had occupied some subordinate position now found themselves translated to the position of a departmental head, and many of them are still enthroned there to this day. But this start from scratch also has its positive side— the drive of every new beginning. The visitor to Karachi and Delhi in 1947 found a totally different atmosphere in the two countries : in Delhi independence had been followed by a kind of hangover. For what had happened ? A few British

ual dance at
Hindu festival
Quilon,
rala.

*Satyagraha in front of the Government building in Trivandrum, Kerala. As a p[...]
against the Communist Government men lie down across the drive to obstruct traffi[...]
court mass arrest.*

o-existence of deities at Kerala : Stalin, Gandhi, Nehru, and the god Krishna.

Communist propaganda painted on a road surface in Kerala. In the background, chil on their way to school.

Communists—in this case the Communist-led All Indian Trade Union Congress—
ond of using traditional spectacles for their demonstrations in order to attract the
public eye.

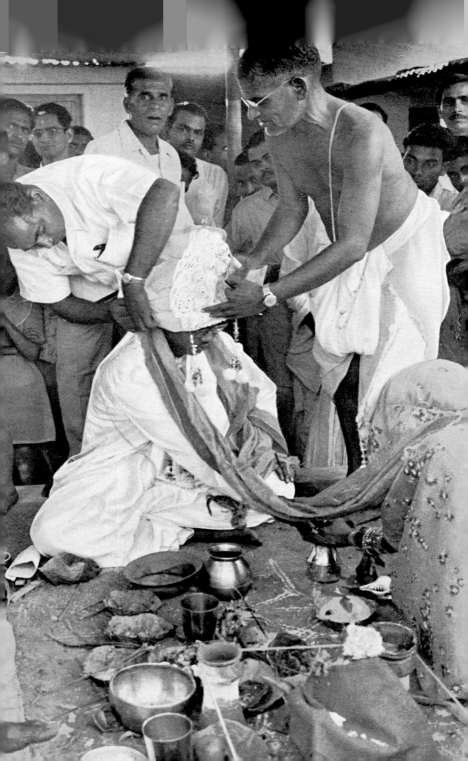

ɔve) *Unanimous vote for Tara Singh : a meeting of the Akalai Party, a Sikh secession movement.*

) *A brahmin wedding : the final act of the ceremony. The couple clasp hands and are tied to each other with a shawl.*

*Pakistani girls at the atomic physics laboratory in Lahore wear their traditional colo.
Punjabi costumes. The highest posts are to-day open to women willing to tak
science as a career.*

...awar, Pakistan.   *Clash of two worlds : a woman in purdah below a poster
advertising a Brigitte Bardot film.*

ove) *Ambush in the streets of Katmandu : passers-by are given an injection against cholera by a team of the W.H.O.*

ft) *Cow droppings for briquettes. They are dried and used for fuel.*

Street in Katmandu, Nepal. The houses are decorated with fine wood-carvin

sahibs had departed, and the Indian officials next in order of succession had moved up into their posts—and everything remained much the same. Pakistan, on the other hand, was still permeated by the exhilaration found in every country after a revolution : there was an exuberant optimism in the air.

Subsequent developments have shown the danger of relying on first impressions. In India, in spite of all progress achieved, the mood has remained almost the same. People criticize and grumble about the snail-like progress, about corruption, and heaven knows what else—but all the time the country makes steady and undramatic progress. It is the weakness of evolutionary development that it takes place unspectacularly. Fortunate nations, as everybody knows, have a dull history. Pakistan, in its dynamic optimism, reaped the fruits of its inexperience. The death of its founder and first president Jinnah shortly after the partition was an act of God ; the death of Liaquat Ali Khan, his successor, by assassination was almost in accordance with the normal pattern of a country torn by violence, ridden by irresponsible politicians, and undermined by corruption. The country seemed to be breaking apart in the same spirit in which it had been founded : in a chaos of irrational emotions, in a morass of incompetence.

Pakistan means ' land of the pure.' Before long it had become the plaything of all that was most impure in the world. *Qui veut faire l'ange, fait la bête,* says Pascal. To be an employer meant unbridled exploitation and 300 per cent. profit. To be an official meant trade in licences and contracts, baksheesh all along the line, from the Minister down to the postman who will not hand over a letter unless tipped. To be a landowner meant smuggling your crops across the Indian frontier and selling the foreign currency at black-market rates. Pakistan, that rich agrarian country, had to import grain. Its currency was wasting away as if consumptive.

When I came to Karachi again toward the end of 1959 the mood was the same as in 1947—that of a new beginning. Again the foreigners were saying : This is better than India ! What *deus ex machina* had changed the country's fortunes so suddenly ?

It was a general from the north-west province, Ayub Khan, a
man whose round, pink face, twirled moustache, and pleasant
smile make him look more like an Englishman than an Indian. In
the entire miasma of Pakistan the army was the only organized
group which had remained more or less clean. To this day it
lives, in accordance with British colonial tradition, separated
from the rest of the population, in its cantonment lines outside the
cities.   Moreover, as in other under-developed countries, a large
number of intelligent young people who find no vacancy in the
Civil Service or in an as yet undeveloped industry choose the
career of an army officer. The result is that the army becomes a
kind of nursery of thinking rebels.   When the rottenness in
Pakistan had reached a degree which jeopardized the existence of
the state these martial puritans resorted to action.   Ayub Khan
chased away Parliament, suspended the Constitution, banned all
parties and trade-unions, and proclaimed a state of emergency.
And then began a cleaning-up drive on a gigantic scale. It began
quite literally with brooms : the streets which had been blocked
with vendors' stalls, hawkers, beggars, and various scum were
swept clean of rubble and humans, and handed over again to
proper traffic.   " May we see your books, please ? " the tax
officials asked the industrialists who had never paid any taxes—
or only symbolical ones into the private pockets of the collectors.
Price lists appeared in the shop-windows, and woe to the dealer
who overcharged his customer by even a penny.   The punish-
ments for transgressors were Draconic : the prisons filled rapidly
with gentlemen who but a day before had been riding about in
Cadillacs.   The Pakistani Navy fished up tons of gold from
coastal waters, where alarmed smugglers had sunk it. Vast stocks
of wheat and other foodstuffs, hoarded by speculators and black
marketeers in the hope of forcing up prices, were brought out
from hiding-places.   Corrupt officials were being shaken out of
Government departments like ripe apples from trees. Reporting
of offenders was made compulsory by law ; failure to report was
made punishable as complicity. The order of the barrack square
was introduced in Pakistan. Democracy was dead, stone dead.

And yet all decent people to whom I spoke were happy. And in spite of the state of emergency not a single drop of blood had been shed. " We merely lent emphasis to the existing laws," a senior officer told me simply. " That was all."

Once order had been established in the country it became possible to tackle those problems which had until then been forgotten in the chaos of demagogy. A land reform, sabotaged throughout ten years by big landowners playing at politics, was put into effect. Unrealistic industrial castles in the air, the dreams of state planning authorities, were buried, and private initiative, including foreign capital, was given the green light instead. Not only morality, but reason as well, had suddenly made its appearance in Pakistan. The unique feature of this dictatorship was the fact that realistic entrepreneurs and honest businessmen were given a degree of freedom and chance of economic expansion which aroused the envy of any red-tape-fettered businessman in democratic India. Thus Ayub Khan could face with confidence born of a clear conscience the storm which broke out in neighbouring India, right up to the highest posts, over the ' suppression of democracy ' in Pakistan. Democratic institutions, he explained with his soldier's logic, if they are to work presuppose a minimum educational standard : where the overwhelming majority of a people can neither read nor write the ballot paper becomes a farce. This was simple soldier's logic—perhaps a little too simple. Yet the military coups which swept at the same time through other Asian countries sick with democracy prove that Ayub's revolution was not a localized incident, but represents a necessary phase in the political development of these nations. That, indeed, is the reason for Delhi's violent reaction : there are many people who believe the Indian patient to be equally ready for a surgical operation with bayonets.

CHAPTER NINETEEN

The Land of the Pure

*W*HY DO YOU EXIST AT ALL?" THIS ISSUE TOO
Ayub Khan had tried to clarify. In the official designation of
Pakistan as 'Islamic Republic' he simply deleted the word
'Islamic'—and that reflected an entire Government programme.
It meant an avowal in favour of a secular, liberal state, where
everybody was free to worship as or whom he chose. He
thereby put a spoke in the wheel of the mullahs and other
religious fanatics and demagogues who wanted to see Pakistan
ruled by the clergy in accordance with the ancient laws of Islam.
On my first visit I had had a conversation with the Pir of Manki,
at that time one of the most dangerous powers behind the scenes.
A close-buttoned man, both mentally and in his dealings with
others, anything but brilliant, with a beard and immovable
stonelike features and smouldering eyes, he had uttered, even
through his interpreter, nothing beyond a few platitudes. On
my present visit to Lahore I visited another religious man, one
whose education and open-mindedness put him in an entirely
different category. The Koran Research Centre, of which G. A.
Parwez was the head, was accommodated on the ground floor
of a house in the suburb of Gulberg, among the homes of
film stars and other earthly creatures. To judge by the mixture of domestic utensils and manuscripts, it did double duty
as his office and bedroom. The old gentleman, a former
civil servant, had a face lined by intensive study and sleep-
less nights ; his steel-framed glasses and white hair lent him
an intellectual severity tempered to some extent by his dreamy
eyes. Piety to him clearly was not withdrawal from the world,

but a deliberate attempt to change the world into the likeness of God.

The country was at the time in the throes of a public discussion on the land reform. No private property was to exceed 500 acres in future. Was that not very mild compared with the maximum of 30 acres envisaged in India ? The severe old gentleman nodded eagerly. " Private ownership of the means of production ought to be abolished altogether," he lectured. " In accordance with the Holy Koran, all land is a gift of Allah, just as are air and sunshine, and should not be owned by any individual any more than air and sunshine should ; it ought merely to be made available to everybody in accordance with his needs. You must understand that Islam is concerned not only with the future bliss of the believers, but also with their present earthly requirements. In accordance with the Holy Koran, it is the responsibility of the state to see that every citizen has all his basic needs : food, clothing, shelter, medicines, and education. Yes : the responsibility of the state ! That is a tremendous task, and can be realized only if all the means of production are owned by the state." I was listening to the quiet, unemotional professorial lecture with growing astonishment. " Are you—I hope you don't mind my asking—are you a Communist ? " I asked cautiously. He shook his head triumphantly. " Many people ask me that question," he said almost grimly. " Certainly a good many things demanded by the Holy Koran resemble the ideals of Communism. But the really essential thing—the ultimate aim —is fundamentally different. For if our state provides for each citizen all his basic needs, then this is not an end in itself : this liberation from hardship is designed to give him strength and leisure to develop all that is best in him, his whole personality. Communism, on the other hand, thinks only of the satisfaction of a man's physical needs at the expense of human individuality. But it is this fully developed individuality, made possible by the social order of the Koran, that survives death and marches forward to bring all latent possibilities to full fruition."

The old man's speech had turned into that prophetic rhetoric

which rules out all discussion ; arguments no longer penetrate
into the magic circle within which the thoughts of the fanatic
move about as in a cage. " But how do you hope to realize this
social order of the Koran ? " I ventured to object all the same.
" Solely by conviction, not by violence ! " he answered quickly.
" But if the state is to take over all the means of production this
would mean in effect the establishment of a bureaucracy of
hundreds of thousands—and after your country's experience so
far, surely you cannot assume that the practices of these bureaucrats would be very much in line with the Koran ? Your
programme could be realized only with angels ; but man is not
so good. . . ." It was clear that Parwez had merely been waiting
for such a generalized statement in order to avoid facing up to
less fundamental but real problems. " Man is neither good nor
bad by nature," he interrupted. " It all depends on how he
realizes himself, and the Koran helps him to choose the good."
I sighed. " Islam is the highest form of rationalism," the old man
went on. " Every individual must choose for himself. I quite
understand that as a Christian you find it difficult to comprehend
the greatness of this idea, for your Christ has relieved you of
your responsibility by his death ! What an immoral absurdity,
that remission of sins of yours—to let some one else suffer for
one's own trespasses ! " I endeavoured to get the conversation
back to a more realistic basis again. " How many followers
have you got ? " I asked. " No mass following," Parwez
smiled. " I must expect opposition rather than approval for my
ideas, opposition from both sides : from the modern unbelievers
who want to turn Pakistan into a secular country like any other,
and from the mullahs who have not even read the Koran
correctly, and who are furiously defending a tradition which is
neither holy nor viable. My ideas are not for the masses, but
my books are read by intellectuals, and through them much is
translated into reality." " And when may we expect to see the
realization of the social order of the Koran ? " I continued my
questions. " In your own lifetime ? " The old man shook his
head. " I know that the world at the moment is imperfect, but

I also know that my efforts to improve it will be taken up and continued by hundreds of others. Some day, in a hundred years, or perhaps in a thousand years, the kingdom of God will be realized. If I can contribute to this end, however slightly, I am satisfied."

We have spoken of God and gods, of traditions and philosophical systems. But how does the outsider, the visitor, experience the different atmosphere in India and Pakistan? To characterize this difference let me relate the story of my visit to the two famous hydro-engineering projects which are springing up on the edge of the Himalayas. The Bhakra Nangal Dam, the second highest in the world, is being built on Indian territory to divert the water of the Sutlej river which flows into the basin of the Indus. The Warsak Dam, built with Canadian aid, spans a gorge near Peshawar, where the Kabul river enters the plain from Afghanistan. Both projects have assumed for the native populations an almost magical significance. Unending masses of people stream out to both building-sites. " Have you seen Bhakra Nangal ? " I was asked throughout India, in much the same way as the traveller in Egypt is asked whether he had already seen the pyramids. In actual fact there is nothing very much to be seen at either building-site—apart from the vast mountains of cement, they are just rather depressing gorges. But these heaps of cement embody great hopes, for they will provide electric power for industry, water for the fields, and prosperity for the people. In India excursions to the Bhakra Nangal site are simply and boldly described as ' pilgrimages ' : the dam has become something in the nature of a holy place, a temple of the new technical god of prosperity.

Perhaps it is because of this strange and almost religious reverence which the Indians feel for their technical miracles that to take photographs is as strictly forbidden there as in the holy of holies in a temple. Even when they are being built by foreign engineers—in the case of Bhakra Nangal, by Americans—and in accordance with foreign plans.

When I entered the Public Relations Office there, brandishing my Press card and asking for a photograph permit, the officials looked very doubtful. To do that, they declared, I ought to have brought a permit with me from Delhi ! Nonsense, I tried to laugh it off ; surely a dam is no strategic object ? So what can there be secret about it ? The officials entrenched themselves behind their telephones. The Indian engineer-in-chief was not in his office. The deputy engineer-in-chief declared himself unable to take a decision which only the engineer-in-chief was authorized to take ; but he would do his best to track him down. Would I please wait ? A quarter of an hour later the telephone rang again. Sorry, but the engineer-chief could not be found any-where. No photographs !

At the Warsak Dam, on the other hand, I arrived without warning, and I did not even have my Press card with me. This building-site is open to visitors only on Sundays because other-wise they might get in the way of the work ; moreover, this site, strange as it may sound, really is a strategic job. All along the surrounding hills stand fortress-like watch-towers. For the territory of the Pathan tribes begins almost within sight of the turbines, and their ancient customs are as yet unreconciled with hydro-power projects. Not that a chieftain would be interested in a turbine, but there are other things, more easily stolen and carried away, at the building-site of a giant power-station. Hence the fortifications on the hill-tops.

True, there are also legal ways for a warlike character to profit from a hydro-power project. Many Pathans have taken on jobs as pneumatic-drill operators or as watchmen to prevent their fierce fellow-tribesmen from thieving. The young man who stopped me at the barrier was clearly one of the latter. He was positively sparkling with gay vitality, and his way of treating me was clearly that of a free man. " Let's see," was his reply when I told him of my request. He snatched the telephone from the wall. No reply. " Public Relations aren't there," he said laconically. " Let's try Security." A surly voice came through the instrument. " He says No," the young man interpreted.

" Sorry." " Pity," I said, " especially after I've come such a long
way." " Wait," the young man said. " I'll ring them again."
" Listen," he said into the telephone, " why can't we let the
foreign gentleman in ? " A furious howling came through the
telephone. The young man flung the receiver back on the cradle
as if it were a piece of wood. " We'll try the engineer-in-chief
now." The engineer-in-chief proved amenable. " Take no
notice of Security ; just drive on," the young man advised me.
Fifteen minutes later I stood at the building-site, among the sparks
of the welding equipment and the roar of the concrete-mixers.

This is just one example of the easier accessibility of people in
Pakistan. I could quote many more. With a little observation
and experience you can tell a person's religion at sight, so clearly
is the different mental attitude of Moslems and Hindus reflected
in their features. The Moslem is simple, reasonable, and unam-
biguous. Allah, like the Christian God, is a being that one can
talk to. From this dialogue relationship arises the possibility and
necessity of decision. The Moslem's eyes are always flashing—
sometimes with aggressiveness. His speech is yea and nay, and
even though he frequently is a rascal his rascally deeds are somehow predictable and calculable. But with the Hindu you cannot
even look properly into his eyes : there is something bottomless
in them, and if you immerse yourself in them you enter a realm
that is both eerie and wonderful. Oh, the endless trouble of
getting a concrete grasp of a Hindu, intellectually or spiritually !
" Sometimes I nearly go out of my mind," a German architect
who is employed by the Government in Delhi confessed to me.
" I feel as though I were in a world of Kafka's. There is a new
project that I am to take over, so I demand to see the preliminary
studies. Nothing, blank looks, vacant stares, among superiors
and subordinates : nobody knows anything about them. Like
a madman, I get down to the job : I calculate and design
everything from scratch ; and when I then submit my plans after
working day and night for a fortnight the departmental head
will look up with a smile : ' Oh, but we've had these plans here
in our filing cabinet for ages ! ' I don't know if the people are

so thoughtless or if they are committing secret sabotage, or if
the two are intermingled in their unconscious mind. Certainly,
a white man wrecks his nerves here completely." I can confirm
his experience. Whenever I arrived in an Indian town and called
on officials or colleagues—there were always the same strange,
absent unfathomable looks, as equivocal as Shiva with her many
arms, as the whole mythological jumble that fills the Hindu
temples and can be unravelled only by a scholar. I know that
this world of gods represents, as it were, the entire universe, and
that the multiplicity of this universe can never be framed in a
monotheistic system or reduced to a simple logical principle.
But what does a man want the whole universe for in everyday
practical life ? How can he shape a personality if contrasts become
one, if everything indeterminate appears as supreme wisdom and
anything definite as unphilosophical philistinism ? To return to
my own position as an inquiring author : only on the rarest of
occasions have I ever learnt anything interesting from a Hindu
acting spontaneously. Sometimes I would read in the papers that
a particular city where I had looked for this feature or that did
in fact possess this feature in its most typical form—but nobody
ever told me. Nor did it often emerge from casual conversation :
dialogue with a Hindu is like a game of tennis in a fog. You
demand precise details and facts : the Hindu will evade them by
lengthy general disquisitions. As fundamental and as imprecise
as possible. Trying to nail him down, you feel like a police
officer questioning a delinquent. But where everything merges
in the All-One the separate things all become equally relevant
and hence irrelevant. Our Western concept of ' interesting ' is
alien to most Indians ; they lack a sense of psychology.

I do not want to imply that the Pakistanis altogether lack the
unpredictability and vagueness of the Hindus—witness my conversation with Parwez. After all, they have sprung from the
same soil. But they are more fathomable for our probing spirit,
and in one's human relations with them one is more likely to
achieve results. It is no accident that Pakistan has concluded an
alliance with the West. Islam belongs within the emanation of

the Mediterranean, as we all do—and that determines its affinity. Pakistan makes sense even to such extrovert people as the Americans ; in Delhi they are at sea. In India, as I have said, the white man becomes a nervous wreck : in Karachi he will only get bored, for reasonable people are not interesting. Maybe this is the reason why most Westerners tend to side with Pakistan in the quarrel between the two warring brothers. As if world history were written by reason ! For that it is far too interesting.

CHAPTER TWENTY

Neither Funeral Pyre nor Veil

THE MANAGER WAS ENGAGED : WOULD I MIND waiting a few minutes ? I did not mind in the least, because it gave me a chance to chat with the young receptionists—most of them pretty—who were operating the telephone switchboard with skill and assurance. Some of them were a little shy when questioned about their private affairs, but others were quite forthcoming. Though not, perhaps, quite so frank as the young Burmese girl who had left her country and found employment with the Bangalore Machine Tool Factory. " Burmese men are too weak," she said laconically when I asked her why she preferred India to Burma. Quite apart from the pleasure, conversation with these girls was exceedingly instructive : most of them, strictly speaking, ought to be called young women. One of them was the wife of an army officer ; until he got promotion she would help in this way to supplement his pay. But India also has another great innovation—divorced women living on their own. Every Indian town of any size now has its ' Working Girls' Hostel,' where they can live inexpensively, chaperoned by some old dragon. It has only been possible since 1955 for an Indian woman to leave her husband—since a new code of civil law, the so-called Hindu Code, had not only granted to sisters the same right of inheritançe from their father as was enjoyed by their brothers, but had also emancipated a wife from the whims of her domestic despot. The cruel custom of widows ' voluntarily ' following their dead husbands to the funeral pyre had been made a crime as early as 1829, under the Governor-Generalship of Lord William Bentinck, and is only very rarely practised to-day in remote parts of the country and in the greatest secrecy. Even so, the Indian Press has been able during the past few years to report some six or seven successful *satis*, and about the same number of successfully prevented ones. But although this dramatic aspect of a wife's worthlessness has now practically disappeared, it continues to be only too obvious in a number of undramatic everyday features. In the street the old-fashioned Hindu wife will walk, not by the side of her husband, but humbly behind him. She must not speak unless spoken to, she must not contradict her husband, or even interrupt him. He addresses her in the familiar form, like a servant girl, but she honours him with the formal mode of address ; when she calls him she uses not his name but the form ' Gharrwalla,' which means ' Master of the house.' She watches him in the attitude of a servant while he takes his food, and she herself eats what is left over. When the new godless Hindu Code became law in May 1955, against the violent opposition of the orthodox groups, they replied by organizing a five-day festival in Lucknow in honour of the God Vishnu, the symbol of the ideal husband. There the women present addressed themselves to their husbands with the following words : " Oh my merciful husband, incarnation of God, if I have offended, knowingly or unwittingly, pray forgive my offence." But that, of course, is old-fashioned. The young Indian woman of to-day has every means of getting herself treated with respect—at least, if she wants to. No more secondary wives : the Hindu Code has abolished polygamy. Virgin widows will likewise soon be a thing of the past : those girls who, while still in the cradle or at a tender age, used to be married to another child, and on that child's death had to share the unhappy fate of all uncremated widows—living with the family as a kind of old maiden aunt, dressed in a white shroud, her head shorn of all hair, without jewellery, a sexless being marked by an evil fate.

All these little acts of cruelty, though not quite as rare as a widow's death on the funeral pyre, have to-day been relegated to the shrinking circle of rigid orthodoxy. Even if widows and divorced women do not find happiness in another marriage, there are posts for them in an expanding industry, and a well-paid secretary with her own flat and telephone can exude quite a considerable sex appeal for an honourable young man. While we are on the subject of sex—one does not see a great deal of it in India, but behind the puritan façade simmers hot blood, and because a woman has been divorced or left a widow this does not necessarily condemn her to a nun's existence. Paradoxically enough, the very fact that marriages are based on solid, durable family agreements rather than evanescent emotional relationships leads to a good deal of freedom. Frequently when I was a guest in an Indian home I noticed my host quite unconcernedly poaching outside his own preserves: doctors with their reception-ists, businessmen with their secretaries—and by no means surreptitiously but, it seemed to me, with the full knowledge and the willing or unwilling approval of their ageing wives. In point of fact, they really were unable to compete—those dignified fat ladies enthroned like broody hens among their numerous crowd of children. They were not raving with jealousy— nothing of the sort. After all, this very crowd of children that had played havoc with a wife's physical charms has made her secure against the passing whims of her husband. Let him amuse himself, for none of these charming young girls could prevail against that which endured : the family, the lady of the house, the mother in her armour of almost divine inviolability. And what good and selfless creatures these girl friends are, on the other hand ! A tall, strapping Sikh told me that he handed over nearly his whole salary to his wife to support the family. For his personal requirements he received 100 rupees pocket-money a month from his young mistress, who was a hospital nurse and not allowed to marry, and who wished in this way to repay his love and his wife's tolerant attitude. The little gold-digger of the Western type hardly exists in India ; she is the product of an industrial society and the resultant—if I may coin a new word—hetairarchy. Because their strong ties prevent them from sliding into amoral anarchy, the Indians with all their complicated relationships are in some respects freer than we whose entire lives are based on the individual conscience. On the other hand, when they shake off their fetters—men and girls alike—they lack that sense of a limit that would preserve them from anarchy. Thus freedom is frequently interpreted as total indiscipline. That is the drawback of woman's emancipation, not only in India but in all ancient civilizations undergoing transformation: it is bought at the price of security. Courtship replaces respect, youthful charms are rated higher than maturity, and the teenager is glorified instead of the mother.

India, however, has not yet advanced very far along this road, and it is my impression that the Indian women have some deep instinct that the change has not brought them advantages only. It is significant that emancipation in India came without militant suffragettes, but as a thief in the night, that nothing is enforced prematurely but everything is allowed to grow and mature, and that if struggle is necessary—as with the introduction of the Hindu Code—this struggle is fought out by the men. This slow and gradual growth of equality for women has not prevented outstanding women from stepping effortlessly into the highest political posts in the land. I am thinking not so much of the spectacular case of Indira Gandhi, the daughter of Nehru, whose election to the chairmanship of the Congress Party in 1959 may have been a tribute to her father rather than to herself. A more impressive case is the career of the Mayor of Delhi, Mrs Aruna Asafali, who during the struggle for independence was in charge for a while of terrorist activities, but who once India had gained her independence felt too independent herself to be satisfied with a career as a prominent member of the Congress Party. She chose the far more difficult road of a non-party public figure, at times sympathizing with the Communists. As Mayor of Delhi her warm-hearted championship of the cause of the poor earned her such an enthusiastic following that she was re-elected to her post against the opposition of her former party. She combines a mother's kindliness and undemanding humility with the visionary fire of a social idealist : in the last century she would have been

described as a beautiful soul. Many other women have like her
risen to prominent political positions.

It is characteristic of the different atmospheres of India and
Pakistan that in the latter country the emancipation of the women
had to be achieved in a much harsher and more decisive manner,
almost as a struggle.

Anyone near the entrance of the orthodox Ismalia College for
Women in Lahore at nine o'clock in the morning can witness an
almost depressing spectacle. Slim, tall figures arrive from all
directions. They chat merrily together, and the sound of their
voices and the silver ring of their laughter betray a youthful mind
still expectantly open to all the wonders of life—caressed and
troubled by yearnings just as any teenager in Europe. But only
their voices betray them. For across their faces is drawn a black
veil which they hastily pull down the moment they leave the
protection of their parental home and step out into the street.
Not till they reach the courtyard of the College are they allowed
to take it off : here no man's glance can penetrate, and only
women teachers come near them. This parade of black veils
seems gloomier than the same spectacle in primitive Afghanistan,
because there the veils are a brilliant interplay of colours from
mauve to olive-green, allowing the girls some womanly self-
expression even in hiding. The girl students of Ismalia College,
by way of contrast, look like a congregation of mourners.
Equally uncanny are the orthodox ladies of an older vintage who
are occasionally met in the market-places of the old towns :
white canvas hoods are tipped over their heads, and only a coarse
netting in front of their eyes opens on the world. These *burka*
are reminiscent of the protective masks worn during the outbreaks of plague in the Middle Ages by the carters of the dead.
The first time you see them a shiver runs down your spine, just
as it does at the sight of the black-veiled teenagers.

On the other hand, there are the truly modern women, such
as Razia Ghulam Ali, whom I met in Karachi. Indeed, there is
no shortage in Karachi of ' modern ' ladies, provided you write
modern in quotation marks. They are found at the headquarters

of the All-Pakistan Women's Association—elegant, soignée women in expensive saris, who maintain sewing-rooms for refugee women, propagate hygiene and other information in Mothers' Clubs, and make grand speeches about the rights of the women in Pakistan. In reality these Begums are not half as progressive as they make out, considering that their fine saris are paid for by their husbands, and that they can afford to spend the day in good works only because those same husbands maintain a big household with many servants. The wealthy men in Pakistan have, moreover, developed a taste for a different kind of freedom since Pakistan's independence : in increasing measure they avail themselves of the possibility of adding to the wilting charms of their Begums the yet unspoilt ones of a second wife, as the Prophet permits. The circumstance that this right is qualified by the condition that they must divide their love equitably between the two wives has never greatly worried the amorous Moslems : men in love forget their prayers. Needless to say, there was an outcry of indignation among the Begums as this practice began to spread, and when in 1955 the then Prime Minister Mohammed Ali—who had been married to Begum Hamida for fourteen years and had five children—took his attractive secretary as a second wife the Pakistan Women's Association called for a social boycott of the offender. A lot of noise was made at the time, but after a while the excitement died down and the boycott was forgotten. Mohammed Ali to this day enjoys his two wives, and if he has vanished from the political scene this was due not so much to the indignant women as to rebellious generals. " All these Begums," a clever Englishwoman who is married to a Pakistani told me, " skate around the central question of women's emancipation. Women who are luxury wives and economically dependent on their husbands cannot fight for their rights but can merely talk, or at best apply to certain sore spots the mitigating ointment of good deeds. Genuine emancipation of women can arrive only by way of careers for women, and our first step must be to ensure for them economic and social equality with the men. Do you know how

much a schoolmistress or a hospital nurse earns ? Sixty, or at
most eighty, rupees per month. We must fight for equal pay.
All other problems will then be solved automatically. Once a
wife can leave her husband because she no longer needs his money
a man will think twice before marrying a second wife."

Similar views were expressed to me by Razia Ghulam Ali,
whom I mentioned before—and she not only made speeches but
had for her own part achieved this independence. She happens
to be the leading manufacturer of concrete pipes in Pakistan—
rather a strange profession for so charming a lady. She had
started off with no more than her good common sense and an
eye for business. " My husband used to be an engineer on the
Bombay railway," she told me. " When partition came we had
to give up our property, and from a Hindu—who for his part
had to emigrate from here—we bought a property with a modest
house. In the backyard stood an abandoned pipe-casting machine.
Although I did not understand much about it, I began, really
mostly for the fun, to play about with it. Our experiments
turned out well beyond expectation, and I realized that an
expanding young capital such as Karachi would need a vast
quantity of pipes. Thus, almost without doing anything about
it, I became a pipe-manufacturer." To-day Razia Ghulam Ali
has moved from the small, dusty office in which her extraordinary
career began into spacious and comfortable premises, and on the
open ground behind there are sheds upon sheds with machinery
which she has bought up over the years. Some 2000 workmen
are employed there at present, and when this energetic woman,
carrying her parasol like a sceptre, walks through her empire her
employees greet her respectfully like a goddess. She is also one
of the most active members of the Club of Career Women,
which is fighting for equal rights for women in jobs. " We are
not finding it easy," she explained to me. " Even though in our
progressive Karachi the veil has disappeared, it continues to be
present, as it were, in an invisible form. I am fortunate in having
a generous husband who not only places no obstacles in my way
but, on the contrary, is my best collaborator. But most men

consider having a wife in employment to be undignified or even improper."

The invisible veil : I was reminded of the phrase when I met a modern young girl, Asmi, at the house of Begum Rahim. Begum Rahim is another one of those women who have cast off the veil and advanced to economic freedom—not from necessity, since her husband earns a considerable income as one of Karachi's leading doctors—but because her tremendous drive needed an outlet or a hobby. She found it in fashion. To-day she owns Karachi's leading fashion salon, and has already begun to export to America. For inspiration she does not have to travel to Paris. Whereas the women of Japan have rushed full-tilt into Western fashions—presumably because the kimono is one of the most expensive and least practical garments in the world—in Pakistan, just as in India, the native style is holding its own with only slight modifications. There can scarcely be a more convenient female garment than that of the Punjab : loose trousers in a light material, with over them a shirt split down the sides and mostly in a different colour, which gracefully follow the wearer's movements as she walks along. And there can hardly be a more majestic-looking garment than the sari, which imparts to every woman something of the sweet exultation of a Murillo Madonna. True, neither garment gives much scope for sex appeal : in the former the woman remains a work-mate, in the latter she becomes an idol. But even in Karachi feminine independence has not quite reached the point it has in Bombay, where saris can be had with provocative low necklines. To get back to the modern girl Asmi whom I met at Begum Rahim's salon as she was choosing an evening dress. " Don't you think I look like Elvis Presley ? " she asked me boldly the moment we had been introduced. " I have copied his hair-style. Certainly we dance rock ' n ' roll and cha-cha-cha at our parties—we young people don't live on the moon, you know." But when I tried to aim my camera at this Pakistani teddy-girl she suddenly became as shy as a young nun. " You want to take a photograph

of me ? " she asked in horror. " And even publish it ? But I
would first have to ask Papa's permission." The invisible veil :
it is not only the men who enfold their Begums and daughters in
it ; it is also present in the women's mental make-up. Fundamentally, they merely act modern. When I asked the young girl
to write down her name and address in my notebook, so that I
could send her the picture, she merely wrote ' Asmi.' " Please
don't ask any more."

CHAPTER TWENTY-ONE

Kashmir: an Expensive Holiday Playground

*W*HEN I DROVE INTO SRINAGAR, THE CAPITAL of Kashmir, I thought I had fallen among thieves. No sooner had I turned the car towards the embankment along Lake Dal than the road on both sides seemed transformed into a racing-track, with panting, arm-waving men tripping over one another and elbowing each other away from the open driving-window. Alarmed, I stepped on the accelerator, but the crowd simply leapt up on the running-board, the wings, and the bumpers. "Nice houseboat, cheap houseboat," they all cried together. "My houseboat is best!" When I stopped the car, perplexed by the noise and the unsolicited load, one of the rascals simply tore open the door, triumphantly flopped into the seat beside me, and, as if he were my lord and master, assumed command. "My boat's up there in front—the *Golden Streak*, with flushing W.C. Just drive straight on." I had no choice but to bow to my fate. The moment I signalled my surrender by a resigned nodding of my head the turmoil around the car vanished as if I had uttered an exorcism. The *Golden Streak* with flushing W.C. was one of those houseboats which any romantically inclined visitor of this Indian Venice chooses as a residence. She was tidily moored in the straight line which, divided from the road by a canal, stretched for mile after mile through shallow waters, half land and half sea. Most of them are powerfully built, broad-beamed, flat-bottomed craft, rather like Noah's Ark but without the lions, regular floating houses with large windows, spacious verandas, pretty curtains, and—we must not forget them— W.C's. The W.C. appears to play a tremendously important

part with the Kashmiris : its existence is advertised immediately
below the very poetical names of the boats, in large letters, legible
right across the water : " *Silver Moon*, with guaranteed flushing
lavatory," " *Fragrant Rose,* with most modern toilet," " *Happy
Bird*, with all hygienic comfort," "*The New City of Paris*, with ... "
and so on.   Anybody omitting this proud title of nobility thereby silently admits his backwardness—which consists in the fact
that the guest must perform his private business on one of those
wooden thrones with a lid on top and a chamber-pot fitted inside,
a piece of furniture also found in the more old-fashioned hotels
in the Indian plain.   It is the technical perfection of the W.C.'s
which determines the official grading of the houseboats : a boat
belonging to the luxury class because of its well-functioning
flushing cistern costs twice as much to hire as the more modest
chamber-pot models.

With or without W.C., a holiday on a houseboat is delightful.
Strictly speaking, it is not a case of *one* houseboat : there are in
fact three.   The big, beautiful craft with a saloon furnished in the
European taste, where a visitor can sink into a club chair and
study albums filled with the glowing praises of earlier visitors, is
only for the guest.   The proprietor and his family live on a
smaller boat, made fast alongside, without carpet, tables, beds,
or W.C. : everybody there lives and sleeps, procreates, and dies
on the bare planks.   " We are poor, master," the owner of my
boat, Dandu, used to complain to me.   " Our entire country is
poor—nothing but mountains and barren soil. I own nothing
except this boat.   When we have guests we eat our fill.   In
winter, when the tourists stay away, we are hungry.   But I
always have charming guests, generous guests.   Last summer I
had a British colonel. . . ."   And now followed a story of unparalleled benefactions, of entire wardrobes which had passed
from great gentlemen to the poor Dandu.   " I saw it in your face
at once," was the invariable refrain at the end of these stories ;
" you too are generous, very generous."   The only defence left
to me was the hackneyed old story of the poor author who lives
on dry bread and can show his generosity, much to his regret,

only in his feelings. I felt like an aphis visiting an ant. I lived alone aboard my luxurious craft with flushing W.C., while Dandu shared the smaller boat with his aged father, who cease-lessly smoked a pipe, his wife, and three boys ; recently the household had further increased by a younger brother and his new wife. How were they going to manage on the little boat if their family, as might be expected, continued to grow ? Dandu's carefree face just beamed at me : the future was in Allah's hands, who had always sent him such generous guests. The master of the third boat was Hassan, Dandu's eldest son, whose narrow boat provided the means of communication between the family and guest on the one hand, and the mainland on the other. He was permanently hovering near my ark, and the moment I called out he slid alongside, crouching in the stern, whipping the water with a short paddle. Like him, countless boatmen were scurrying about between the houseboats all day long. The first caller in the morning used to be the flower-vendor who would knock at my window to offer delightful bunches of lily of the valley. " How lovely ! Simply gorgeous ! " he would coo in a high falsetto with the melodious intonation of an English lady. He was almost impossible to get rid of. He would be followed by a tailor who simply boarded my ark and began to measure me for a suit, by a photographer, and by a fruit-vendor with tasty apples and those tree nuts which are typical of Kashmir. To all these ants I was an aphis, a pampered and much-wooed giver of sweetness, much smiled at and cheated. The moment Hassan brought me ashore I would be totally surrounded by the merchants who lie in wait for prospective customers everywhere, and who cannot be shaken off by any amount of cunning. " I merely want to show you my factory—you need not buy anything at all." If you agree you will find yourself hauled off to some dark shed, called a ' factory,' where children are weaving carpets on heavy looms, where papier-mâché is shaped into plates and lamp-stands, and where sandalwood is carved to make over-elaborate boxes and coffers. Throughout India the products of the craftsmen of Kashmir are sold in souvenir shops, but anyone hoping to find true folk-art here will be sadly disappointed. Nowhere else has folklore been frozen into such shameless clichés and mass production. The best things are the fabrics of gossamer-fine wool, so delicate and soft that a shawl a yard wide can be pulled through a ring. But the prices of these masterpieces are correspondingly high—around 60 rupees. As a result, when these eager businessmen crept up to me like hyenas, whispering, " Want to see my factory ? " I used to reply with a resolute and curt, " No, I don't." And that was that.

Only one of them succeeded in trapping me with a trick. I was ambling along the promenade which follows the Jumna river, watching with the malicious pleasure of the confirmed non-buyer the contortions of cunning and salesmanship with which the countless tourist stalls tried to lure their customers— one of them is called " Suffering Moses," the proprietor explaining this original name by the numerous police fines imposed on him for overcharging—when suddenly a sly-looking young man appeared before me. " You're a journalist," he whispered, conspiratorially looking all round him, " follow me unobtrusively to my shop." I smiled. " What are you trying to sell me ? " I scoffed. " Nothing ! " he answered solemnly. He stepped quite close to me. " My business is political ! " he breathed into my ear. " But how do you know that I am a journalist ? " I asked. " Our secret service . . ." he said importantly. " Besides, you've got it written all over you." Flattered, I followed Mahmud to a wooden shack where an assortment of downright hideous carvings in a modernized folklore style, a kind of streamlined primitivism, were offered for sale. He pulled the curtain—" On no account must we be seen ! "—and sat down by my side.

I told him he could save himself the political introduction. I knew very well what Kashmir had suffered as the bone of contention between India and Pakistan. Perhaps the reader will allow me to review briefly those events which at the time filled the columns of the world Press, and which are to-day no nearer solution, although the world has got too used to this particular tragedy to be unduly disturbed by it any longer. At the time of partition it had been agreed that the maharajas, who were not subjects of the British Crown but nominally independent sovereigns, should have the right to decide which of the two states they wished to join—although, of course, it was expected that the Moslems among them would choose Pakistan, and the Hindus India. But what was to happen to those states whose rulers and privileged upper class belonged to one faith while the overwhelming majority of the population belonged to the other? In the case of two states where Moslem maharajas ruled over a Hindu population Nehru was quick with an answer: surely a ruler, whose days of domination were counted anyway, must be democratic enough in such a case to follow the will of his subjects. When the Nawab of Junagadh and the Nizam of Hyderabad violated this principle Indian troops presently moved into their territories and the issue was settled, though not exactly by non-violent means. But what about Kashmir, where a Hindu despot so arbitrarily tyrannized over a population which was 80 per cent. Moslem that it had been in a permanent state of rebellion against his authority even before 1947? It was perfectly obvious that not only its religion and Islamic tradition but also its geographical position among the headwaters of the Indus basin must earmark Kashmir for Pakistan. There is some doubt about what precisely went on behind the scenes during those fateful days in October 1947. The fact is that the people of Kashmir, alarmed by rumours that the Maharaja was negotiating about association with Delhi, once more rose against him, and were once more cruelly crushed by his troops. The Pakistanis thereupon tried to forestall what they assumed were India's plans by creating a *fait accompli*. Not by means of regular troops, but, to avoid diplomatic complications, by means of 'volunteers.' That was an unforgivable mistake. To the wild Pathans of the north-west frontier, who were entrusted with the operation, war meant a jolly campaign with murder, rape, and rich booty. Their advance to Srinagar terrified the Hindus and Moslems of Kashmir alike. The Maharaja asked for Indian troops to save his country from the berserk invaders. When airborne Indian troops arrived and halted the marauders the whole of Kashmir was grateful to them. But one devil had been driven out by another—possibly a more decent devil, but a devil nevertheless. The saviours made themselves at home, and although Nehru, following mediation in the United Nations, undertook to hold a plebiscite, he subsequently shirked the implementation of his promise with one lame excuse after another.

"We are an occupied country," Mahmud declared sulkily. "The place is swarming with police informers, and anyone speaking out against the Indians is jailed and tortured." "Dreadful," I said. "You too?" Mahmud nodded tragically. "A few months ago an American correspondent came to Srinagar. He'd been invited here by Nehru. He was being shown around by men from the Information Office, and could not talk to the people at all. But I went to see him—right into the Government guest-house. I didn't care that there was an Indian official with him. 'They're all lying to you,' I told him to his face. 'If you want to know the truth come with me.' He later ordered this box from me, an order worth nearly one thousand rupees!" "Splendid," I said. "And for that you were tortured." Mahmud looked tragic. "The day after his departure they came for me," he confirmed sombrely. "They interrogated me; they tried to squeeze the names of my friends out of me. I gritted my teeth and remained silent. I was beaten unmercifully. . . . That bookshelf over there costs twenty rupees, but this tray is a better bargain. . . . I was covered with blood all over. . . . How do you like this cigarette-box? It was five weeks before they discharged me. You can have it for fifteen rupees—why don't you buy it?" I did not like anything. "Would you like me to get you some documents of our resistance movement?" Mahmud continued, undismayed by my refusals. We stepped out into the open and after a short walk entered another shop which had 'London Tailor' written over it. "This gentleman is interested in our work," Mahmud introduced me to the tailor. Before my

surprised eyes he immediately began to unroll bales of cloth.
"You can have your first fitting to-morrow morning," he said.
"Complete with documents," Mahmud added. I did not need a
suit.

I continued this game with my high-powered salesman-martyr
and his friends for days, without succumbing to his pressure.
Whenever we met in his shop or in a café I would put him off to
my day of departure. He made great play of warning me against
Dandu. A Government spy, he said. If I wanted to buy a shawl
or a carpet I must certainly not let Dandu buy it for me, but
consult a good patriot. After a week Mahmud got tired of my
delaying tactics. He received me with well-mimed despair. "I've
been warned," he groaned. "Warned by several people. I've
been seen with you. The police are going to pick me up again."
"I should like to relieve you of your martyrdom," I consoled
him. Without making a purchase.

In fairness to Mahmud, it ought to be said that his atrocity
stories, skilfully though he used them for his commercial purposes,
contained a good grain of truth. A sensible man in Kashmir
prefers not to discuss politics. I tried in vain to sound Dandu :
he answered all my questions evasively. However, I got a fairly
clear idea of the real feelings of the Kashmiris on the occasion of
the great Idgah Festival, when hundreds of thousands of people
stream into Srinagar to mark the end of the month of fasting. I
arrived in Dandu's company, and while he merged like a small
drop into the vast ocean of the faithful who were listening to
the address of the mullah I cautiously edged my way forward.
Immediately in front of the mullah, in the first row, knelt the
Moslem Ministers of the Government—dignified elderly gentlemen with pointed beards. Among them a short younger man
with a black lamb's-skin cap caught my eye by his imperious
manner. He was, as I subsequently learnt from Dandu, the
leader of the pro-Indian party, a nephew of Gulam Mohammed
Bakshi, the Premier, who was then on a visit in Delhi. He
seemed to be expecting something or other, for he was moving

his head about excitedly, looking back over his shoulder at the
crowds behind him. The moment the mullah had finished his
speech the young man rose to address the crowd himself. But
his imperiously raised arm, demanding silence, had the opposite
effect. A threatening murmur arose from the crowd ; many of
the faithful had leapt to their feet and were shouting. " We
don't want to listen to you ! " they called out. " We've come
here to pray. Shut up ! " Once more the arrogant young man
tried to subdue the tumult by gestures. Without success. Like
a whipped dog, he sat down again among his colleagues, and
presently friend and foe were bowing their foreheads to the
ground, in veneration of the One beyond all politics. But the
moment prayers were over politics once more raised its ugly
head. Outside the Hindu Ministers were waiting for their
Moslem colleagues in a tent, and as they embraced each other in
brotherly greeting a small number of those near by burst into
cheers for the Bakshi Government. But the spark from these
hired supporters did not set fire to the crowd : their vivats died
away in an icy silence. In the square outside vendors were
offering pictures for sale : I could scarcely believe my eyes when
I recognized the portrait of Ayub Khan, the military dictator of
Pakistan. " That is our leader, not Nehru," a young man
whispered to me. I was surprised at the boldness of the demonstration ; subsequently I was told that the police, when they
discovered the treasonable portraits, had torn them up and
beaten up the vendors.

A few days later I climbed the dusty narrow wooden stairs to
the party secretariat of the Plebiscite Front, which for several
years had been unsuccessfully pressing Delhi for a plebiscite.
Since India must permit at least a semblance of a democratic
opposition, there is another party active besides this Front—the
Political Conference, which demands outright association with
Pakistan. The only snag is that all its important members, all
those who could have provided a lead for this organization, had
long vanished into prison without a trial. Including that Sheikh

Abdullah who, as a socialist, a friend of Nehru, and the Kashmiri Premier at the time of partition, was largely responsible for his country's accession to India. A little later, when, disillusioned and disappointed by India's policy, he reminded his friend Nehru of the promised plebiscite, and even toyed with the idea of making his contested country into an independent state, he was overthrown in the coup staged by the Indian Army in 1953 and imprisoned. In January 1958 he was released, but he was hurriedly locked up again in April when the Indians saw that he was not prepared to reduce his demands in the slightest, and that the people who had previously hated him because of his friendship with Delhi—just as they are now hating Bakshi—hailed him upon his release as a national hero.

On the mountain road from Jammu to Srinagar I passed a car which was pulled up by the side of the road. One of the men in it addressed me : he spoke excellent English, and had markedly aristocratic manners and beautifully moulded features. He turned out to be Abdullah's son-in-law, G. M. Shah, who likewise had been conditionally released after six years' imprisonment without trial, and was now being taken home by friends. During his imprisonment he had lost several pounds in weight, because the inmates had to share their rations with their warders. Worse than these privations had been his complete isolation from the outside world. Only by means of telegrams had he been able to keep his family informed of his condition, and his perpetually changing places of detention. Why he had been arrested, and why he was now being released again, he did not know himself. Shah invited me to visit him at his home in Srinagar. In the evening, when I passed through his gate, I found about two dozen political friends of his sitting on the lawn outside his house ; they had come from neighbouring villages to welcome him back. There were many happy exchanges and manly embraces. Most of these people had likewise made the acquaintance of prison cells, even though not for such long periods as their host. A man's time of detention is like an honourable title, and was being used in introductions : " This is Sheikh Abdul Hamid, three years' imprisonment ; this here is Dr Rashid, two and a half years." Some of them had been imprisoned on the strength of entirely fabricated charges, such as theft, murder, or even indecent assault.

It is not pleasant to have to report such things from the country of Nehru, who has become, in the eyes of so many Westerners, the champion of the oppressed, and as it were the voice of the world's conscience. The situation in Kashmir may be less dramatic than that in Algeria, or in other African colonies—but the reason for that is not so much a lesser degree of oppression (the number of people killed in 1953, when the Kashmiris revolted against the arrest of Sheikh Abdullah, is estimated at 1500) as the complete muteness to which this nation has been condemned. In Kashmir no paper of the Plebiscite Front is allowed. All the correspondents of the Indian papers are creatures of the Government, so that even the Indian public has no idea of what is going on in Kashmir. There is no such paper in India as the Paris *Express* or the London *Tribune*, which would pillory the excesses of its own authorities in these oppressed areas. As a result, there is only a minute number of independent minds in India who are able to see the events in Kashmir for what they really are—a gigantic piece of folly.

In Kashmir itself the truth cannot remain hidden. " Not one of the Indian officers who were guarding us," Shah told me, " believed any longer in the justice of their cause." A foreign journalist does not have to talk for long to the Indian propagandists to realize how unsure they are of their own arguments. There is no point in listing all the legalistic subtleties with which they are trying to gloss over Nehru's breach of faith : the demand that the Pakistani aggressors must first withdraw from the part of Kashmir occupied by them, or the rather Reddish argument that Pakistan's membership in an aggressive military bloc was compelling India to keep Kashmir, that strategic key position between China, India, and Russia, free from imperialist bomber bases. To a critical mind these arguments are downright

untenable. When I shook hands after hours of fruitless discussion
with the Information Officers one of them—the most honest
among them—said, " I spoke to you as my duty demanded."
There was an undertone as if to say : " Surely you don't think I
am idiotic enough to believe my own arguments ? " Then
abruptly his face was clouded with anxiety. " And how do you
think it will all end ? " he asked. " End ? " I replied. " It will
never end ! Neither Nehru nor the Pakistanis will give in. The
bloodstained frontiers of to-day will remain, and with them
hatred and bad feelings. . . ." " That's what I think," said the
officer.

An even more hopeless view is expressed by many Indians in
Kashmir, especially by the intellectuals. " Here in Kashmir we
never had the religious conflicts which divided India," a student
told me. " We always lived as a minority in harmony with the
Moslems, and could have continued to do so if this unfortunate
policy had not artificially created the clash. We Kashmiris, no
matter whether Hindus or Moslems, are totally different from
the Indians in race and mentality—we are nearer the Persians than
the Indians. As a province of India we have no future : Delhi
will always treat us as a colony. Already the Indians have
captured 80 per cent. of our trade, and the rest is shared among
the B.B.C. What is the B.B.C.? Well, it's what we in Kashmir
call the family of our Premier : Bakshi Brothers Corporation,
a clan which controls the most profitable offices and the most
lucrative posts. There are seven brothers, not counting all the
nephews and friends. They used to be civil servants and school-
teachers earning 45 to 60 rupees a month—and to-day they are
millionaires. There is only one salvation for us : independence.
Why not have a Kashmiri buffer state—like Afghanistan, Nepal,
Sikkim, and Bhutan ? Or if we can't have independence, then
we'll join Pakistan. Even we Hindus believe there's more hope
for us in Karachi than in Delhi."

There is one thing the student forgot to mention : Nehru is
a Kashmiri by birth. This, according to the few Indian critics of
his policy, is the reason for his obstinate intransigence. Nehru's

native land must never be part of the accursed Pakistan : family sentiment at the root of a world conflict. One injustice begets another. Because of the Kashmir issue both India and Pakistan are spending 40 per cent. of their limited means, not on urgent development projects, but on unproductive armaments. The price paid for this holiday playground is already far too high.

Admittedly, India is doing all she can to soothe her guilty conscience. Kashmir is being positively flooded with money from Delhi's exchequer. It is the well-known colonial method of trying to overcome irrational opposition with money, the building of schools, hospitals, power-stations, etc. Kashmir, a poor country, is to forget its annoying Islamic solidarity amid economic progress. But so far these intellectual hopes have not been fulfilled by its simple men and women. Man does not live by bread alone.

CHAPTER TWENTY-TWO

Nepal : Front against China

IN APRIL 1959, WHEN THE SOVIET AMBASSADOR IN Delhi landed in the capital of Nepal to sign one of those famous aid agreements with which the Soviets had already blessed a number of other countries, his aircraft very nearly overshot the runway and pulled up just a few yards in front of a precipice. No better spot was available for an airfield in this mountainous country, and to this day every landing is a test of the pilot's skill. Possibly the Nepalese would not have been at all sorry if the Soviet envoy had started on his descent into hell in their country. For at that time things did not look at all pleasant along the northern frontier. Tibetan refugees were streaming across the passes over the Himalayas, and Red Chinese troops were pressing forward behind them. Nobody was quite sure whether Nepalese territory had also been invaded—there are no roads or telephones to the frontier areas, and a messenger would take a good week for the journey to the capital. Admittedly, there were posts equipped with radio telegraphy on the frontier passes, but these were manned by Indians, and sent their reports straight to the Indian Embassy at Katmandu. If the Nepalese Government asked very politely the Indians would graciously inform them whether their territory was still inviolate.

Tibetans and Nepalese have been linked for centuries by brotherly love and enmity ; Tibetan Buddhism is widespread in Nepal, side by side with Hinduism. Since they defeated the Tibetans in a fratricidal war in 1870, the Nepalese enjoyed a number of contractual rights—for instance, that of having their army march through Tibet, and Customs exemption for all

Nepalese merchandise.   The children of mixed marriages were regarded as Nepalese, and could only be judged by Nepalese judges in Tibet.   Finally, Tibet paid an annual tribute of 10,000 rupees to Nepal.   Since 1950, when Peking first extended its hand towards Lhasa, Nepal had waived these privileges ; in return, China had paid her a 'grant in aid' of 12,000,000 dollars.   If these inexperienced mountain people believed that they had pacified the dragon by yielding they now had a rude awakening.   The peace of the Himalayas was gone, and the hermits of world history suddenly found themselves in the front line of an inexorable clash.

Until a few years ago Nepal had been barred to the curious foreigner almost as inhospitably as is its eastern neighbour Bhutan to this day.   In 1956 the Indian Army eventually built a road from the plain to Katmandu, winding its way across romantic mountain passes in vertiginous hairpin bends.   The journey is easier and pleasanter by air—in spite of the risk in landing—and a plane of the Indian Air Lines makes the connexion from Patna every day.   Through the windows you look out on wild valleys without roads ; only narrow paths climb up to the terraces where the mountain-dwellers wrest their daily bread from the mountain. You can take it all in at one glance : a poor country, untouched by the blessings and the curses of progress.   It is symbolical that the clocks in Nepal are ten minutes fast without any astronomical justification, and that, similarly without religious justification, Sunday is observed on Saturday—just as if the population were Jews.   But in spite of its poverty Nepal is not a sad, tragic country like India, but a country of laughter.   It is a curious characteristic of the Mongols that they always seem to be in a good temper, and I really believe that this is true of the Nepalese.   Did not Buddha, a native of Katmandu, teach that sufferings spring merely from unsatisfied desires, and that in order to attain happiness all vain wishes must be scattered to the winds ?   It seems that the Nepalese have in their poverty found a self-sufficient happiness.

When I speak of the Nepalese I ought really to qualify this

term : like most visitors to this country, I only know the little nation of the Newars who inhabit the valley of Katmandu. They are a mixture between the Bhotias in the north, kinsmen of the Tibetans, and the Terais in the flat jungle country along the Indian frontier, whose dark skin scarcely differentiates them from the Indians. Then there are the Gurkhas in the west, famous for the heroic mercenary regiments which they have made available to the British and the Indians, and various other types of humanity in the inaccessible corners of the Himalayas. What is known as Nepal is therefore not so much one nation as a conglomeration of various but tenuously linked regions and groups with local potentates, whose relations with the King in Katmandu differs a great deal from one another. There is, for instance, a Nepalese currency with beautifully printed banknotes ; but in certain regions only the Indian rupee is accepted in payment, and in others you have to have a bearer to carry on his back a huge load of silver coins. Anyone wishing to travel about Nepal can leave his car behind. Passes and valleys are crossed on foot. Many of the rest-homes and, even worse, the bridges which were built some 30 years ago, are now dilapidated, and it may frequently take a day's march to circumvent a gorge which might have been crossed in ten minutes by suspension bridge. Natural obstacles are matched by those in the minds of the bureaucrats : anyone wishing to move out of the capital requires a special permit. If you want to take a perfectly harmless walk the gentlemen in the Government building will make sour faces as though you planned to blow up Mount Everest. In a sense their mistrust is understandable : once a man has crossed a mountain he is beyond their reach. When Dr K. I. Singh, an *enfant terrible* of Nepalese politics, started a conspiracy in another valley the Nepalese police were unable to get at him. They had to request the Indians to penetrate into the particular valley from their side and to catch the offender. But what does it matter if the visitor's radius of action is limited ? The valley of Katmandu is the jewel of the country. One really has to draw on the language of fairy-tales to describe it. Once upon a time there were three kings. Their

kingdoms were so small that their capitals were only a few miles
from each other, and they could look into each other's cooking-
pots. And as each of them was anxious to own the most beautiful temple and the most beautiful palaces, each of the kings was
spurred on to ever greater efforts by the splendours of the other
two. But there also sprang up envy, distrust, and strife, so that
the small kingdoms exhausted one another in cruel wars until a
neighbouring Gurkha prince was able to pocket them all. The
descendants of this conqueror rule the country to this day. But
still the three capitals of Nepal testify to the three splendour-
loving kings, and it would be difficult to say which of them is the
most beautiful—Katmandu, Patan, or Bhadgaon. Just as the
Newars unite in themselves Mongol and Indian traits, so their
architecture is a blend of the strange beauty of both civilizations.
As I stood in front of the Nepalese temples I was reminded in
turn of the golden roofs of the Forbidden City in Peking and of
the most impressive temples in India. The Chinese element is
present in the curved, stacked pagoda roofs, in the primary red
of the walls—half blood and half soil—in the barbarian splendour
of the gateways with their real gold, with winged lions and other
mystical beasts on their friezes, and the bells below them which
whisper melodiously at every breath of wind. The Indian
element is present in the delight in invention, in the sensuality
which twines in jungle-like profusion around every window-
frame or supporting beam—in motifs so strange and daring that
ladies blush as they look at them. Naturally, there are magnificent monuments of antiquity all over the world. But whereas
elsewhere an alien modern life clashes all around them, the Middle
Ages here are still alive in the people's soul : human beings and
architecture are still at one. To the Nepalese peasants these
temples do not represent a venerable past, but are articles of
direct everyday magic use. This practical relationship with the
beautiful has its advantages and its disadvantages. The good
people will not understand why they should not repair the defec-
tive roof of a magnificent temple with corrugated iron, or why
they should not, to prevent the general defilement of the place,

instal a public lavatory in the temple wall, immediately next to the gateway. That is the danger besetting all genuinely primitive people : as soon as they step outside their traditional forms they lose all sense of taste or caution, and, indiscriminately as a child, pounce on anything that is new to them.

Many a strange story is told by the foreign experts brought to Nepal to guide it in its first steps into modernity. Nepal has, perhaps fortunately, only inconsiderable mineral wealth—not enough to justify extraction. But no sooner had a geologist discovered a few thousand tons of coal and some iron ore than an impressive mining company was formed, and people began to talk of a steelworks. When a Swiss expert founded a school to instruct the young Nepalese in the most elementary technical skills it was not long before the money ran out. What the Nepalese really wanted was not a technical school but a University.

Of course, such childish mistakes—impatience to take the second step before the first—are common among all under-developed people. In fairness to the Nepalese it must be admitted that they have not shown themselves at all slow at learning. It was only in 1950 that their King overthrew the so-called Ranas who had ruled the country as despots since 1847 ; it was only in 1959 that he gave his country a modern Constitution, and that the first elections were held—a real feat in a country without roads and telephones. And already the people have responded to these first steps in democracy with a zeal and maturity of judgment that might well serve as an example to more highly developed Asian countries. Monuments of the past rule of the Ranas are to this day the magnificent palaces which they had built in Katmandu and the monuments they put up in all public squares, showing themselves on horseback, with a yard-long plume of bird-of-paradise feathers trailing from their heads. They were great gentlemen, these Ranas who, like the Shoguns in Japan, raised themselves in 1847 from their position of servants above the heads of the weak kings and for the next hundred years ruled the land in the part of hereditary Prime Ministers, inter-marrying freely with the royal family. Many of them were good fathers of their country, and if they are to-day being abused as 'reactionaries,' this refers merely to the fact that they had been reluctant to upset their people by modern experiments : they were themselves very progressive gentlemen, educated at English universities, and living in palaces which still testify to their cosmopolitan outlook. When they lost their power most of them left the country with their possessions, although they had nothing more to fear than the land reform with which the new rulers threatened their landed property. I visited the brother of the last Prime Minister, a courteous elderly gentleman who had all his life concerned himself more with ancient manuscripts and a huge modern library than with intrigue and power. When I asked him for his opinion on the political situation he replied with a sly smile, " When the new politicians who to-day speak so ill of the Ranas have become as rich as we are they will also be driven out and slandered."

This danger of corruption through power is present also in the mind of the man whose Nepalese Congress Party has emerged victorious from the first elections. Their outcome had been awaited with some suspense, and even anxiety, as it was not known how an electorate that was up to 90 per cent. illiterate would react to this unaccustomed experiment. Would the Ranas not stage a comeback thanks to the loyalty of the ordinary people ? Or would not the small but superbly organized Communist Party promise the moon to the unsuspecting peasants? But the Nepalese seemed to have taken to democracy : in vast numbers they streamed to the polling-boxes in February 1959, waited patiently while strange officials examined their identity papers and, to prevent abuse, marked their hands with indelible ink. The women proved to be even more ardent politicians than their menfolk. At one polling-station a dispute arose when an illiterate lady turned up first with the identity papers of her husband and then again with those of her son. " Next time you'd better put on trousers," the official advised her.

Everybody was therefore pleasantly surprised when the most

sensible party of the lot, the Congress Party, won an over-whelming majority. B. P. Koirala, the youthful Prime Minister, is one of the most engaging politicians I have met in Asia : an idealist without losing himself in the clouds, a socialist without radical jargon, a man who knows what a risky undertaking it is to lay hands on a century-old social structure without causing the whole edifice to collapse. Above all, a convinced anti-Communist, not from political calculation but from common humanity. And, what is more, a man of great integrity. " I have insisted that my Ministers should remain poor," he told me. " Our revolution is a real step forward only if the old exploitation comes to an end. To modernize Nepal we must save—and we in the Government must set an example."

At least, the Nepalese do not have to foot the whole bill for their progress themselves. There is a whole army of international experts in their capital—from the F.A.O., the Ford Foundation, and the United States, British, and Indian Governments. I saw Swiss dairy experts set out for remote valleys to instruct the Nepalese peasants in the manufacture of cheese. Gruyère made in Nepal is very popular in India. One day in the streets of Katmundu I saw a team of the World Health Organization, armed with hypodermic syringes, waylay the passers-by and pounce on them with an anti-cholera immunization before they knew what was happening to them. The most recent arrivals are some Russians, who are building a power-station, a hospital, a sugar-refinery, and a cigarette factory for Nepal ; they are also planning to build a road along the Indian-Nepalese frontier, a road which Nepal has long wanted. The few existing roads all run from north to south—that is, out of the mountain valleys towards the Indian frontier, where they link up with the Indian roads. Communications from one part of Nepal to another are therefore frequently across Indian territory, and the Indians are not at all displeased to continue in the rôle of protectors of Nepal, a rôle inherited from the British. Besides, how was a primitive little country of 8,500,000 inhabitants to resist the grip of 400,000,000 ? Even the technical assistance given by the Indians

has a curiously selfish character. When the Nepalese wanted to
divert their rivers to irrigate the arid lowlands the Indians turned
a deaf ear, because they would much rather divert the waters on
their own territory. An Indian ' military mission ' of 1000
people caused a good deal of nervousness among the Nepalese
before it was reduced to a more sensible scale. In 1950 Delhi
persuaded the inexperienced Nepalese to conclude a trade agreement which handed over to the Indian authorities all Nepalese
Customs rights, practically cut off Nepal from the outside world,
and made her economically a province of India. As a result,
unscrupulous Indian businessmen have succeeded in gaining a
monopoly of the timber trade and, acting in complicity with
corrupt officials, carrying out extensive and harmful timber-felling
far in excess of their concessions. Until recently the Nepalese
Post Office was not entitled to carry letters across the frontiers ;
it was only in April 1959 that the little country finally became a
member of the World Post Union, so that it can now send out
into the world its pretty postage-stamps. Until then letters for
abroad had to be taken to the post office at the Indian Embassy.
In short, the Indians occupied, and still occupy, a privileged
position in Nepal which has given rise among the Nepalese
intelligentsia to the slogan of ' Indian colonialism '; the victorious
Congress Party had struck out hard at the unpopular Indians in
its election propaganda. But what grain of wheat has ever
successfully revolted against one of the millstones between which
it was being crushed ? So long as the sufferings of their brethren
on the far side of the tall white mountains are so insistently
before their eyes, the Nepalese are unlikely to quarrel overmuch
with a fate that has made them dependent on India. At least, not
for the moment.

It is never very pleasant for a small country to find itself in the
front line—least of all on a frontier which has been experiencing
the icy breath of the cold war ever since the spring of 1959. As
the frontiers between India and China had never been accurately
drawn the Peking rulers have tried to advance their borders in
the west as well as in the east—in Ladakh as well as in Assam.

Here, on Indian territory, the Indian Army might bar their way. But the small princely states of Nepal, Sikkim, and Bhutan, timeless and powerless in their Himalayan valleys, have yet to get used to their new rôle of being No Man's Land.

However, it is not only advancing armies that decide a nation's victory or defeat. When the more spectacular tensions have ebbed away there remains a radiation of political power which, working silently and unnoticed, creates and marks off zones of influence before the statesmen realize what has happened. There is much discussion in the West about the fundamental significance of this competition, of this rivalry between two economic and political systems. India, it is argued, is virgin land which the free West might cultivate in a less precipitate but more organic manner, and without the tyrannical sacrifices which are being exacted from the Chinese by their Communist masters. I do not think that the West should have any great illusions about the outcome of that rivalry. No one who has travelled in both China and India can have the slightest doubt as to which of the two will gain eventual hegemony in Asia. Let us not talk of systems. Let us instead talk of people, for it is the human beings behind the ideologies that matter in the end. My recollection of China is that of an antheap, of a vast workshop roaring and throbbing, of infinitely hard work and vibrant vitality. India, by contrast, is a scene of holy tranquillity and unholy indolence, of officially enforced progress, of doubts and despair. Some might call this an exaggerated and unfair picture ; they might even try to refute it in this or that respect by adducing statistics and examples—but as a general impression it cannot be denied. It may even be that the atmosphere of freedom that one experiences in India, in contrast with the despotism of China, is an expression not so much of Western (prosperity-based) humanism as of that lethargy which, despite all its aspirations, invariably shrinks from seeing things through to the end. Whether a Communist government in India would change this basic attitude to any marked extent is more than questionable, just as it is questionable whether, on the other hand, this fundamental attitude could tolerate for long the radicalism of a far more rigorous regime.   One need only recall the lesson of Kerala ! Besides, the prestige of Communism throughout the world is altogether based on false pretences : what masquerades as the success of an ideology is in fact no more than a biological phenomenon, the natural achievement of two nations of great vitality, the Russians and the Chinese.   The lethargy of India, I very much fear, cannot be overcome by any political revolution. Surely it is no coincidence that India's most forceful resurgence, the movement of Vinoba, runs its course outside the country's political life and within a limited circle of the elect.

Yet this great tranquillity need not be regarded as something altogether negative.   It might yet prove an effective bar to Bolshevism by depriving suffering of its revolutionary dynamism and confining its upsurge within the dykes of traditionalism. There is enough inertia in the present pattern of India to serve, for several decades and perhaps even centuries, as the basis of a gradual evolutionary development such as is really much more in line with the temperament of this people.   But the pressure of rivalry, the menacing presence of the northern neighbour, have rudely shaken the Indians out of their tranquillity, driven them into hectic development, and undermined their social fabric even further.   The cry of " Peking at the gates " has upset the international as much as the social blueprint for India.

To this fundamental threat—which does not depend on day to day developments, on the concentration or withdrawal of troops in contested frontier areas, but which hangs in the air as an ever-present disaster—Nehru answers with the idea of neutralism. What is the difference between neutralism and neutrality ?   The latter, as expressed in the traditional attitude of a small country like Switzerland, is based on the humble recognition of one's own weakness, on the realization that to keep quiet and to duck are the demands of realistic self-preservation.   Neutralism, on the other hand, is anything but humble.   Just as non-violence in effect aims at a higher form of violence, so neutralism is a disguised claim to political influence on a world scale.   The refusal to take sides in the cold war is not due to a sense of being above the parties. But the clash between America and Russia is reduced for a spiritual mind to the scale of a regrettable squabble between two philosophically inferior materialistic beings, each of whom is more blinded than the other. The irrelevance of all earthly contradictions *sub specie aeternitatis,* this principle of Hindu metaphysics, is alive also as a political axiom in the secularized minds of the Indian statesmen. As a result of his nation's century-old tradition of wisdom, as well as the legacy of Gandhi, Nehru assumed the rôle of an *arbiter mundi*, a world conscience, called upon to speak out as soon as one of the great Powers uses force against a weaker country. But his own guilt in the matter of Kashmir is bound to impair his judicial impartiality in the eyes of the world. Since on this issue he needed Moscow's diplomatic support, many of his judgments have betrayed a surprising clemency towards the sins of the Soviets. Suez was a crime, but Budapest only a lapse. It needed Peking's brutal aggression in the Tibetan frontier areas, it needed the indignation of a whole country, before a hesitant Nehru, almost reluctantly, adopted a somewhat firmer attitude.

More and more, neutralism has lost its moral halo and revealed itself as a policy of expediency. The fact is that India's vast population is a source not of strength but of difficulties ; she is not, for the time being, a great power either militarily or economically—only a potential great power. Nor is she—in spite of a preconceived idea widely held throughout the world— morally superior to others. There is in her social make-up far too sharp a clash between idealism and undisguised private advantage, between loyalty and betrayal, between wisdom and emptiness. Anyone seeing only the one aspect or the other fails to do justice to this country. Nowhere else in the world, with the possible exception of Spain and Russia, do good and evil clash so harshly as unconnected extremes, without blending. It is in this, in this profound dichotomy between the divine and the diabolical, that the initiated sees the true soul of India.

INDEX

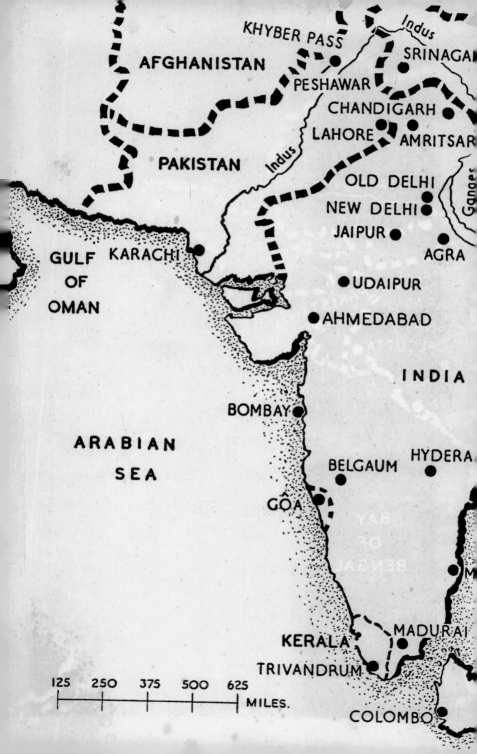